Childcare, Choice and Class Practices

How do parents find and choose childcare for their young children?

The contentious issue of childcare has enjoyed a recent and meteoric rise up the social policy agenda. The topic is frequently in the media spotlight, and continues to spark heated debate in the UK and around the world. *Childcare, Choice and Class Practices* is based on the findings of a substantive study which investigated the childcare markets and the choices made by middle-class parents in two London localities. In this account of the research the authors explore the complexities of the relationship between locality, childcare choice and childrearing. They highlight processes of social reproduction, the continuation of gendered responsibilities and conceptions of 'good' parenting.

The book considers the development of the UK government's childcare strategy from 1998 to the present day, and highlights the critical debates surrounding middle-class families' choice of childcare. In doing so, a number of themes develop, including:

- how parents balance paid work with the responsibilities of childcare
- what role modern fathers play in caring for and organizing care for their children
- how the childcare market operates, and what kind of care is available
- whether it is possible for parents to find care that complements their own views on childrearing
- the similarities and differences between middle-class fractions in relation to the care and education of young children.

This important study will be of great interest to anyone concerned with understanding the development of the childcare market and the fears and aspirations of middle-class parents.

It offers invaluable insights into a complex subject, and will be essential reading for all those working in or studying early years provision and policy, and students of sociology, class, gender and work.

Carol Vincent is Reader of Education at the Institute of Education, University of London.

Stephen Ball is the Karl Mannheim Professor of Sociology of Education at the Institute of Education, University of London.

Childcare, Choice and Class Practices

Middle-class parents and their children

Carol Vincent and Stephen J. Ball

Routledge
Taylor & Francis Group

LONDON AND NEW YORK

To Madi and Daniel

First published 2006 by Routledge
2 Park Square, Milton Park, Abingdon, Oxon OX14 4RN

Simultaneously published in the USA and Canada
by Routledge
270 Madison Ave, New York NY 10016

Routledge is an imprint of the Taylor & Francis Group

© 2006 Carol Vincent and Stephen J. Ball

Typeset in Bembo by
GreenGate Publishing Services, Tonbridge, Kent
Printed and bound in Great Britain by
The Cromwell Press, Trowbridge, Wiltshire

British Library Cataloguing in Publication Data
A catalogue record for this book is available from the British Library

Library of Congress Cataloging in Publication Data

ISBN 10: 0-415-36216-4 (hbk)
ISBN 10: 0-415-36217-2 (pbk)

ISBN 13: 9-78-0-415-36216-0 (hbk)
ISBN 13: 9-78-0-415-36217-7 (pbk)

Contents

Tables

Acknowledgements

First of all, we would like to thank all the mothers, fathers and providers who very generously gave up their time in order to talk to us about childcare, work and family. We are enormously grateful to them, and hope that this book reflects their concerns and experiences.

Sophie Kemp, Soile Pietikainen and Polly Radcliffe, the research officers on the project, played an invaluable role in the conduct and completion of the research. We are indebted to them for their hard work and the understanding they brought to our analysis of the data. We also owe thanks to the Economic and Social Research Council for funding this two-year project (award number R000239232).

A large number of people read and/or discussed parts of this book with us. Particular thanks must go to Tim Butler. We have found his work extremely useful, and have had regular and constructive conversations with him about the metropolitan middle classes, which we hope will continue. Peter Moss has shared his ideas about the future of provision for young children and we have also learnt from him. We would also like to thank Wendy Ball, Stephen Burke, Annette Braun, Simon Duncan, Claire Frost, Michele Harrison, Sarah Neal and Jayne Osgood for their comments, their help and their support. Lise Obi did a great job of proof-reading the manuscript.

Stephen would like to thank Trinidad for helping him cope and keeping him sane. Carol would like to thank Ian for being a particularly evolved and involved 'juggling dad', and her children, Madi and Dan, who were, for her, the inspiration for doing this research and writing this book.

Earlier versions of some of the material in this book have appeared in the following journals:

- Parts of Chapter 3 have appeared in an earlier version as 'The "childcare champion"? New Labour, social justice and the childcare market', *British Educational Research Journal*, 31 (5): 557–70 (2005).
- Parts of Chapter 4 have appeared in an earlier version as 'Middle class fractions, childcare and the "relational" and "normative" aspects of

class practices' (with Sophie Kemp and Soile Pietikainen), *The Sociological Review*, 53 (4): 478–502 (2004).

- Parts of Chapters 4 and 7 have appeared in a earlier version as 'The social geography of childcare: the 'making up' of the middle class child' (with Sophie Kemp), *British Journal of Sociology of Education*, 25 (2): 229–44 (2004).
- Parts of Chapter 5 have appeared in an earlier version in 'Metropolitan mothering: Mothers, mothering and paid work' (with Soile Pietikainen), *Women's Studies International Forum*, 27: 571–87 (2004).

All material has been reworked for this book.

Abbreviations

ACORN	A Classification of Residential Neighbourhoods
B	Battersea
CAB	Citizens Advice Bureau
CACE	Certificate in Adult and Continuing Education
CPI	Consumer Price Index
DfES	Department for Education and Skills
ESRC	Economic and Social Research Council
EOC	Equal Opportunities Commission
EPPE	Effective Provision of Pre-School Education
HE	Higher Education
HMT	Her Majesty's Treasury
IT	Information Technology
LEA	Local Education Authority
NCT	National Childbirth Trust
NGO	Non-Governmental Organization
NDNA	National Day Nurseries Association
NS-SEC	National Statistics Socio-Economic Classification
OECD	Organisation for Economic Co-operation and Development
Ofsted	Office for Standards in Education
SN	Stoke Newington
SPSS	Statistical Package for the Social Sciences
WTC	Working Tax Credit

Chapter 1

Introduction

Childcare today

MPs want affordable care for all
(*Nursery World*, 16 September, 2004, p. 8)

Parents pay inflation-busting cost of childcare
(Press release dated 27 January 2005 from the Daycare Trust
on their annual cost of childcare survey. Over the last year
costs had risen three-and-a-quarter times the rate of inflation.)

Nurseries peg pay to NMW (National Minimum Wage)
(*Nursery World*, 5 August, 2004, p. 4)

Day Nursery market grows 20 per cent in one year
(*Nursery World*, 17 March, 2005, p. 4)

Private nurseries are valued at £2bn
(*Nursery World*, 12 August, 2004, p. 4)

This is a book about childcare, but it also a book about families, social class, gender, education markets and education and social policy. We explore these wider issues through a focus, through the lens, if you like, of the choice and management of childcare arrangements. Thus this book has three interrelated themes. One highlights substantive issues around childcare choice: how parents make a choice, their views on different forms of childcare, the relationships they develop with carers, how they 'juggle' the demands of their children with other domestic and workplace demands, and how mothers and fathers experience this 'juggling' to different degrees. In a second theme we analyse policy around childcare, and situate it within a wider policy context of markets and education. A third theme highlights a set of sociological concerns around social class, particularly the middle classes, and gender, particularly the gendered division of domestic labour and childrearing. These three themes may seem to appeal to very different audiences, but we argue that they need to be thought about together, in order to gain analytical purchase on the role of the state, the market and the family in caring for young children, and the classed and gendered nature of 'family practices' (Morgan 1996).

We first discussed researching childcare in 1997. At the time it was possible to agree with Denise Riley (1983) when she noted that childcare was not seen to be a glamorous or exciting policy issue; indeed 'the very term "child care" has a dispiriting and dutiful heaviness hanging over it … it is as short on colour and incisiveness as the business of negotiating the wet kerb with the pushchair' (cited in Brennan 1998, p. 3). However in the eight years that have passed between our preliminary discussions and the writing of this book, childcare has been transformed as a policy issue. It has shot up the government agenda, with the National Childcare Strategy appearing in 1998, and the first ever Ten Year Strategy for Childcare being published in December 2004. Childcare became a key issue in the 2005 general election, receiving the attention of the Prime Minister Tony Blair and the Chancellor Gordon Brown, both eager to draw the electorate's attention to the expansion in childcare places, the government's attempts to increase parents' access to 'affordable, good quality childcare' (Baroness Ashton, cited in Mooney 2003a, p. 112), the promises of moves towards a universal offering of childcare through Children's Centres, as well as a number of other changes (increased maternity leave, increased levels of child tax credit: see Chapter 3) which will result in what Gordon Brown, Chancellor of the Exchequer, called 'a welfare state that is truly family friendly for the first time' (Brown 2004). As we discuss in Chapter 3, childcare as a policy issue has been the subject of increased attention under New Labour because of its apparent ability to address a number of New Labour concerns: increasing social inclusion, and in particular combating child poverty, revitalizing the labour market, and raising standards in education. The provision of childcare is seen as having the potential to bring women (particularly those on benefits) back into the workforce, modelling childrearing skills to parents understood as being in need of such support, and giving children the skills and experience they need to succeed in compulsory education. It thus plays a key role in both New Labour's economic agenda (the maintenance and improvement of a skilled workforce) and its social agenda (especially its pledge to end child poverty).

As indicated earlier, a study of childcare also encompasses a number of other policy issues, in particular, the respective roles of the private and public sectors in providing social provision. Until the advent of Sure Start[1] and Children's Centres, public sector provision in childcare was under the auspices of the local authorities, aimed at three- and four-year-olds only, and was usually minimal (although with considerable variations between authorities). Thus the expansion in childcare places during the 1990s has been in the private and voluntary sectors, with particularly rapid expansion in the former, leaving the UK with a large private sector relative to other modes of provision (for more details, see

Chapter 3). The OECD has raised questions about the likelihood of achieving accessible and equitable care in a private market (OECD 2001). However, the current government shows no signs of departing from its commitment to a mixed economy of private, state and voluntary sector provision.

Whilst this blaze of policy activity and recognition is clearly welcome, the question of why childcare as an issue took so long to come to prominence also deserves attention. Jennifer Marchbank (2000) notes that feminists have been slow to organize around childcare issues, unlike the sustained attention given to equal pay, or abortion rights. She argues that there are a number of reasons for this: that in the late 1960s and early 1970s some feminist writing displayed an ambivalent attitude towards motherhood, seeing it as a source of women's oppression, that younger women activists may not have had children, and that motherhood itself leaves little time for campaigning. She further argues that women's views on 'appropriate' childcare are highly differentiated, and also that many women are ambivalent about seeming to relinquish family and domestic responsibilities which appear to be a source of female power.

Later chapters in this book show clearly the ways in which responsibility for children, and for organizing and managing childcare, continues to lie with the mother, illustrating the robustness and longevity of traditional gender roles. Indeed this became one of the key sociological concerns of the project. Initially focused more on the operation of the pre-school market and the ability of middle-class consumers to engage with that market, the experience of doing our first round of interviews led us to focus more attention on the gendered division of labour around domestic issues, the role of mothers and fathers in childcare and childrearing more generally, and the efforts made by parents to achieve a work/life balance with which they were more or less happy.

A convergence of theoretical interests led us to focus the research on middle-class families. We were interested specifically in ideas of class fractions within the middle class, 'in practices of distinction and closure' (Ball 2003, p. 175) *within* class groups, and the relationship between class and space. There was also a practical rationale for focusing on the middle classes, namely, that in order to access the private childcare market in inner London, families had to have the levels of income normally available through employment in middle-class professional/managerial occupations.

We turn now to consider the structure and content of the book.

The structure of the book

This introductory chapter explores why we see childcare as being a key issue in both contemporary policy making and sociological terms. **Chapter 2** describes the qualitative research on which this book is based. We consider the respondents in terms of their education, occupations and place of residence. The two London settings for the research – Battersea and Stoke Newington – are described and the reasons for choosing them explained. The literature on the gentrification of urban areas, particularly work on the gentrification of London by Tim Butler and colleagues, is used to justify the importance placed on locality in the study. The final section of this chapter contains a reflexive account of the research process. **Chapter 3** focuses on policy. It draws on theoretical frameworks offered by Esping Anderson which seek to analyse and compare post-industrial welfare regimes. Such analyses emphasize the extent to which childcare in English-speaking countries, particularly the USA and the UK, has been regarded as a private, not a public issue, one to be resolved by individual households (except for those in extreme situations of need). In the second part of the chapter, we ask what effect the vigorous policy focus on childcare, maintained by the UK government, is having. Thus we consider the development of New Labour's National Childcare Strategy, from its birth in 1998 to the time of writing (summer 2005), noting that the major role played by private sector 'for-profit' providers is unlikely to change. We link national developments with the provision in our research localities. We identify the characteristics of the two local childcare markets in Battersea and Stoke Newington, and consider how the development of provision on the ground relates to the aspirations of national policy makers. In **Chapter 4** we turn to consider class theory and analysis, focusing on the middle classes. The key debates here turn on the extent to which there is a unitary middle class or a set of distinct fractions marked off from one another by values, lifestyle and political preferences and social relations; whether, if these differences are significant, they relate back to occupational divisions – professionals and managers, state- and private-sector employees and so on. In this chapter we briefly review the literature in this field, and argue that a focus on individuals' occupations alone is too blunt an instrument to provide a correlation with values, attitudes and lifestyles. Drawing on our earlier focus on locality (see Chapter 2), we consider how this can be productive in mapping nuances of difference and similarity between middle-class fractions.

The following chapters (5–7) go on to consider the differences and similarities between the middle-class respondents of Battersea and Stoke Newington, focusing in particular on their choice of childcare and education, but also considering the gendered divisions of care responsibilities within households. In **Chapter 5** we demonstrate the key roles of mothers in choosing childcare, and the sense of responsibility and anxiety that pervades the process. We also analyse the respondents' attempts to reconcile the demands of paid work and childcare, and consider the position of those within our sample who chose to stay at home full-time. Finally, we focus on the fathers, to try to understand their attempts at finding a balance between their work and family commitments. We conclude that despite the social and economic advantages of the respondents, despite the cultural power of the 'new man', that these mothers and fathers are not in the main presenting a serious challenge to a traditional understanding of family relationships. In **Chapter 6** we explore parents' experiences of childcare and their relationships with carers, using data from both parents and carers. The relationship has a potential fault line, as carers are required by parents, and also by their own occupational and professional cultures to show affection for their young charges, a very intense form of emotional labour. However, the interaction is also a financial one, and love and money are at times in tension with each other. In this chapter we also consider the extent to which parents feel they can exercise their 'voice' and achieve a 'fit' of values between themselves and the carer concerning the care of the child. In **Chapter 7** we argue in accordance with Stephen Ball's (2003) earlier work that education is of prime importance to the middle classes. Educational success ensures social reproduction of the middle classes as a whole, and offers individuals access to the 'right' universities, and particular points of entry into the labour market. As such education is an investment against 'the fear of falling' (Ehrenreich 1989), a mechanism through which the middle classes can close themselves off from the working classes. In support of this argument we offer three types of settings with which middle-class families engage in search of social reproduction: nurseries, primary schools, and 'enrichment activities'. With regard to the first two we identify local differences between the middle classes of Stoke Newington and Battersea and the types of nursery and school with which they feel comfortable. Finally we draw attention to the role of the increasingly ubiquitous classes and drop-ins in music, sport, art, drama, and dance, and their role in 'making up the middle-class child'. In **Chapter 8** we review the issues arising from our study; in particular the role of childcare in attaining social advantage and in maintaining social divisions, the contribution of our work to the understanding of middle-class fractions, the effectiveness of a mixed-market system of childcare in satisfying families' needs, future developments in childcare policy and provision, and the view of contemporary gender relations which emerged from the research.

Chapter 2

Contextualizing the study

Making and maintaining arrangements for childcare is not a simple process; indeed it is more like a volatile chemical reaction that may or may not settle down into a stable state of equilibrium

(Uttal 2002, p. 5)

Introduction

This chapter describes two aspects of the context to the research. In the first section therefore we give the reader some factual information about the respondents in the research, where they lived, their occupations and their education. We also briefly describe our research method: how we identified the respondents, conducted the interviews and analysed the data. The second section has a more experimental tone; in it we try to place ourselves within the research and reflect on how different aspects of our own personal and professional identities affected how we understood the data.

The study, the respondents, the localities

We are interested in the developing and dynamic pre-school education and care market, and the interactions of parents with that market. We are focusing on professional and managerial middle-class users, sometimes referred to as members of the 'service class', a sizeable group of users in the formal childcare market place where the costs involved in accessing care are high, especially in London, the setting for our research. (The Daycare Trust's 2005 Childcare Costs Survey reports *average* London costs of £197 per week for a full-time place for a child under two. That is nearly £10,000 per annum.) The research involves interviews with a respondent group of 57 mothers and 14 fathers (from 59 families); 20 of the mothers were re-interviewed to track changes in their care arrangements. In addition 21 providers were interviewed including nursery staff, childminders and nannies. They were selected for interview from amongst those used by respondent families. Five relevant 'others' including LEA personnel and representatives of provider organizations were also interviewed. In total we conducted 109 interviews, involving 101 individuals.

Table 2.1 The respondents

Respondents	Mothers	Fathers	Providers	'Others'
Stoke Newington	30	8	6 group settings 5 home-based carers (3 nannies and 2 childminders)	2 LEA personnel 2 from provider organizations 1 nanny agency
Battersea	27	6	7 group settings 3 home-based carers (2 nannies and 1 au pair)	
Total	57	14	21	5

We located the research within two inner London areas: Stoke Newington in North London, and Battersea in South London (of which more below). The respondents were recruited in a number of ways: we placed adverts in child-friendly shops and cafés in the areas and in local area parenting newsletters and those of the National Childbirth Trust. We attended music groups and library story-time in order to make contact with parents. We also 'snowballed' from our original respondents to others. Our original contact was in all cases but one with the mother, but in the later stages of the project we sought to include fathers' views, by interviewing them alone or as part of the re-interview with their partners (as they chose).

Only two families interviewed did not meet the criteria for Goldthorpe's (1995) 'service class' membership, and these were held as additional to the sample referred to here. The parents were a singular group, being largely white (except three) and in heterosexual relationships (except one), and all were highly educated. Amongst the mothers 42 per cent (25) had a first degree as their highest qualification and 46 per cent (27) had post-graduate qualifications. Amongst fathers 51 per cent (30) had a first degree as their highest qualification, and 37 per cent (22) had post-graduate qualifications; 20 per cent of the mothers (12) and 31 per cent (18) of the fathers had studied at Oxbridge (see Tables 2.2–2.5).

Table 2.2 Mothers' further/higher education qualifications

	PhD (or several post-graduate qualifications)	Masters (or other post-degree diploma)	First degree	No degree but diploma	Other qualification	Total
Battersea	6	11	8	1	2	28
Stoke Newington	5	5	17	2	2	31
Total	11	16	25	3	4	59

Table 2.3 Fathers' further/higher education qualifications

	PhD (or several post-graduate qualifications)	Masters (or other post-degree diploma)	First degree	No degree but diploma	Other qualification	Total
Battersea	3	11	13	0	1	28
Stoke Newington	2	6	17	2	3	30*
Total	5	17	30	2	4	58

* One respondent is a single mother and we do not have data on her child's father

Table 2.4 Mothers' studies in Oxbridge universities

	Yes	No	Total
Battersea	8	20	28
Stoke Newington	4	27	31
Total	12	47	59

In terms of their schooling, the parent sample was fairly evenly split between those who had received state schooling and those who had been to at least one private school (usually secondary). There were two marked examples of area-based differences: 61 per cent (17) of the men in Battersea were educated at private schools and 39 per cent (11) at state schools compared with the women in Stoke Newington of whom 68 per cent (21) were educated at state schools, compared with only 32 per cent (10) in private schools. The Stoke Newington women were also the group least likely to have been educated at Oxbridge, and most likely to have a first degree as their highest educational qualification. These differences are comparable with our later observations about the characteristics of the middle-class populations of both areas, and specifically about their occupational positions (see Tables 2.6 and 2.7).

All the families had at least one pre-school child at the time of the first interview. Family size varied between one and three children, with the majority in both areas having two (see Table 2.8).

Table 2.5 Fathers' studies in Oxbridge universities

	Yes	No	Total
Battersea	8	20	28
Stoke Newington	10	20	30*
Total	18	40	58

* One respondent is a single mother and we do not have data on her child's father

Table 2.6 Type of school attended by the mother (includes primary and secondary schools)

	State only	State and private	Private, day school only	Private, also boarding	Total
Battersea	15	6	3	4	28
Stoke Newington	21	4	4	2	31
Total	36	10	7	6	59

Table 2.7 Type of school attended by the father (includes primary and secondary schools)

	State only	State and private	Private, day school only	Private, also boarding	Total
Battersea	11	4	8	5	28
Stoke Newington	13	4	8	5	30*
Total	24	8	16	10	58

* One respondent is a single mother and we do not have data on her child's father

We interviewed most parents in their homes with a small number choosing to be interviewed at their workplace. We asked them about their current and recent childcare arrangements, why and how they chose the care setting/carer, what they liked most and least about the arrangement. We asked what the children did whilst in the care setting and about the parents' relationship with the carer. Another theme was whether the mothers were in paid work or not and why they had made those decisions. Further questions focused on the division of domestic labour and childcare between the mother and father, their thoughts and plans for choosing a primary school, whether the children took part in any 'enrichment activities', and parents' perceptions of their local area.

All the interviews were semi-structured in nature and lasted between one and two hours. They were fully recorded, transcribed and loaded into NVivo, a computer software package designed to help with analysis and data management. Generally the parents were very forthcoming, but occasionally conversation about the children became very emotive, and we endeavoured to respond with sensitivity. As noted, we planned to re-interview a proportion of our sample to track changes in care as circumstances changed. In fact these

Table 2.8 Family size frequencies

	Families with 1 child	Families with 2 children	Families with 3 children	Total
Battersea	8	13	7	28
Stoke Newington	10	17	4	31
Total	18	30	11	59

interviews became very important in also allowing us access to fathers (in some cases) and to follow up and develop themes which emerged strongly from the first round of interviews (particularly the gendered division of domestic responsibilities and work/life balance).

The analytical work undertaken was of three main kinds.

1   We conducted search counts and categorizations using NVivo and an SPSS frame. By loading all the interview materials into NVivo we were able to identify, examine and count examples of particular practices or concerns or uses of language across the sample. For example, all references to 'luck' and 'chance', etc. could be traced; all references to the 'nightmares' involved in making childcare arrangements were collected and examined; all mentions of childminders, nannies and so on were gathered together for further perusal. This allows for a form of 'constant comparison' within NVivo codes (see Strauss 1987). The SPSS frame enabled us to identify and record the complex and changing childcare arrangements organized by the families and trace these back to the localities. The trajectory of each family's changing arrangements could thence be tracked, examined and compared with those of others.

2   Hand coding was conducted as a means to identify key themes and issues. Using Straussian techniques (Strauss 1987), this was begun early in the research process, and we built up a portfolio of themes and issues which was subject to continuing review and revision. Each transcript was coded separately, usually by more than one team member. Some transcripts were coded by all team members and codes were compared and discussed. In some cases detailed code notes were produced and discussed and some typologies were developed. Our forms of coding were similar but styles differed. Careful comparisons were undertaken within the data and a fine-grained examination of particular issues (e.g. social mix, mothering, gender roles, communication with providers, future planning) was conducted. These 'astringent' codes were typically discussed at length by the team and were the basis for writing. Most of the project writing was done by Vincent and Ball with one or other acting as lead writer for different topics.

3   We also carried out document analysis of provider publicity, and of local and national developments in the childcare market and a detailed content analysis of the *Nursery World* magazine. We collected publicity from all the providers we interviewed and others in the localities of the sample families. The families and providers were also located and marked on large-scale area maps – enabling us to see the use of space and the distribution of supply. We also collected policy documents on childcare issues. *Nursery World* provided a useful overview of the 'childcare industry'. All of these materials were treated systematically as well as providing general background reading for the research.

The localities

One of the aims of our study was to investigate the possibility of normative and relational differences between middle-class fractions; the research design was influenced in respect to this by the work of Tim Butler on the spatial distribution of the middle classes in London (e.g. Butler with Robson 2003). Using his detailed findings we identified Battersea and Stoke Newington as areas likely to offer an interesting contrast in middle-class populations with Battersea having large numbers of financial-sector professionals and managers, and Stoke Newington being home to more welfare/voluntary sector professionals and media workers. These assumptions were borne out in the sample as we indicate below.

The nub of Butler and Robson's argument is the importance of locality. They draw on Savage's work on the heterogeneity and diversity present within the middle classes (see Chapter 4), and consider how best to further understand the clusters of subtle differences and distinctions. Their valuable contribution to this debate has been to foreground locality.

> Savage's approach [to middle class fractions] which we broadly endorse ... ignores the issue of space and is not sufficiently sensitive to some of the nuances of difference within the middle class; many of which are expressed spatially ... Middle class people identify with neighborhoods where they perceive 'people like us to live'.
>
> (Butler and Robson 2003, p. 1792)

Butler and Robson write about the way middle-class individuals and groups, particularly those in dual-income households with children, have reacted to the effect of globalization on their lives generally and their careers specifically. The uncertainty that now affects some previously stable middle-class occupations, and even more importantly the *perception* of uncertainty, 'the basic insecurity of an increasingly flexible world' as Butler with Robson (2003, p. 24) put it, and resulting concerns about the reproduction and transmission of their social advantages, has contributed to anxiety amongst the metropolitan middle classes. In response to this, 'as [they] have increasingly lost a sense of place-based rootedness at work, they have struggled to replace these in their domestic and residential lives' (Butler and Robson 2003, p. 1791). Such middle-class groups, they continue, 'desire to build a local community within the global city that maps onto their particular set of values, backgrounds, aspirations and resources' (Butler and Robson 2003, p. 1795). As a result distinctive areas have been created, with particular 'styles' or characteristics, which reflect the 'lifestyle' differences within the middle class and which are attractive to different middle-class groups (Butler and Robson 2001, p. 2148). Place is then a dependent variable; local 'cultures' arise from class choices, but these choices are in part also driven by material concerns, such as house prices. What we have here is not a set of neat patterns but rather a concatenation of factors which have effects and consequences in terms of the realization of class, and class identities in particular settings.

We have responded to this, together with a focus on occupation, household arrangements, and to an extent, lifestyle, in the design and conduct of our study. As noted earlier, we have located the fieldwork in two distinctive middle-class localities in London: Stoke Newington in the north London borough of Hackney, and a less clearly bounded area in the south, mostly within the London borough of Wandsworth which covers parts of Clapham and Battersea, extending down to Balham, a triangle sometimes referred to as 'Nappy Valley', in acknowledgement of the abundance of families with young children in the area.

Stoke Newington and Battersea: perceptions of Stoke Newington by respondent mothers

There are whole swathes of the middle class who work in the media around here.

(Madeleine)

I wouldn't want to live anywhere else in London ... mostly because Stoke Newington is the closest I am going to get to San Francisco in England.

(Madison)

A bit of an artisty type of feel and it's very ethnically diverse, so that's what probably attracted me.

(Caroline)

We were squatters in our early days ... half of Greenpeace live around here, and half of Friends of the Earth live around here.

(Mia)

I notice the dirt and I notice, you know, the weirdos. But then we have fantastic restaurants, we have shops that are open all night making croissants.

(Connie)

Stoke Newington and Battersea: perceptions of Battersea by respondent mothers

[We] moved from a childless area to 'Buggy Jams'

(Margot)

Perfect for children – it's not called Nappy Valley for nothing

(Lynn)

Both people we shared [our nannies] with were accountants, they're all accountants round here ... Both of us are very committed to state education which is very unusual in this area ... It has changed, and obviously an awful lot of estate agents where there used to be shoe menders and things ... you can't buy proper food now really in the market so much as you used to, it's all olive stalls and basket making and things like that.

(Linda)

Well, all our neighbours are similar, in this little strip it's nice because everyone's similar minded. Even though they've mostly moved to be near Goldwater [School] ... it means the people here are close and friendly.

(Jill)

In their book *London Calling*, Tim Butler with Garry Robson (2003b) use ACORN (A Classification Of Residential Neighbourhoods) classifications of particular areas. These data give an indication of consumption and lifestyle patterns of people living in a particular postcode. Summaries are available on the website www.upmystreet.com. On the basis of these data (which include census and various market research/lifestyle data bases), 17 groups are identified, containing between them 56 specific 'Types' (see www.caci.co.uk/acorn). ACORN is regularly updated and the classifications have changed from those used by Butler and Robson. They identified the central Battersea area of 'between the commons' (as estate agents term it) as Type 20, 'gentrified multi-ethnic'. The 2004 data clearly acknowledge the area's increasing gentrification, with the predominant types being Type 13, 'well off professionals', and Type 15, 'affluent urban professionals'. For Type 13 the likelihood of children is high, unsurprisingly for an area which is part of 'Nappy Valley'. Among families categorized in Type 15, there is a predominance of young children under five years of age. These patterns are reflected in the respondents' descriptions of their localities. People of both types share a very high tendency to be interested in current affairs, and a very high likelihood of being educated at least to degree level. Both are in professional and managerial positions at work, with higher managerial/professional positions clearly dominant, particularly amongst Type 13. People categorized as Types 13 and 15 share many interests including theatre, classical music, opera, cinema, foreign travel, gourmet food, skiing, and reading historical works. Type 15, also to be found in Stoke Newington, provides a level of commonality between the two areas.

Conducting the same exercise with ACORN data in Stoke Newington (a larger geographical space than 'between the commons') results in two main classification types: Type 15, 'affluent urban professionals', and Type 18, 'multi-ethnic young'. The appearance of Type 18 suggests a lower level of affluence amongst these Stoke Newington families. Unusually for an area recently voted in a national Sunday broadsheet as the number one place to be a parent (Templeton 2004), the two Types predict the likelihood of being a parent to be low. However, children in Type 15 families are likely to be under five, which suggests that a proportion of families move out of the area as children get older. This accords with our data (although our families tended at least to start primary school in the locality). In other respects the three Types (13, 15 and 18) are similar in terms of their behaviour and preferences, indicating a certain broad commonality of interests across the middle classes, although there are differences related to income, as well as age and therefore position in the life cycle. Whilst our research respondents are all in their thirties and forties with children, Stoke Newington and Battersea also clearly attract younger professionals who can afford to live in those areas (many houses are converted into flats), and who appreciate their liveliness. People in the two Stoke Newington Types (15 and 18) share a likelihood of being in professional or managerial jobs, although for Type 18 the likelihood of being in either a higher or lower managerial or professional position is much more equal, whereas for Types 13 and 15, there is an overwhelming likelihood of being in a higher position. Those in the two Stoke Newington Types share a high or very high tendency to be interested in current affairs and to be educated to degree level or above. Additionally, they share a tendency to use public transport and to read the *Guardian* or the *Independent* (although Type 15 people may also read *The Times* or *The Financial Times*). People in Type 15 and Type 18 share an interest in sport and exercise, theatre and arts. A Type 18 person has a high level of interest in education and self-improvement, not so noticeable in the other two Types, but loses their marked interest in skiing and classical music. Indeed the interests of the three Types appear to become increasingly close to Savage's 'liberal ascetics' as we move up the scale (i.e. from Type 13 to 18) (Savage *et al.* 1992). (Chapter 4 contains more detail on Savage's classifications of the middle classes.) Below we comment on the occupational categories to which our respondent parents belong; we can see that there is a correspondence between the lifestyle descriptions offered by ACORN and the parents' forms of employment, with Stoke Newington families, especially the mothers, having slightly lower status occupations and the families being relatively less affluent.

Although Stoke Newington inhabitants are relatively less affluent than their Battersea counterparts, the majority of our respondents in both areas are from middle-class populations which fit into just two of ACORN's 17 groupings. Type 13 is part of the 'prosperous professionals' group, whereas Types 15 and 18 are 'educated urbanites'. Both broad groups fit into what ACORN refers to as 'urban prosperity', and in this the lives of our respondents are in strong contrast to other much less affluent groups living just a few streets away in Wandsworth and Hackney. Indeed Butler with Robson note that 'the visibility and influence [of the middle classes] far outstrip its physical presence – even in the most gentrified parts of inner London boroughs ... the middle class is rarely in a majority' (2003, p. 8). As a cororally, they report that despite a stated commitment to multiculturalism in some of their gentrified areas, the friendship groups of the gentrifiers were largely white and middle-class, leading to limited cross-class and ethnicity networks.

Thus Battersea and Stoke Newington appear to offer an interesting contrast of localities, one area that has been subject to long-term but gradual gentrification (Stoke Newington) versus the other that has experienced more recent, but quickly established change (Battersea). Butler and Robson chose Battersea as one of their research areas because 'we felt that "between the commons" in Battersea would approximate to the notion of a corporate indistinctive section of the middle class' (Butler and Robson 2003, p. 1797; see also Chapter 4). Butler also conducted research in Stoke Newington in the late 1980s.

> Stoke Newington was the centre of much of the counterculture of the early 1970s … alternative living seemed over represented here … By the 1980s, however, gentrification was in full swing, with prices rising rapidly, and Stoke Newington was losing its 'alternative-y' nature …
>
> (Butler 1995, pp. 194–5)

As we shall see, these qualities have not been entirely lost in Stoke Newington and we identified the area as one in which we might find a significant number of 'liberal/ascetic', welfare professional families, or 'postmoderns' (see Chapter 4).

Battersea residents are described by Butler and Robson as a 'well bounded and distinctive group … from very solid professional/managerial backgrounds … most likely to socialise with people like themselves … [who] display high levels of employment in self employed and private sectors' (2003, p. 1799).

> 'Between the commons' has become a carefully cultivated 'urban village' in which young professionals can conveniently educate their children, work in the metropolitan economy and enjoy the pleasures of central London before moving on to still more desirable parts of Wandsworth or the southern home counties.
>
> (Butler and Robson 2001, p. 2154)

In the central area of 'between the commons', the houses are mainly three- or four-bedroom Victorian terraces, restored in the 'original' style and extremely well maintained and often 'extended'. House prices have risen exponentially in the area over the last ten years, and currently the terraced houses go for £500,000–950,000. Thus the residents are strong in economic capital, and this can be seen in the type of shops and restaurants that flourish on the main thoroughfares, and the proliferation of private schools in the area. The respondents in our study who lived in Battersea, when asked what attracted them to the area, mentioned the presence of many other families with young children, the array of child-friendly activities that has developed to cater for families, and the 'good' schools. The latter, as we shall see, are especially important, as these families with pre-school children have an eye on their educational future. Butler with Robson (2003, p. 59) describe the area as 'clearly corporate/City country'. They note the large numbers of women and children out and about during the daytime, the proliferation of four-by-fours, the perception by residents that the area is safe, the striking homogeneity of the population in the immediate area of 'between the commons', and the invisibility of other more disadvantaged communities living just a few streets away. Their overall picture is one of an 'enclaved' or cocooned population, living in, but not of the metropolis. A light-hearted column entitled 'South London tribes' in a local magazine recently identified the 'Northcote Road housewife' (Northcote Road is the main shopping thoroughfare in the 'between the commons' area), describing these middle-class mothers as 'swarming round the fresh bakery stall, jamming doorways and insisting restaurants rearrange furniture to accommodate them … You'll see their slip knotted scarves are flecked with organic salmon puree and their eyes are tired' (Etherington 2005, p. 11).

Our respondents in Battersea also demonstrated a different occupational pattern to those in Stoke Newington. Just over half of the Battersea fathers (54 per cent, 15 individuals) and 18 per cent of the mothers (5 individuals) worked in the City, whilst only 3 per cent (1) of the Stoke Newington fathers did and none of the mothers. However 42 per cent of the Stoke Newington mothers (13) and 17 per cent of the fathers (5) worked in welfare professions or the voluntary sector, compared with 28 per cent (8) and 4 per cent (1) of the Battersea mothers and fathers respectively (see Tables 2.9 and 2.10).

Tables 2.11 and 2.12 show that 64 per cent (18) of the Battersea mothers were or had been in higher managerial and professional occupations, compared with only 29 per cent (9) of the Stoke Newington mothers. Thirty-nine per cent (12) of the Stoke Newington mothers were in lower managerial or

Table 2.9 Financial sector jobs in the City

	Mothers	Fathers	Total
Battersea	5/28 (18%)	15/28 (54%)	20/56 (36%)
Stoke Newington	0/31 (0%)	1/30* (3%)	1/61 (1.6%)
Total	5/59 (8%)	16/58 (28%)	21/117 (18%)

* One respondent is a single mother and we do not have data on her child's father

Table 2.10 Welfare and voluntary jobs only

	Mothers	Fathers	Total
Battersea	8/28 (28%)	1/28 (4%)	9/56 (16%)
Stoke Newington	13/31 (42%)	5/30* (17%)	18/61 (30%)
Total	21/59 (36%)	6/58 (10%)	27/117 (23%)

* One respondent is a single mother and we do not have data on her child's father

Table 2.11 NS-SEC classification of mother

	1.1	1.2	2	3	4	5	6	7	8	Information insufficient to classify	Total
Battersea	5	13	6	1	1	0	0	0	0	2	28
Stoke Newington	1	8	12	3	1	0	0	0	1	5	31
Total	6	21	18	4	2	0	0	0	1	7	59

NS-SEC classifications (using the 8-class classification)
Class 1   Higher managerial and professional occupations
              1.1 Large employers and higher managerial occupations
              2.1 Higher professional occupations
Class 2   Lower managerial and professional occupations
Class 3   Intermediate occupations
Class 4   Small employers and own account workers
Class 5   Lower supervisory and technical occupations
Class 6   Semi-routine occupations
Class 7   Routine occupations
Class 8   Never worked and long-term unemployed

Table 2.12 NS-SEC classification of father

	1.1	1.2	2	3	4	5	6	7	8	Information insufficient to classify	Total
Battersea	10	7	7	0	1	0	0	0	0	3	28
Stoke Newington	4	8	8	0	3	0	0	0	0	7	30
Total	14	15	15	0	4	0	0	0	0	10	58

* One respondent is a single mother and we do not have data on her child's father

professional occupations compared with only half that number in Battersea. In Battersea, 61 per cent (17) of the men were in higher managerial and professional occupations, compared with 40 per cent (12) in Stoke Newington. Those who were self-employed (see Tables 2.13 and 2.14) included business and education consultants in Battersea and, in contrast, artists, freelance translators and an aromatherapist in Stoke Newington.

All this points to a relatively less affluent group, working in slightly lower status occupations in Stoke Newington than in Battersea. As for the area itself, the Hackney Council website in 2002 described what it called 'Stoke Newington Village' as follows:

'Stokie' is becoming one of London's most fashionable areas; yet has retained its village atmosphere and unique identity ... Its array of open space and good local facilities give Stoke Newington more of a community feel than its Islington neighbour; ideal for families wanting to put down roots.

Table 2.13 Sectors of current or last employment (mothers)

	Public	Private	Voluntary	Self-employed	Other	Total
Battersea	12	11	0	4	1	28
Stoke Newington	14	4	5	6	2	31
Total	26	15	5	10	3	59

Table 2.14 Sectors of current employment (fathers)

	Public	Private	Voluntary	Self-employed	Other	Total
Battersea	3	15	1	9	0	28
Stoke Newington	4	10	4	10	2	30*
Total	7	25	5	19	2	58*

* One respondent is a single mother and we do not have data on her child's father

As with Battersea, our respondents mentioned the presence of other families with children as a factor that attracted them to the area, as well as the local, well-equipped park, the cafés and shops. However, there are differences between the two areas. House prices are cheaper in Stoke Newington: a small three-bedroomed Victorian terrace house is likely to sell for £350,000–400,000. The area has perhaps a more distinctive identity than Battersea. As can be seen it has a nickname, and until recently it hosted an energetic annual midsummer street festival. The original 'pioneers' of gentrification seem to have been welfare professionals who valued the area for its multiculturalism. Some features of that past identity remain in the idiosyncratic shops, and easy availability of alternative therapies. The area is less homogeneous than Battersea, more multiracial, and has a more urban 'edge' to it. Parents in our study often used the word 'community' when talking about the 'feel' of the area. This is perhaps what Butler with Robson refer to as a 'village in the mind' (2003), although this 'village' is actually a small area of relative white middle-class affluence in an extremely socially and economically deprived borough. Although most of our families lived in comfortable circumstances, and some in very spacious houses, it was only in Stoke Newington that we found instances of families living in clearly cramped accommodation, often small flats in converted houses. Again this is a reflection of the differences in families' financial capital across the two areas.

Thus we have argued here that in Battersea and Stoke Newington there are demonstrably different middle-class groups. However, having identified some differences between the two areas, we wish to end this section by noting that there are also similarities between the two localities and their populations. In this, we agree strongly with Butler with Robson that we should be wary 'of being too eager to map out patterns of closure and cohesion where they may only tenuously exist, and to bear in mind the possibility of important but easily overlooked commonalities among middle-class groupings' (2003, p. 43). In the following chapters (especially Chapters 4, 5, 6 and 7) we endeavour to identify shared practices, values and attitudes between the two areas, as well as pointing out differences. This raises the typicality of the areas in relation to other middle-class localities, especially those in other parts of the country. Butler with Robson (2003) identify what they term the 'metropolitan habitus' – a set of specificities embedded in the structure and experience of London living for the middle classes. Indeed this is a premise rather than a problem in terms of our research. What we are highlighting here is the specificity and peculiarity of locality. There is clearly a need for further research in different middle-class settings (see for example, Wynne 1998, and Bagnall, Longhurst and Savage 2003).

A reflexive account of the research process

In this final section of the chapter we make some brief observations about the research process. We are interested particularly in the way in which we as a research team responded differently to the interviewees' accounts depending on our own histories, lifestyles and values. We feel such attempts at reflexivity are a key part of the research process, as researchers 'acknowledge one's involvement in one's work and [achieve] some level of honesty in writing about that involvement' (Krieger 1996). Similarly Coffey argues that:

> Emotional connectedness to the processes and practices of fieldwork to analysis and writing is normal and appropriate. It should not be denied nor stifled. It should be acknowledged, reflected upon and seen as a fundamental feature of well-executed research.
>
> (1999, pp. 158–9)

Clearly the researcher is not separate from the act of doing research, but rather always positioned in certain ways in relation to the research, ways that need to be made explicit. The researcher's frameworks may be a result of his/her particular biography and/or a commitment to a particular theory or epistemology and need to be made explicit. As Bourdieu and Wacquant (1992, p. 225) argue, 'the most "empirical" technical choices cannot be disentangled from the most "theoretical" choices in the construction of the object'. Thus throughout this chapter we are attempting to produce an account of the research that is 'fallibilistic (Seale 1999), that is, it contains enough contextual and reflexive material for the audience to be able to judge how convincing it is' (Mason 2002, p. 192). A 'fallibilistic' approach to research is one that requires 'the willingness to imagine one's own results as fallible' (Seale 1999). It requires critical and reflexive practice. Reflexivity itself constitutes a 'self-conscious process of constructing knowledge' (Scott 2000, p. 58). We recognize however, that 'confessional' accounts, attempts to 'tell it like it was', are, despite appearances to the contrary, also selective and partial reconstructions of the research process, whereby we, as authors, remain the arbiters of what we disclose and what we do not, and of how such disclosures are framed and presented for public consumption. They play their own part in the claims made for plausibility and authenticity. In writing such accounts, 'we rarely resist the opportunity to invite sympathy, to paint a favourable portrait. Research is paved with deceits and conceits – the researcher's more than the researched' (Reay 1998, p. 3).

Much recent writing about the processes by which respondents are represented in qualitative texts has sought to tease out dilemmas that have arisen as a result of the 'crisis of representation'. Driven by 'the postmodernist turn' many qualitative researchers have been concerned to problematize the way in which much research seemingly presents 'real', detached and objective accounts of the social world, whilst paying little attention to the way in which such accounts have been constructed by researchers, filtering data through their own world view and their own sets of (theoretical and empirical) concerns (e.g. Cotterill 1992). 'Crafting authoritative texts is not an "innocent" objective process of representation, rather it is a highly subjective process of representation as we forge "our story of their story"' (Limerick *et al.* 1996, p. 450)' (also Coffey and Atkinson 1996, p. 72). Furthermore, as Coffey states, 'the re-recognition of the rhetorical features of lived experience, and therefore its representation, emphasized the narrative qualities of social life. That is, the ways in which 'reality' is textually constructed to render it socially meaningful' (1999, p. 142). In the light of this, we offer the following as a series of observations on our (differing) relationships with the respondents and the data.

Researcher–respondent relations are frequently discussed with reference to a 'powerless' group of research subjects (relative to the researchers), although Scheurich (1997) notes the ability of any interviewee to resist and reinterpret the goals, intentions and meanings of the researcher. The men and women we spoke to are however, for the most part, a privileged affluent group, articulate, confident, and we suggest, extremely capable of constructing rational, morally adequate narratives, and producing coherent, reasonable interview 'selves' for the purposes of that exchange (see also Jordan *et al.* 1994). Jordan and his colleagues comment that many of the 'public accounts' (Cotterill 1992, p. 595) of the middle-class couples they interviewed in their study of decision-making produced narratives that were somewhat bland: 'orderly, organised, reasonable and rather like each other' (1994, p. 56). They contrast this majority with the few (all male) respondents that were either 'heretics' (giving jokey, irreverent answers) or 'fundamentalists' (giving minimalist answers). Our women respondents fell between these two extremes; they were certainly neither bland nor dry in their accounts, but nor did they produce sustained heretical or fundamentalist accounts. The tone of their narratives was generally fairly organized, coherent and reasonable, but underpinned with the intense emotion – both positive and negative – that small children inspire. These emotions were for the large part 'managed' and only in one or two cases did we hear sustained accounts of very raw emotions engendered by motherhood. This management was, we suggest, part of a desire to present themselves as 'good mothers' in an encounter with a stranger (see Bagnall *et al.* 2003 for examples; Ribbens 1998, p. 33, talks of her own automatic moral monitoring, where the care of her own child is concerned).

Implicit in how we constructed, conducted and analyzed the research are many of the basic tenets of feminist researchers (see for example Smith 1988; Stanley and Wise 1993). As the majority of our respondents were women, we were extremely concerned to address women's lives in their own terms, and ground the theory used in their 'lived experiences' and everyday worlds. As Jane Ribbens notes, the question then arising is, 'how are we to conceptualise women's lives in ways that both value women's perspectives within the private sphere, yet also allow for critical insights from outside?' (1994, p. 33). Ribben's answer is that 'insider' and 'outsider' perspectives are necessary; we have sought to keep these two approaches in a (hopefully) productive tension.

The majority of the interviews feature (middle-class) women interviewing (middle-class) women. Although the matching of class (in broad terms) and gender does not automatically and necessarily mean that the respondents could 'place' the researcher,[1] we felt that the rapport evident from reading the transcripts meant that this had happened in most cases. Sophie Kemp, in particular, who did much of the interviewing, had an very informal, conversational style, and we feel that many of the transcripts tap into the tone and style in which these women discussed children, work, and childcare with their friends. We are not suggesting of course that we achieved the same level of intimacy in one or two meetings with the respondents, but rather that the issues we discussed offered them a familiar tone and style in which to respond. As interviewers we sought not to be friends but to be 'sympathetic listeners', aware that as researchers we would 'eventually walk away' (Cotterill 1992, p. 604). Some of the fathers were quite different in their style, and offered more rational and impersonal accounts of choosing and maintaining childcare (see Chapter 5). The ten interviews with couples produced a somewhat different dynamic again, involving exchanges between the parents which in some instances elicited divergent accounts of childcare responsibilities. We had hoped that repeat interviews would give us an opportunity to develop stronger relationships with respondents, but changes in the team meant that the original and repeat interviews were conducted by different researchers, although of course, the respondents were more familiar with the substance of the research the second time around.

Considered as a team, our individual relationships to the data and the respondents were both different and similar to those of other members, influenced by our gender, the differences in our lifestyles (the biggest being whether or not we had children), our embeddedness in the metropolitan middle classes, and the empirical and theoretical frameworks with which we worked. This raises the issue of the equivalence between interviews. Are the interviewers' styles so different that the respondents were offered radically different experiences which elicited different data? (The interviews would not of course be exactly the same because they were conducted as semi-structured interviews allowing the respondents to introduce issues that were important to them.) We consider below the differences and similarities in the interests, priorities and histories of three of the research team. We also addressed this issue in our analysis comparing across transcripts. Whilst not wishing to dismiss the differences, and on occasion, it is clear that a particular interviewer developed a particular rapport with a respondent, we believe that we maintained a fundamental commonality in how we explained the research to the respondent, the themes covered, how we conducted ourselves and the sort of rapport we endeavoured to build.

The data 'lived' with five people. Polly Radcliffe and Sophie Kemp were research officers on the project from its inception in November 2001. Polly moved out of London and academia in January 2002, and Sophie in April 2003. They conducted the bulk of the first round of interviews. We were joined by Soile Pietikanen who conducted the re-interviews and contributed towards the final analysis until May 2004 when the project ended. The original proposal and the idea for the project were the joint conception of Carol Vincent and Stephen Ball. Having one day each allocated to the project, Carol and Stephen carried out only a small amount of data collection. This, together with the changes in research officer which brought Soile into the project at a stage when the thinking about the data was fairly well-established, resulted in a somewhat traditional and hierarchical research team, whereby research officers collected the data which was then, in large part, analysed by the project's 'directors'. This was, to varying degrees, unsatisfactory for everyone concerned. We decided that one way of illustrating the various differences and similarities of approach was for Stephen, Carol and Soile to write a brief account of how we engaged with the data and the data collection process.

Carol: In terms of time, I was committed equally to another research project whilst we worked on the childcare research. In terms of emotional commitment however, there was little contest. I had co-written the proposal, and was deeply interested in the main themes of the middle classes, care for pre-school children, discourses around mothering, gendered divisions of domestic labour, and work/life balance. I have two young children of my own, am now middle-class (although as Stephen comments later, perhaps I share more affinities with the 'professional' middle class of Stoke Newington than the 'managerial' fraction ascendant in Battersea) and live in inner London. In some ways it was like researching my own life and that of my friends, and for a while whenever I talked informally about my own childcare, I would visualize my words reproduced as if on a page of transcript (with an omnipotent researcher's highlighting pen poised, to deconstruct my thoughts). That sense of being a subject, or even an object for manipulation in another's research, informed what will seem to many to be a self-interested stance. Namely, that I was keen to balance the necessary requirement to analyse critically, to take apart commonsense understandings, to show the aggregate effect of individual decisions, with a sympathetic and careful handling of the pieces of their lives handed to us by our respondents. This may seem an obvious ethical requirement of all research, but it seems to me that data gathered amongst the white middle classes are sometimes subject to a critique from which that sympathy is lacking. The structural differentials between researcher and respondent are absent, so the duty of care may seem less pressing.

A close identification with respondents can play a powerful role in the research process. Conle (2000) describes the 'resonance' which results when an element of experience described by a respondent 'reverberates with us so strongly that ... we are struck or hit emotionally in such a way that our awareness of the phenomenon is heightened and we can "see" things previously "unseen"'. An example of this was my growing appreciation of the complexities of the relationship between mother and carer. Lynet Uttal (2002), in the preface to her study of childcare choices amongst American mothers, states that as a mother she had always sought a degree of intimacy with the carers who looked after her own children and that she failed to understand why some of her respondents did not do so. In contrast, I became very aware of how difficult and fraught this relationship can be, and therefore why many mothers and carers manage and limit the possibilities for dissensus by conducting a working relationship which does not go beyond the necessary basics (although still held to be a 'good' relationship). The silences and absences in both the relationships we studied and in my own with carers became very clear to me. We have considered these issues further in Chapter 6. On the other hand, a close identification with respondents is also potentially problematic for a researcher. Lynet Uttal (2002) cites Lincoln and Guba (1985) on the subject. In situations one has personally experienced, tacit knowledge as well as professional knowledge is used in order to understand what is being studied. Tacit knowledge is always influential and therefore its impact needs to be considered (2002, p. xi). I had several arguments with Stephen in the course of writing this book about how we should (re)present the data, and often my position was I think affected by being a mother of small children, and his by being a man without children (which doesn't mean I was any the less likely to be 'right' of course!). One example was over the role played by guilt, anxiety and doubt in the transcripts of working mothers. To what extent did these emotions 'grind down' the mothers, or to what extent did they manage them? These debates served to challenge our original analyses, and make us both return to the data to further examine the respondents' words.

Soile: When I took over from Sophie on the childcare markets project I was a less experienced research interviewer. This affected the style of my interviewing compared with Sophie's. She had a very easygoing style about her inputs in the transcripts. She was skilled at accommodating the respondents' concerns alongside those we had highlighted. She asked follow-up questions very naturally and adeptly fitted her questions into the interviewees' narratives. I became more adept in these respects as I became more familiar with the project. Before starting the re-interviews, and during the first months of interviewing, I read carefully dozens of her transcripts. In light of the reading I decided it would be wiser to adopt a little more detached style that would allow me gradually to build confidence and avoid risk-taking. With hindsight, this meant that respondents interpreted the conversations with me probably in more formal or professional terms and consequently emotional encounters were rare. Sophie had reported that she had found some interviewees difficult to communicate with and in some other cases half way through the schedule her conversation sounded like old friends chatting away. There was probably less variation between my discussions with different respondents. It is impossible to say definitively what was lost or gained, and many of the mothers may have had preferences for one style or another. In one re-interview the mother told me afterwards she preferred the less personal style I had.

Carol and Stephen comment here on the similarities between their own class position and those of some of the respondents. My position was different from both of theirs. Each of the two European societies that formed the geography of my life prior to my recent move to England (Finland, Italy) has a distinct kind of social stratification; different markers convey particular class positions and practices. When I started the childcare markets interviews I had a very vague perception of what those markers might be here in England. Indeed, regardless of now having learned a great deal more about the class system in England, I am still unable to imagine how my interviewees might have interpreted my own class background, and the degree to which I may have been perceived as 'people like us'.

I did have one particular source of commonality with the mothers. When I was doing the fieldwork I was in late pregnancy with my daughter. However this appeared to help the mothers 'place' me (Mirza 1998) to only a limited degree. Interviewees often commented on my pregnancy and asked if this was my first child. On being told that I already had a two-year-old son they tended to react with surprise that seemed to be linked to my perceived young age. This does underline the point that the women in the research sample had children 'later' rather than 'earlier'.

The single issue that strikes me most now, a year after finishing the interviews, is the power relationships between the spouses as performed during the joint interviews. Women tended to do the main storytelling, sometimes asking small 'wasn't it?' questions and looking for eye contact with their partners to check on their agreement with the 'official' narratives. The interviews that I found slightly more challenging were those where partners were interviewed together and where tensions emerged in the interactions between them, as differences in the way they accounted for their childcare arrangements and choices became visible. There seemed, however, to be only one, perhaps two, instances where this seemed to suggest that there might be difficulties in the partnership and the official façade of the happy family was being transgressed.

Stephen: This research makes sense for me and in relation to me in a number of contexts. One is that I have been researching class issues for a long time and issues of family choice for a long time. I have been involved in studies of secondary school, FE and HE choice with both working-class and middle-class families. I have been interviewing parents and young people about such choices almost continuously since 1991. I came to this study then with the benefit and limitations of those experiences. I was also, during the study, finishing a book about the middle class and education markets (Ball 2003).[2] None of this could be erased from my head when thinking about this project. On the other hand, not having children of my own meant that this was my first meaningful encounter with issues of childcare. As a market I found childcare fascinating. It prefigures one future scenario for compulsory education – a mix of state, private and voluntary providers, highly segmented and stratified. The insights that the study provided into the educational life of families were also fascinating and theoretically important. As Bourdieu argues, 'Academic capital is in fact the guaranteed product of the combined effects of cultural transmission by the family and cultural transmission by the school (the efficiency of which depends on the amount of cultural capital directly inherited from the family)' (2004, p. 23). In other words, in order to come fully to grips with the distribution of academic capital we must look at the work done inside the family in the transmission of cultural capital and in particular 'in its earliest conditions of acquisition … through the more or less visible marks they leave' (2004, p. 18). OK, but I also come to the study, the families and the data, as a man with no children, and most of the interviewees were mothers. As things worked out I could not get involved in interviewing fathers, which is perhaps a pity. It is difficult to know what a difference absences make. I know being a man and being childless meant that some possibilities available to the rest of the team in their interviews were not available to me. Certain sorts of interactions were excluded but I was able to use my naïvety as a tactic in the interviews – and not a particularly contrived one – and ask for explanations. But reading the transcripts it is not apparent that all of my interviews are so very different from all of the others conducted by the women interviewers: some are; some are not. I did have other kinds of shared experience which I could deploy in the interviews which I will come on to in a moment. In many respects the interviews were easy; the respondents were articulate, self-aware and only too willing to take the opportunity to talk about their children. I did not have to work hard to make the interviews work. But in saying these things I am not trying to minimize the difference I made but rather that what that difference might be is not all that clear in the data.

The other important context is the setting, or rather one of them. I live in the Battersea research area and have done since 1991 – pre-dating most of the respondents. I moved from Southfields, not far away, in the early stages of gentrification in Battersea, and watched the road in which I live and the local high street change around me. The 'financial' middle class moved in, with their estate cars and four-wheel drives, their skips and house extensions. We acquired a Starbucks, three children's clothes shops, two children's shoe shops, a children's café and hairdressers. My mixed-class and mixed-race road became monocultural. Is there a slight antipathy in all this? To be honest, yes. Maybe I would be more comfortable in the 'professional' middle-class enclave of Stoke Newington. Certainly this sense of fractional difference that I felt personally may have fuelled my interest in looking for such differences in the data and I pursued some aspects of difference in the analysis but this did not work to obscure the other important commonalities across the localities and the fractions. There were also antipathies expressed by the some of the respondents, again mainly from the 'professional' fraction towards the 'financial' 'others'. But the differences I felt also served to produce a kind of ethnographic strangeness and a distancing from the respondents to whom I might otherwise have been too close, although on the other hand I was able to discuss the locality with them and recognize the places they referred to. Did my antipathies make me unsympathetic? Well, yes and no. There were things in the data that made me wince, but not that many, and only once during my interviews (I interviewed eight of the mothers) did I experience a sense of real class estrangement. My interaction with the women I interviewed was pre-eminently as mothers rather than as class agents. But the data, as it is with data, became increasingly more detached from the particularity of the people in the interview encounter. The people become in our account 'working mothers', 'new middle class', 'men with careers', etc. and indeed with five of us conducting the interviews most of the transcripts were of the words of people we had never met. And as it is with research, like them or not, I still regard 'my' data and 'my' sample with some affection. Nonetheless, I am left wondering whether my antipathies and resentment have actually made a difference in the analysis and reporting of the work – for it is not 'my' research, it is a team effort and as a team we have argued through our analyses and interpretations. But like Carol says, however I felt does not mean that I was not right anyway!

The conundrum which remains, perhaps, is whether this account of involvement and fallibility – and indeed the earlier more factual account of the project's numbers, and the respondents' social characteristics and locations – makes a difference to you as reader, either in how you read the research account which follows or in illuminating some kind of relationship between the substance of the confession and the form or content of the account. We are certainly not clear what that relationship might be or whether it is of any great importance. Our confessions may simply serve a kind of tropic function as, in relation to the authoring of the text, we became more human as the producers of the research, and thus as a result you are more or indeed less confident in the reliability and plausibility or our account.

Chapter 3

Childcare policy
International, national and local perspectives

If, in pursuit of higher rates of growth, economic policy makers seek to move people's time from the unpaid economy to the paid economy, the desired outcomes will not be achieved unless the full ramifications are recognized, planned and budgeted for. Ignoring the unpaid economy encourages the view, which does not accurately reflect even men's lives, that all time outside employment is a costless resource for economic policy to exploit

(Himmelweit 2002a, p. 54)

Introduction

In this chapter we discuss and illustrate the framing of families' childcare choices within aspects of national social policy, setting national and local patterns of possibility and constraint within a broad political, economic and social context. While we acknowledge the enormous progress made in childcare provision over the past ten years we identify a number of problems and omissions within the current policy approach. The chapter concludes with data on the local London markets as experienced by the respondents in our study.

International perspectives

In this first section we seek to locate childcare provision and policy in England within a broader international context, thus demonstrating the similarities and differences with other countries, and highlighting the particularities of English provision and the underlying discourses which support those patterns of provision.

Esping-Anderson (1990, 1999) argues that the welfare states of different nations are not 'merely passive by-products of industrial development; but have become 'powerful societal mechanism[s] which decisively shape the future' (1990, p. 221). His argument is that there are three ideal type welfare regimes in 'western' countries, although no one country displays all the features of the ideal type. The first is the liberal welfare state in which means-tested assistance, modest universal transfers or modest social insurance plans predominate. Entitlement rules for benefits for those who do not work are strict and claiming them is often associated with stigma. Thus for those who can afford it, welfare services, beyond the minimal, must be purchased from the market. The USA, Australia and Britain are seen as examples here (1990, p. 27), although as Esping-Anderson later notes, Britain was a late arrival to this category, an example of 'regime shifting' (1999, p. 86) with a period of neo-liberalism in the 1980s and 1990s after the social demo-cratic post-war years. The second regime type is more common in continental Europe, where the welfare state is strongly 'corporatist'; although the granting of social rights has never been strongly contested, the state has also preserved status differentials, thus limiting its re-distributive potential. There is notable support for traditional gendered divisions of labour, and family benefits encourage mother-hood. Esping-Anderson suggests Germany, Italy and Austria as examples (1990, p. 27), with France a more maverick member of this group. The third 'regime clus-ter', the social democratic welfare states of Scandinavia, sought a 'welfare state that would promote an equality of highest standards not an equality of minimal needs as was pursued elsewhere' (p. 27). Individual incomes are protected even if people do not work. However, because the costs to the state of individuals not working are so high, the state requires as full employment as possible. Thus in Sweden for example, the state provides universal childcare and the vast majority of mothers are in the workforce.

Esping-Anderson claims that welfare state structures are systematically linked to labour market outcomes and spends some time looking at rates of women's employment and sectors of employment to illustrate his argument.

> Welfare state policies may not explain the entire story, but differences in the provision of child care and related services will affect women's supply of labour and so will absenteeism programmes (how quickly wages are withheld when the employee is absent) and tax policy.
>
> (1999, p. 159)

However, the Anglo-Saxon countries with liberal welfare states also have rela-tively high rates of female participation in the workforce, but the direct effect of the welfare state on female participation is marginal. In many of these countries, including the USA and the UK, the market and voluntary sectors have stepped forward, certainly in relation to the provision of childcare ser-vices, and it is only within the last five years that this has been changing in the UK as state interest and then intervention in childcare has grown (see below; also Moss 2001). In his later work (1999) Esping-Anderson introduces a con-tinuum of 'familialisation'. A familialistic welfare regime is one that assigns a maximum of welfare obligations to the household; de-familialisation policies, on the other hand, lessen an individual's reliance on the family (1999, p. 45). It is clear that to date, the Nordic welfare states are the only ones where social policy is explicitly designed to maximise women's economic independence and de-familialise childcare:

> Welfare states have responded in radically different ways to the double challenge of women's employment and family instability. Active de-familialisation of welfare burdens in the social democratic regimes; essentially passive or at the most targeted assistance in the liberal, and a policy of sustained familialisation in continental Europe - much less in France and Belgium, much more in Italy and Spain.
>
> (Esping-Anderson 1999, p. 161)

This work has been extended with reference to childcare by other commentators. Ros Edwards (2002) cites Pfau-Effinger's work on notions of 'good' childhood as understood differently in particular welfare regimes. She contrasts 'the male breadwinner/female part-time carer provider' model (e.g. Britain, New Zealand, Switzerland and the USA) with 'Dual breadwinner/state childcare provider' model (eg Norway, Finland, Sweden). This means that even for those women who work, the carer is a mother substitute in the former category of welfare policy regimes. This is referred to by Edwards as 'familialisation' rather than 'institutionalisation' (also Leonard 1997, p. 38). As part of familialisation practices, care is organized by individual households and often in individual homes, rather than in state institutions. Even when in the more public realm of nurseries, familialisation leads to a preference for the small and intimate care setting.

It is possible that the UK, given the current policy focus on childcare and the Labour government's pledge of universal childcare (starting from three years of age), is again an example of a 'regime shifting', moving along Esping-Anderson's continuum away from familialisation towards de-familialisation. Nonetheless, it remains to be seen whether even if universal childcare becomes a reality the ideology of familialisation as the best form of care will loosen its hold to any marked degree across the population as a whole. In a variety of ways childcare provision, and the way in which it is used, affect and are affected by situated values of childrearing as well as the material circumstances of families.

Peter Moss argues that Britain's current and planned expansion of childcare offers a potential opportunity to move away from the dominant idea of care as 'creating substitute mothering for young children (with the implicit recognition that "real" mothering is obviously best, and something that women are essentially capable of doing) to an idea that children can manage, indeed thrive, in parallel but different environments' (personal communication 2004). The virtues of formal childcare are argued by the Italian pedagogue Loris Malaguzzi, describing the experience in the famous early childhood centres in Reggio Emilia:

> The children in Reggio understood sooner than expected that their adventures in life could flow between two places. [Through early childhood institutions] they could express their previously overlooked desire to be with their peers and find in them points of reference, understanding,

surprises, affective ties and merriment that could dispel shadows and uneasiness. For the children and their families there now opened up the possibility of a very long and continuous period of [children] living together [with each other], 5 or 6 years of reciprocal trust and work.

(Malaguzzi 1993, p. 55, cited in Dahlberg *et al.* 1999, p. 52)

In England there may be a substantial inconsistency in the dominant values of childrearing and the changing needs for provision. Moss suggests that

The problem, as I see it, is that parental employment practices have changed without yet a commensurate change in ideas about children and upbringing – we don't have a way of thinking about or talking about non-parental upbringing which does not take parental upbringing as a point of normative comparison.

(personal communication 2004)

The 'vision' of the role of childcare settings, their contribution to the holistic development of young children, their relationship with the child's home, and with compulsory schooling is of great concern to researchers and many practitioners (see, for example, Moss and Penn 2003 and Moss 2004b on children's spaces). National policy-makers however appear more focused on access, a stance that becomes apparent when we look at national policy in more detail.

New Labour childcare policy

As we noted in Chapter 1, childcare was overlooked in policy terms until New Labour came to power in 1997. It was understood to be a private family matter, too dull and apparently insignificant an issue for public policy. However, the rising number of mothers with small children who were returning or wanting to return to the labour market was a phenomenon that demanded a response: the 2004 Ten Year Strategy for Childcare cites figures of 64 per cent maternal employment (54 per cent in London), with 40 per cent of mothers working part-time (Her Majesty's Treasury 2004, paragraphs 2.33–2.34). In addition, and importantly, early years care and education is a productive policy area for New Labour. As we noted in Chapter 1, initiatives here can theoretically address several agendas: increasing social inclusion and in particular combating child poverty, revitalizing the labour market, and raising standards in education. The provision of childcare is seen as having the potential to bring women back into the workforce, thereby increasing productivity as well as lifting families out of poverty, moving families, and particularly allowing single parents to move from welfare to work, as well as modelling childrearing skills to parents understood as being in need of such support, and giving children the learning skills and experiences that will help them to succeed in compulsory education. As the Fabian Society concluded, 'Children and families are now more central to public debate than for many generations … It is now widely recognized that "investing early" is essential to any meaningful anti-poverty strategy' (Diamond *et al.* 2004, p. 1). It is worth noting however that these different agendas are only partially complementary.

We now turn to the changes the childcare sector has recently experienced, starting by considering the growth in the private sector, which the government has encouraged to develop as part of its strategy for increasing the overall number of childcare places. We then discuss in some detail the government's recent policy for childcare. Until recently, and as is the case in the USA (Uttal 2002) the private childcare sector has been the major beneficiary of the increasing number of women returning to work. In the period between 1990 and 2000 the UK day nursery market quadrupled, and day nurseries account for about 30 per cent of registered places. The day nursery market is worth £3.26 bn (Laing and Buisson consultants 2005a) and during 2004 grew by more than 20 per cent. The sector is currently experiencing a period of mergers and acquisitions among the larger operators, with Nord Anglia buying two other major chains, Leapfrog and Jigsaw, in 2004, making it the market leader in terms of size (102 nurseries and 10,318 places in March 2005). Asquith Court, the former market leader (114 nurseries and 6,847 places in March 2005), and Kidsunlimited also announced a merger over the summer of 2004 to form the Nursery Years Group. However this was then called off as being 'commercially unviable' (statement from Kidsunlimited, reported in *Nursery World* 11 November 2004).[1] Despite this, more mergers and acquisitions are likely to follow, resulting, eventually, in perhaps four or five major players dominating the market, paralleling the history of the residential care sector (although independent small businesses are unlikely to completely disappear; currently more than 40 per cent of the market belongs to small businesses offering 40 places or fewer (Laing & Buisson Consultants 2005a)). Currently then, the private day nursery sector remains a competitive, fragmented market. Providers with three or more nurseries account for only 9–15 per cent of places, depending on the source of figures (compared with 33 per cent in the residential care market), although Laing & Buisson Consultants (2005b) comment that 'for-profit nursery groups (major providers) are gaining market share and this trend is set to continue'. The voluntary sector is larger and more diverse than the private sector, and is also ready to expand (Curnow 2005b). The Pre-school Learning Alliance, for example, currently supports 15,000 community pre-schools in England. Over half of these are sessional pre-schools, offering a three-hour session.

There are clearly also some tensions emerging between the goals of the Ten Year Strategy and the commercial interests of private providers. Currently, private sector providers, particularly those outside London, are complaining that their viability, in a period of falling birth rates, is further at risk from government funded Sure Start initiatives scooping up the limited numbers of children and staff in particular localities (Vevers 2004b).[2] The plans to extend maternity leave may also ease demand. In a conference in early 2005, William Laing, the director of Laing & Buisson Consultants, reported that two-thirds of private nurseries saw the government's early years initiatives as a threat, and only one-quarter as an opportunity. In particular, capital costs were quoted as a major factor which made it difficult to 'compete' with maintained provisions. And while some providers are keen to engage in partnerships with local authorities, through the Neighbourhood Nurseries Initiative for example (which subsidizes capital costs), others are wary of the increasing regulation and 'management' of the childcare market (Laing 2005). Even so, the business property agents Christie and Co. reported in a promotional leaflet in the spring of 2005, that 'The year 2004 proved to be a phenomenal year for care property transactions … and … a surfeit of buyers across all market sectors and increased activity by financial investors'. Private equity investors in particular clearly see the nursery and other care markets as good investments.

As for state provision, through the National Childcare Strategy (DfEE 1998) and the new Ten Year Strategy (HMT 2004), 'New Labour is committed to affordable, accessible, good quality childcare' (HMT 2004, p. 1). This is to be achieved through a plethora of initiatives, particularly directed at disadvantaged areas and lower income families. However, the rhetoric is increasingly of universal childcare (as evidenced in Prime Minister Tony Blair's speech to the 2004 Labour Party Conference, Vevers 2004c), with services being provided through Children's Centres (integrated services on one site eventually planned to be in every local community, but initially in the most disadvantaged areas).[3] The pace of expansion quickened markedly in 2004. As part of the Spending Review, the Chancellor announced that 2,500 Children's Centres will be open by 2008, and the 2005 Labour Party manifesto promised 3,500 Children's Centres by 2010 ('a universal local service', Labour Party 2005, p. 75). This is likely to be based on a 'graduated model' ranging from a 'full offer' in the 30 per cent most disadvantaged areas to a 'universal offer' in the 30 per cent most advantaged areas.[4] The Daycare Trust noted that 3,500 centres across England would mean one centre for every 800 children under five (Vevers 2005a, p. 5). The DfES five-year plan published in 2004 also talks of a vision of integrated 'educare'. The emphasis following the Children Act 2004, and the policy programme, *Every Child Matters*, is clearly on one stop provision drawing together a range of health, education and welfare and care services available eventually to all families. There is, of course, a considerable body of literature on the difficulties of inter-agency collaboration. (For one recent review, see Campbell and Whitty 2002, and an account of the successes of one Sure Start local programme, Bagley et al. 2004.) The umbrella for these many projects is Sure Start[5] which now incorporates Children's Centres and the Neighbourhood Nurseries Initiative (designed to bring affordable care to disadvantaged areas). The future of Sure Start is however contested (see Glass 2005; Hodge 2005) but it seems clear that local programmes will be wound up within the next two years as Children's Centres appear. Glass (2005) asserts that 'little [of the Sure Start philosophy and ways of working] will remain but the brand name'.

The Ten Year Strategy of December 2004 (HMT 2004) announced Labour's key proposals. The strategy takes account of earlier criticisms that Labour's plans were directed primarily at adult workers rather than children, by emphasizing the benefits of pre-school education for children, and acknowledging 'a policy that gives too much emphasis to helping parents work could come at the expense of the needs of children' (HMT 2004, paragraph 2.4). The strategy lays out plans for the extension of paid maternity leave to nine months from 2007 with a planned extension to twelve months by 2010. Some of that leave may be transferable to fathers. Children's Centres should number 3,500 by 2010 (one in every 'community'), although they will be at their most numerous and most extensive in disadvantaged areas. Three- and four-year-olds will receive a phased extension of their free provision up to 15 hours a week (for 38 weeks a year) by 2010, with an ultimate goal of 20 hours a week. There is no mention of universal provision for one- and two-year-olds however. The government has also made tax credits available to lower income families to enable them to access the private and voluntary sectors ($£175$ for one child and $£300$ for two in 2005), and from April 2005, an extension of the childcare voucher scheme offered working parents in participating companies income relief on the first $£50$ they earn each week. With regard to planning provision and ensuring well-trained staff, the local authorities have been given the role of developing and supporting local provision. There will be a Transformation Fund from 2006 which will contain $£125m$ to 'help raise quality and sustainability'. A new training and qualifications structure is already being planned. $£5m$ is to be invested in pilot schemes in London in recognition of the capital's particularly high childcare costs.

In recognition of the government's focus on and investment in childcare, the Chancellor Gordon Brown was hailed as a 'childcare champion' in 2004 by the pressure group and childcare charity the Daycare Trust. However, concerns have been expressed in relation to funding, the timescale of the expansion, and staff recruitment and training (Vevers 2004a, p. 10; National Day Nurseries Association (NDNA) 2004). Affordability is likely to remain as a stumbling block to access. Even with the various subsidies and funding streams in place, childcare costs are still high, especially in London, with parents bearing 75–85 per cent of the costs.[6] The *Guardian* (27 January 2005), reporting the Daycare Trust's Childcare Costs 2005 survey, noted that during 2004 the costs of childcare in the UK rose 'over three times the rate of inflation' (5.2 per cent as against a CPI of 1.6 per cent) with parents in London paying $£197$ per week on average for a full-time nursery place for a child under two, compared with an average of $£141$ per week across the country as a whole. A full-time place with a childminder now averages at $£127$ per week or $£157$ in the south-east. Another recent survey by the Daycare Trust into the impact of the childcare element of the Working Tax Credit on parents and childcare providers in the capital found that the average cost of childcare in London is 'significantly' higher than the rest of the country, meaning that even with tax credits, childcare is unaffordable for many parents (Daycare Trust 2004b). The Ten Year Strategy (HMT 2004) signalled a rise in the childcare element of Working Tax Credit (WTC) up to 70 per cent (80 per cent from April 2006) of childcare costs up to a ceiling of £175 a week (note that the ceiling is less than the London average for a full-time nursery place for a child under two). However, this payment still excludes informal care and take-up is low (Howard 2004). In 2005, the Daycare Trust reported that the average payment through the childcare element of the WTC was £49.83 a week (Daycare Trust 2005b). Tax credits were heavily criticized by two 2005 reports published on the same day, one by the parliamentary ombudsman and the other by the Citizens Advice Bureau (CAB). Both were heavily critical of the tax credit system – which the CAB described in its press release as 'complex to understand and administer' and issuing 'incomprehensible and contradictory award notices' – as well as the Revenue's stringent attempts to recover overpayments (see CAB 2005). Duncan et al. (2004) also cite Hilary Land's argument (2002) that childcare provision, unlike school education or healthcare, is not provided as a free universal service, and thus 'meaningful choice' (Alakeson 2004; Collins and Alakeson 2004) is unavailable to families with lower incomes.

Another common criticism (which the government's proposals will address when they reach fruition) is that childcare options currently depend on where you live. London, our research suggested, was a 'seller's market'; the 2005 Daycare Trust Childcare Costs survey noted that 65 per cent of local childcare information services said parents were reporting difficulties securing the care they wanted (Daycare Trust 2005b). However, as we noted earlier, there are some very recent signs that some providers even in inner London are now beginning to struggle to maintain occupancy levels.

There has also been some concern over Sure Start's targeting of the most disadvantaged areas, the criticism being the same as that for any area-based initiative: families in poverty are also to be found outside the designated areas. One recent example was provided by a street in Newham in London, which was divided by a Sure Start boundary. As a result, services were available to families on one side and not the other. However, the council succeeded in integrating various funding streams and thereby expanding services to all parents within the borough (Curnow 2004).

There are particular difficulties involved in expanding access while maintaining or raising standards of care. The recent BBC programme *Nurseries Uncovered* (August 2004) dramatically illustrated that in three apparently reputable care settings, the quality of carer–child interaction and the levels of hygiene both left a lot to be desired. The undercover reporter found young children, toddlers in some cases, being treated with little dignity by some staff. The issue of staffing in the sector is a crucial one, as acknowledged by the Ten Year Strategy (HMT 2004, e.g. paragraphs 3.34–3.35). There is already a problem with recruitment and retention, as the young women who traditionally make up the bulk of the caring workforce can find better paid employment elsewhere. Presumably in recognition of this, Ofsted now allows providers to count 17-year-old trainees in staffing ratios (Evans 2004). Working with young children is exhausting and draining. Yet nursery assistants in the private sector in 2003 received an average starting salary of £4.50 an hour, going up to £4.80. Qualified nursery nurses earned £4.92, going up to £5.30. Even nursery managers' top rates of pay were little over £8 an hour.[7] Unsurprisingly, there are currently recruitment difficulties, especially at the more senior levels with Sure Start research reporting that 79 per cent of settings have difficulties in recruiting supervisors.[8] As the number of nurseries has nearly doubled in the last five years, the need for new staff is intense. Private providers are concerned that their senior staff members are being attracted away by the higher salaries on offer in the newly expanding state sector. Sure Start estimates that between 175,000–180,000 new staff are needed between 2003–6. Concerns have also been raised about the levels to which staff are trained and the need to professionalize the childcare workforce. Lisa Harker of the Daycare Trust argues that the focus of initiatives needs to be the substance of the child's experiences. 'We have chosen to go down the route of "inspecting out" poor quality, rather than investing in a highly trained workforce that can be depended on to deliver optimal experiences for children.'[9] She draws attention to New Zealand where the government has recently embarked on its own ten-year plan to improve the quality of its childcare provision, by setting a target of 100 per cent teacher-trained workforce by 2012 (Harker 2004). Outcomes here are currently uncertain, as a consultation process on the childcare workforce is under way (see Children's Workforce Strategy, DfES 2005), but the Ten Year Strategy (HMT 2004) recognises the need for improving the training of professionals, particularly in the private sector (paragraph 3.4), which will include increasing the graduate workforce (paragraph 6.8).

Peter Moss develops Harker's point further, arguing strongly for the importance of having a well thought-out answer to 'two critical questions. What is our image or understanding of the child? What is our image or understanding of institutions for young children?' (2004b, p. 2; see also Chapter 8). Clearly our different images and understandings of the child produce different ways of providing services and working with children. Moss presents a strong case for understanding institutions for young children as 'children's spaces', spaces where children are understood holistically, 'the child with the mind, body, emotions, creativity, history and social identity' (2004b, p. 21). Such a vision goes 'beyond childcare' denoting as it does 'an image of "childcare" services as private producers selling a product "childcare" to individual consumers' (2004b, p. 21). It is not clear whether the government, focusing on encouraging adults back into the labour market and producing children geared up for the performative world of primary school, shares Moss's vision, nor indeed has any other clearly thought out ideas about the substance of the children's experience in Children's Centres, beyond the rhetorical mantras of 'quality' and 'educare'.[10] Glass (2005) makes the same criticism in relation to Sure Start, identifying the growing thrust of the government's drive for childcare: to get parents back into the labour market. He notes:

> the early Sure Start documents make very little reference to 'childcare', in the sense of somewhere where children can be looked after to enable their parents to work; it was all about child development ... [However] Sure Start, originally a child-centred programme, became embroiled in the childcare agenda and the need to roll out as many childcare places as possible to support maternal employment.

The Ten Year Strategy (HMT 2004) confirms the recognition from the Labour Party that childcare is a public good, but for most families it is still treated as a private good, something individual parents find for themselves and purchase. As in other areas of education and welfare, New Labour's emphasis is on the individualization of responsibility, based on a notion of individual families sifting possible childcare options (unhindered by concerns with affordability, availability or quality) in order to make an appropriate choice. This is a precursor of the choice process that New Labour sees parents as unproblematically conducting in order to find primary and secondary schools. Our own research demonstrates the private *and* gendered nature of these choice-making processes, understood in the UK solely as a problem of management for individual women (Grace 1998). For childcare is still seen as 'allowing' women, rather than parents, to enter the labour market. It is mothers who return to paid work who have to find care, often pay for it, and then manage the two contrasting locales of home and paid work (see Chapter 5).

Another fundamental issue is that many families, particularly working-class and some black and minority ethnic families prefer informal care, seeing formal childcare arrangements as not offering the 'same degree of flexibility, trust, reciprocity that informal childcare arrangements can and do' (Daycare Trust 2003a, 2003b; Lewis 2003; Land 2002; Scottish Executive 2004; Wheelock and Jones 2002). There is a distrust of leaving young children with 'strangers' which is unlikely to be diminished by programmes such as *Nurseries Uncovered* or the negative media publicity of summer 2004 suggesting that long hours in nursery care lead to emotionally damaged and behaviourally disruptive children, (e.g. 'Are nurseries bad for our kids?' (Bunting 2004), although prominent coverage was also given to the more positive findings of the EPPE project (Effective Provision of Pre-School Education), emphasizing the all-round benefits for children of good quality pre-school experience (Sylva *et al.* 2004)). The preferences of many parents may be being overlooked by the rush to expand nursery provision at the expense of other alternatives. This seems to have been recognized at least partially by government plans to extend paid maternity leave. We do not wish to debate the merits of day nurseries here, but rather to note the remarkable absence of parental voice in the recent expansion of childcare, a point to which we return later.

Research on choice, such as that reported here and that of Simon Duncan and colleagues (e.g. Duncan *et al.* 2003; Duncan and Irwin 2004), shows that parental decisions around childcare are a complex mixture of practical and moral concerns; social relations are as least as important as economic relations. Duncan (2005) supports the point made by Glass (cited earlier) when he argues that childcare policy sees care in economic terms as a mechanism to allow the mother to work. Ball and Charles (2003) make a similar point. In their paper analysing policy discourses around childcare in Wales, they identify the dominance of a 'role equity discourse' which couples childcare with paid work, thereby resonating with a liberal discourse of equal opportunities and economic efficiency, aiming to allow women to operate in the workplace on equal terms with men (Ball and Charles 2003; Marchbank 2000). Duncan and colleagues argue that most families do not, indeed can not, share this view of themselves as purely actors in the labour market, a stance they term the 'adult worker model'. This is a highly limited model which would allow 'little consideration of the wider social, moral and emotional components of parenting or childcare' (Duncan *et al.* 2004, p. 255). Thus they suggest that Labour's childcare policy is in its genesis, a 'rationality mistake' (Duncan *et al.* 2004, p. 256).

> People do not act in an individualistic economically rational way. Rather they take such decisions with reference to moral and socially negotiated views about what behaviour is right and proper, and this varies between particular social groups, neighbourhoods and welfare states.
>
> (ibid.)

Furthermore, as signalled already, research on childcare (e.g. Duncan *et al.* 2003; Duncan and Irwin 2004; Holloway 1998; Mooney *et al.* 2001; Himmelweit 2002b; Uttal 2002) demonstrates that

> it is not just a question of the quantity of childcare but also of its quality and nature, and these judgements about quality and nature will vary socially and geographically. The mere provision of childcare is not adequate as a policy response to the problems of combining caring for children with employment,
>
> (Duncan *et al.* 2004, p. 263)

Whilst we would argue that the government's planned expansion of childcare, 'the new frontier of the welfare state' as the Prime Minister termed it, is too major an intervention to be described as 'mere provision', Duncan *et al.*'s argument points to some central issues in the future development of childcare.

It is clear that the current composition of the market in childcare is likely to be altered if the government's proposals on 'universal' childcare reach fruition. A quasi-market in childcare, similar to those in education and health, may one day be the result, or more optimistically Children's Centres may provide 'a bridgehead for introducing a more social democratic orientation into early childhood policy, holding out the prospect of integrated and inclusive centres as basic provision for all young children' (Moss 2004a, p. 633). That seems a long way ahead. At the moment, given the 'extraordinary diversity in existing patterns of provision' (Randall 2004, p. 4), the operation of local markets is key in determining parents' choice of and use of childcare (Harris *et al.* 2004). Thus, we aim in the remainder of this chapter to give some sense of the 'lived reality' of the childcare market as experienced in our two research areas in London.

A peculiar market

These areas both have very diverse forms of provision, and in Chapters 6 and 7 we briefly discuss some characteristics of the care settings and providers. The most common form of group care in Battersea and Stoke Newington (as used by our respondents) was private sector independent nurseries. The major chains were not represented in the heart of either of the areas we studied.

We focus here on how the formal childcare market works in the two research settings, and we refer to this as a *peculiar market*. The childcare market is peculiar we suggest in a number of different ways. We identify seven here. It does not function in the way that market theory suggests; the services required by consumers are complex and unusual; it is a market suffused with emotion; it is provider-driven; it is a highly gendered market; it is a segmented formal market with a large informal, unregulated sector, and in parts of the market the parents – usually consumers on behalf of the child – become either, in the case of parent-run co-operatives, providers, or, in the case of nannies, employers. We elaborate on these points below.

Our first point is that the childcare market just does not work like markets are supposed to. As a practical market it is very different from a market in theory – and indeed it is a very inefficient market. Second, it is peculiar in as much that the services which are required by consumers are complex and unusual. As our respondents unanimously see it, they want 'safety, happiness and love'. They are willing to pay, in part for an emotional engagement: 'You want someone who will kiss and cuddle them' (Grace, B (Battersea)) and in part for a sense of security, someone you can 'trust'. This is a market which involves putting a price on things beyond price: 'you can't put a price on the safety and happiness of your child' (Grace, B). This is, in a sense, an impossible market. The financial exchange is inadequate as a way of representing the relationships involved, a point to which we return. Trust is at a premium, and doubt, anxiety and guilt abound. It is a market that rests on multiple ambivalences. Our consumer data, interviews with parents, mainly mothers, are *infused* with the language of emotions. That is with expressions of fear, doubt and guilt around the central issue of paying to replace direct parental responsibility for childcare – 'entrusting your child to someone is a huge thing' (Grace, B) – it means in effect giving your child away, in some cases, 'to a complete stranger' (Abby, SN (Stoke Newington)). The emotions involved here are complex and difficult (see Pratt 1997, pp. 168–9), especially those which set the needs or best interests of the child as against the needs of the mother or parents. 'I wouldn't want to be sort of full-time, it sounds awful, but just caring for children all the time, I think it's important to have your own time' (Alice, B). These ambivalences and the attendant feelings of guilt are particularly acute for mothers returning to work, and particularly if the child is 'too young' (Jo, SN; Angie, SN; Rosy, SN); 'I felt very guilty, felt unsafe a little bit, was not quite sure what was happening at home' (Margot, B); 'She was 4 weeks old ... I still feel guilty about it' (Madeleine, SN); 'I occasionally felt guilty that I had left her, you know especially on mornings she does not want to go ... but I know she's happy' (Trisha, B); 'I still feel really guilty that [daughter's] been damaged, you know, that she didn't have the sort of love and stability like [son] has had' (Diane, B); and in the face of this some 'just couldn't do it' (Jo, SN), although others, a small minority, were adamant that they 'don't have any of the guilt thing' (Monica, B).

While unsatisfactory arrangements were terminated and changed, it is perhaps not surprising that positivity is strong in this field of choice; 'good' childcare receives high praise, and maybe this is an important aspect of the justification of choice – self-reassurance. Anything less than good is more difficult to manage and justify emotionally but there were occasions when less than satisfactory arrangements had to be put up with. 'There are ideals that you have for your children and what you actually end up with is very different, very different' (Kathryn, B). What we are trying to stress here is the unstable mix of necessity and emotion that is invested in the market relations of childcare which sometimes confront one another in having to 'sort of make do' (Juliet, B); as this mother explained 'there are things about [nursery] that are very good and things I'm not so happy with ... I would much rather go to a smaller one ... [but] for us a big advantage is the flexibility'. The need to compromise is exacerbated for some families by the impossibility of finding the 'right' kind of care in the childcare market: 'if you really need childcare you turn a blind eye. And I think that's what these people [unsatisfactory carers] depend on ... you have to compromise' (Connie, SN) (see below on supply and demand). In part then compromises are made in relation to what is available in the market: 'you lower your sights ... getting childcare for three children particularly part-time is almost impossible' (Kathryn, B). But also we must not give the impression that all these middle-class families had the same level of disposable income. For some families, it is the cost of care that makes the achievement of an ideal care situation impossible: '[daughter] had a bit of a rotten time actually ... but it's money' (Juliet, B). While these are relatively affluent professional families there are still considerable income variations among them and the cost of their childcare is a source of constant complaint (see below for more on cost).

Third, as should be evident already, this is a market, as Lane (1991, p. 77) put it, 'saturated with emotions'. Emotions are a key aspect of response to the forms of provision on offer. Both positive choices and rejections are usually based on a mix of rational and emotional criteria and typically determined by what is described as 'gut instinct' or 'gut feeling' (Mary, SN). 'I was very wary of it at the start, once you actually meet people you realise that your gut instinct [kicks in] ...' (Elsa, SN). People or places 'seem' or feel right or wrong: 'Teddies gave me not a good feeling' (Monica, B), where the 'heart sank' (Linda, B). This can be a reflection of class or cultural affinities (or dissonances) but is infused with affective judgements – 'how the place felt really' (Rachel, SN). In the case of nannies or childminders, mothers talked about finding people they 'instantly liked' (Katy, SN) or who were 'horrible' (Elsa, SN). But all of this is 'full of doubt' (Grace, B) and can leave the mother feeling 'traumatized' (Connie, SN). The most commonly used term in the interviews to describe the making of childcare arrangements was 'nightmare' – a term which referred to both the practical and emotional demands involved. All of this is beyond the rational. Rationality and calculation are totally inadequate to describe choice here which ultimately rests on a 'leap of faith' (Isabel, B). The key point is 'you're having to make assumptions about people on very little information' (Kathryn, B). The processes involved here are far removed from the concept of market rationality, with its assumption of 'a kind of emotional neutrality' (Lane 1991, p. 58), that is in this case 'totally unrealistic'. Choice of childcare is both very rational and very emotional, as we shall see. Indeed for many families difficult compromises are involved which trade off emotional and rational responses to the market around both sensitivity to price and questions of access and availability. Nonetheless, these compromises are unevenly distributed in relation to the ability to pay. Also as Lane argues, against economic orthodoxy, but again appositely in this peculiar market, the 'final goods' here are 'satisfaction or happiness and human development' (1991, p. 3); although as suggested already, parents are not, indeed can not, be totally unconcerned about efficiency, utility and cost.

Fourth, there is little evidence of 'consumer sovereignty' in these local London markets, partly because of shortages on the supply side, and partly because the consumer is often in a position of relative ignorance in relation to forms of expertise which are part of the purchase of services. As one of our pilot provider respondents saw it: 'Parents are for want of a better term a captive market' (nursery director). He went to describe the providers as 'price-makers' and was critical of what he saw as excessive profits being made by some nursery chains in London. 'Economic theory asserts that producers' behaviour will reflect the nature of the market in which they operate ... A further common assertion is that the strength of competition will be positively correlated with the number of providers in a market' (Davies et al. 2002, p. 93). In both respects, based on the testimony of parents, we should not expect the childcare markets in our two research localities to be particularly responsive or efficient. While, compared with other parts of the country, there is a great range and diversity of provision in these two localities, there is still an inadequate supply overall. Prices are high, as we have already indicated. The shortage of supply applied to nurseries, childminders and nannies. State provision was unavailable to the families in Battersea and heavily oversubscribed in Stoke Newington. The transcripts were littered with very similar complaints and amazement about the difficulties involved in arranging childcare: 'couldn't find a nursery place – waiting lists' (Grace, B); 'It's a seller's market for childminders' (Madison, SN); 'they were fully booked' (Marie, SN); 'the nurseries were full' (Isabel, B); 'I had his name down before birth' (Lynn, B); 'There just aren't many childminders, they are difficult to find' (Mia, SN); 'private nurseries were full ... simply not enough ... waiting lists as long as your arm' (Elsa, SN); 'I was in the market too late at six months pregnant' (Nicole, SN). The families in both localities were unanimous that it 'sounds like a lot of choice but there isn't' (Margaret, B). Indeed, when the mothers talked about 'competition' they did not mean among providers but between choosers – 'everything's so sort of competitive around here' (Grace, B); 'you always hope they will give you preferential treatment on the waiting list because you had a child there before, because it's so competitive' (Madison, SN); 'finding the right childcare is very competitive' (Rachel, SN); 'everything is so competitive around here' (Alice, B). (As we noted above, there may be signs that this is beginning to change in inner London with recent increases in supply soaking up demand.)

The shortage of supply was linked by a number of the mothers to the attitude of providers and a market 'complacency'; 'it was a humiliating experience ... the way they dealt with me ... someone was going to phone me back they never did' (Rachel, SN); 'take it or leave it ... you got the feeling that they couldn't really care whether you went there or not because they knew they had ten more people waiting' (Alice, B); 'they're inflexible ... it's sign up with us otherwise you go somewhere else' (Jean, SN).

> I found them a bit complacent because they're obviously so used, this is the trouble round here, all the schools and everything, they're so used to having people queuing at the door, you tend to get shown round in batches, they're so sure they're always going to be full for years to come
>
> (Alice, B)

This mother went on to say, about the nursery she eventually found a place at, 'I think because it was new they made a lot more effort to be welcoming'.

These accounts of market complacency were confirmed in our interviews with providers. They also talked about over-subscription, waiting lists, parents ringing and being turned away in large numbers. They also offer a glimpse of the inflexibilities that result, including fixed hours and having to pay for sessions not used or needed.

> People come when they're pregnant, looking for baby places ... we have to say 'we can't' and 'there's not going to be anything until this time' ... so it's quite hard because the parents get quite upset, if it's their first child they

don't know anything about the nursery situation … sometimes we may offer parents days they didn't necessarily want. They usually will take them … Usually they are quite understanding – if you offer them a different day or if you say 'if you take two days a third day will come up later on'. For under twos is £42 per day, a full-time rate is £805 a month, and two to fives £38 per day, £624 a month.

(manager, Robin nursery, B)

We could have double, triple the baby places

(manager, Robin nursery, B)

So at the moment, we have new babies who are registering [children start at two and a half, if toilet-trained] and we don't have any places – at the moment on paper we're fully booked up till September 2005 … the morning session is £850 per term, eleven weeks, the afternoon is slightly shorter and they pay £650 per term, they have to pay for a full week whether they use it or not … because the places were in so much demand it was easier…

(headteacher, Chaffinch nursery, B)

We have far too many people to cope with … I'd say we could probably fill the classes three times over at the moment… we have people knocking on the door every morning … telling people who really want the nursery they can't that's the bit I do find quite difficult.

(manager, Sparrow nursery, B)

At one Stoke Newington nursery, parents were expected to ring frequently to monitor their child's place on the waiting list, a tactic devised by the manager to try and contain the list:

We say, 'we don't call you, you call us'. And if they don't call then we just assume that they've found something else … Then there are people who have been – whose children have been attending just two sessions a week in the hope of getting some more sessions. So then, very often, all the places that are released are then taken up internally.

(manager, Garden nursery, SN)

A concomitant of the lack of supply in terms of responsiveness was the view expressed by many working mothers that the opening times and arrangements of many nurseries were not suited to their actual needs; they don't 'accommodate the working mother' (Trisha, B) – either full- or part-time workers – 'I pleaded with [manager] … it's not designed for working people' (Mia, SN). This is a market that does not clear. In that sense, in orthodox terms, it is inefficient. The feeling of the parents was that their custom was not valued, that they were locked into a seller's market. The number of providers has been growing in both locations, but given the density of families with children, this expansion had not, at least during the fieldwork period (2001–4), kept pace with demand. In part this may reflect the high costs of property and building land in the inner London settings of the research.

Fifth, this is a highly gendered market. The main players in both supply and demand are women: 97.5 per cent of the childcare workforce is female (Daycare Trust 2005b). It is very much a woman's world. As Kenway and Epstein (1996) point out, most literature on marketization is silent on gender and also on the role of emotions. Again this challenges the traditional economic assumptions about the theoretical consumer. As Kenway and Epstein (1996, p. 307) suggest, 'the free standing and hyper-rational, unencumbered competitive individual who can operate freely in the morally superior market can only be an image of middle class maleness'. Several of these characteristics simply do not apply here. 'The reality for many families is that childcare is organised by women in order to facilitate their own entry and that of their family members into paid work' (McKie *et al.* 2001, p. 239; see Chapter 5). Another feature of this woman's world is the importance of women's social networks, the giving and seeking of personal recommendations, and opinions from friends and family, what we have called elsewhere 'hot knowledge' (Ball and Vincent 1998). These are experiences that can be relied on, that tell it like it is, 'warts and all'. Hot knowledge can almost always be trusted (and when, on occasion, it fails, this failure comes as a shock, as Angie's experience in Chapter 6 shows). Hot knowledge cuts through marketing presentations to the heart of the matter, 'can I trust my child with this person, this organization'? It is pre-eminently a matter of 'word of mouth'; this term recurred in our accounts of choice as the main and most reliable source of market information. And the importance of this was reinforced in the interviews with providers:

Q: How do you attract parents?
Oh God, word of mouth I think really. Which is very lucky for us. We've got quite a good reputation.

(manager, Goldfinch nursery, B)

Mostly it's just word of mouth. A lot of people know each other in this area, so you get, they know so-and-so who's coming here and they've heard good things. So there's a lot of that, people meeting at NCT groups and things, sharing information.

(manager, Robin nursery, B)

We don't have to advertise. No, we don't do anything ... I think this corner [of SN], to a certain extent, we have cornered the market here

(manager, Garden nursery, SN)

> We don't even advertise our telephone number anywhere because it's all word of mouth. It's completely always been full through word of mouth
>
> (manager, Sparrow nursery, B)

The importance of this kind of market information in making choices cannot be overestimated. There is a considerable and growing provision of 'cold knowledge' (such as Ofsted reports and quality assurance 'marks') assiduously sought out by these parents. However, they are not always convinced of the accuracy and reliability of these. Chance social encounters often superseded the orderly processing of information, of cold knowledge, with many of the respondents mentioning the role of fluke (3), luck (41) and chance (23) in arriving at their childcare solutions. Hot knowledge assuages at least some of the fears embedded in decision-making around childcare, offering shared experience, support, and reassurance. The networks are based on a set of common needs and concerns, what one respondent called a 'grapevine of mothers'. The interviews are packed with examples of these grapevines at work and there were several examples where nannies were literally passed on from one family to another. In two cases families were able to employ childminders who had well-known local reputations. Clearly, not all families have equal access to such networks, but those who fall outside are very much exceptions. The networks are forged within local communities, through friendships, and around nodal points of mothering – like NCT groups, playgroups and children's 'activities', and at the school gates. (Holloway 1998 reports the importance of such networks in her study of middle-class Hallam, as does Mackenzie 1989 in Brighton, and Dyck 1990 in a Canadian suburb.)

Sixth, as mentioned above, this is currently a highly segmented and diverse market, with very many different types of providers, both public and private. The segmented nature of the market is also related to social class and class fractions in terms of different lifestyles, working arrangements, childcare practices and beliefs, and, of course, price. The providers are clearly aware of themselves operating in a hierarchical, classed market; within this market, relations are finely niched, and nuanced, although we suggest in Chapter 7 that the detailed differences between providers are not always so clear to parents. Furthermore, the childcare market also has a very highly developed 'grey market' sector – with many informal, unregistered, 'cash-in-hand' providers. Some of these are avoiding tax, others are newly arrived in the UK. Alongside this, in the population at large, although not in our sample, friends and family members are extensively used to do childcare work. In some respects, then, there is exploitation in this market. However, this social care market, like many others, is regulated by the state: there are (at the time of writing in summer 2005) 48 quality assurance schemes accredited by Sure Start as Investors in Children which are intended to provide reassurance to consumers. All providers in the formal market place are registered, inspected, trained and subject to health and safety regulations. But clearly, as the previous point indicates, only those registered as providers are actually regulated (the efficacy of Ofsted visits as a form of regulation has been questioned, with Ofsted inspectors themselves encouraging parents to inform them if they witness any less than desirable practice), and some parts of the formal market are only lightly regulated, e.g. nannies.

One resort for some families in the research, particularly those in Stoke Newington, was to move outside the regulated market and make use of the 'grey economy' of childcare or more informal 'community arrangements'. This involved such things as: employing women newly arrived in the country, using unregistered childminders, using carers who were in receipt of unemployment benefit or other 'fiddles', and paying 'cash-in-hand'. There is, to a degree, a mutual satisfaction of interests here: 'she was here studying English, she's from Bosnia and she was here on a visa, she sort of originally came as an au pair' (Mia, SN); 'she's not officially a childminder and I just feel so lucky to have met her' (Jackie, SN); 'she'd been cleaning for someone and she was looking for childcare work' (Connie, SN); 'she's an au pair – Swedish, "cash-in-hand"' (Barbara, SN). One Battersea mother (Margaret) turned away applicants who responded to an advert but were 'working illegally' and 'fiddling housing benefit'; she suggested that 'agencies collude' in such arrangements. By definition, the size of the grey economy of childcare in very difficult to gauge, but despite increasing efforts by government to regulate childcare, it is likely to be very large indeed.

Another strategy, a response to both high childcare costs and a dislike of existing forms of provision, was the co-operative nurseries. We found three examples in Stoke Newington, two well-established ones, Butterfly and Ladybird, both with full-time workers who cared for the children, and one much smaller one which met in a mother's house, after a local playgroup closed.

> Ladybird was a crèche … it's basically a co-operative, an unregistered sort of nanny share. It's run by parents, but parents don't look after the children, each parent has a role in the organization. So somebody does the scheduling and somebody does the sick cover and somebody does recruitment.
>
> (Angie, SN)

Ladybird takes place in the house of a parent, considerably reducing running costs, and so moves around the area as people's children come and go. According to our respondents it was started over ten years ago by mothers meeting at an NCT (National Childbirth Trust) ante-natal group. The mothers we spoke to were unreservedly positive about the experience. The advantages for them were the small size (seven full-time places), the intimacy, the opportunities for involvement, the quality of care offered by the main worker, and the cost.

> I like having an input into what's happening with my child when I'm not with her, and it's like, it's not family, it's just so … it's things like they have all the parents make all the food … probably eight years ago there were vegetarians on the collective and it hasn't changed you know. It's got a kind

of political conscience to it, well it inherited one and that's kind of faded now I think. So there's like vegetarian [food] they only drink water there and you know I'm just really comfortable with it

(Ann, SN)

When asked about the 'faded political conscience' Ann responded that although the nursery was white and middle-class now, the curriculum remained multicultural. Additionally, 'it's a non-profit making thing, there's some commitment to it'.

Butterfly was a more recent venture, set up in a spare room by a small group of mothers dissatisfied with available childcare options.

I was terrified when I went to look at this nursery, and the children were ... having their lunch, and they were eating crisps and they were sitting in front of a television, and I just thought, 'oh my God'

(Alicia, founder of Butterfly)

They then went on to lease premises from a church, and won Sure Start funding, which allowed them to employ a full-time worker, supported by a rota of parents. Again parents were responsible for matters relating to premises, finance and so on. There were also regular parent meetings which the founder cheerfully admitted were 'terrible' and had recently been limited to two hours. As at Ladybird, parents were very positive about the care, the intimacy, the size (there were places for eight children at the time), the relaxed nature of the nursery, the cost, and the opportunities for involvement ('we have a say what they should be playing with. It's good, it's challenging, we're not professionals but we're – everyone brings their own experience and then [name of worker] is the professional', Alicia, founder, Butterfly). The same drawbacks were identified at both places: the demands in terms of time, effort and emotion, adding another responsibility to mothering and working:

But you know the downside is that there's no boss, and when there's a problem, someone tells someone, it gets, it can get a bit gossipy ... and people get the nark, you know ... The politics of it can be terribly diffi-cult, but the sharing of ideas and stuff I think benefits the kids.

(Ann, mother, Ladybird)

However, this is not a childcare solution open to all. Many of the Ladybird and Butterfly parents worked part-time or were self-employed, and had some flex-ibility in terms of time. At Ladybird, at least one family at any one time needed a big enough home to house the crèche. Both groups recruit through word of mouth, which meant they attracted a relatively homogeneous group of parents, although as a condition of its Sure Start funding, Butterfly held a parent and toddler group once a week open to all.

We've discussed this many, many times you know, at the end of the day we're very like-minded people, and we're very similar, maybe we should open up, you know, but the more we talk about it the more we think actually that's why it works, because we are like-minded

(Alicia, founder of Butterfly)

When we joined there were lots of architects there. I think it goes through word of mouth, so an architect maybe told another architect … I suppose there are lots, mostly white middle-class people. But in terms of their income, I think it ranged quite a lot … I know because we did the finances … [that some] people struggled to pay … There were some people who were artists and stuff … I mean you know the range of people's occupations is quite broad, but in terms of ethnic origin a lot of them were white.

(Mary, mother, Ladybird)

Co-operatives therefore have a limited applicability in terms of childcare solutions for the general population. However they do offer parental input in a way and to an extent that is unknown in private or state sector nurseries (although see Chapter 7), and it is this aspect in particular that lends them potential. We are uncertain as to how widespread such initiatives are in the UK (although they are better known in parts of the USA and Australia). By their very nature co-operatives are small, highly localized operations, and if unregistered may fight shy of publicity. They are an area deserving of further research.

Our final point about this 'peculiar' childcare market is that parts of it position parents as employers of individual service providers – nannies specifically – to work in their own homes. Again the relations of exchange here are very complex involving both personal/emotional and formal/financial aspects. As Gregson and Lowe (1994, p. 190) put it, 'the social relations of nanny employment are characterised by an elision as fundamental as that between the nanny as childcare professional and as mother substitute … [and] are constructed by and shaped through wage and false kinship relations'.[11] Another complex set of emotions is invested in the relations between parents, again mainly mothers, and female carers, especially where home-based care is involved, as with childminders and nannies. The contradictions and tensions involved in 'paying for love', the 'double construction' (Gregson and Lowe 1994, p. 191) involved in childcare, are both heightened and obscured in these relationships. The nanny is 'in' but not 'of' the family, a situation which Gregson and Lowe (1994) call 'false kinship'. Again, as Gregson and Lowe (1994, p. 199) found, false kinship relations 'made certain forms of intervention difficult for employers, although … far from impossible'. Kathryn (B) was 'really upset' when she felt she had to 'sack' her nanny: 'it's very personal. It was one of the worst days of my life'. Relationships between parents and home-based carers, especially those living in the parents' home, are odd, intense but passing. In most cases the relationship is usually dispensable. We explore these relations between mothers and carers further in Chapter 6.

Conclusion

In conclusion, we wish to make three points about the childcare market as it stands. The first is that it is an imperfect, inconsistent market; we suggest some reasons for this. The second argument is that New Labour's interventions into the market, focusing heavily on increasing access, have been necessary but not sufficient to improve this market. The third point to note is that parental views and opinions have remained unheard during childcare's recent ascent up the policy agenda.

On the first point, our account of the 'lived experiences' of families in Battersea and Stoke Newington suggests that the childcare market is one which does not work as markets are meant to do: it does not guarantee quality or efficiency and it dispenses services in a highly inequitable fashion. As an instrument of childcare policy it is at present deeply flawed. In part we want to conclude by suggesting that these problems within the market are irresolvable in so far as there are important paradigmatic differences between the nature of market relations and the nature of the social relations embedded in childcare. As Anderson (1991) points out, there are five basic characteristics to market relations: impersonality, the pursuit of advantage, the exclusivity of goods, value as personal taste, and the use of exit rather than voice. While as we have suggested elsewhere (Vincent *et al.* 2004) some parents do bring interests in terms of advantage and exclusivity, most, as indicated above, bring emotional investments around the need for commitment and intimacy. While we recognize that the form of such commitment may be to some extent ersatz, the expression of warmth, care and love, is both what is being paid for and is a sought-after aspect of the relationship between carer and child. Pellegrino (1999) makes a similar point about healthcare relationships. The market is in essence a denial of this: it is an exchange relationship rather than a shared practice based on shared values. So many tensions and anxieties arise from this despite the fact that some parents go to some lengths to ensure that their concerns and reasons for choice are understood and shared by the provider. The problem, as Anderson (1991, p. 188) argues, is that the motives for choice 'cannot be traded on the market': the parents' fears and anxieties, their hopes for the child and their sense of the child's individual needs are not recognized within a market exchange. The provider is not really concerned about the reasons for the child's presence, and as Shipman (1999, p. 4) asserts, 'there is a sterility in social relations which ascribe purpose only to that which carries a price'.

This may be not only a peculiar market; it may ultimately be an impossible market, in as much as it can only function either as not a proper market, or, to the extent that it does operate as a proper market, it removes from childcare essential aspects of its social relations, and thereby undermines its integrity (Anderson 1991, p. 202). Many of the dilemmas expressed by the mothers represented in this chapter can be understood as stemming from this removal. There are tensions then between the market solution and delivering 'quality'

affordable childcare to all families. New Labour's emphasis on access, on bringing childcare to those families who did not have such options, is highly
laudable. Given the neglected state of childcare as an issue on the policy
agenda, and the lack of provision available, the government's initiatives have
transformed the landscape of care. However, New Labour's emphasis on the
politics of distribution and redistribution – the concern with access to care –
is not sufficient, we suggest, to render this market less peculiar, less impossible.
A focus on distributive justice, of access to a particular social good is incomplete without an accompanying focus on content and motives. Whilst those
who work in early years care may be able to substantiate the rhetorical assertion of the need for 'quality care', we suggest from the evidence in our research
that parents find it harder to do so. Lacking meaningful information about daily
life in care settings, they find themselves having to 'make a leap of faith'.
Parents' voices have been muted in the expansion of childcare to date (except
in the unusual parent-run settings, like the Stoke Newington co-operatives,
and in some local Sure Start partnerships which have focused on building dialogue with parents). We were struck by the absences and silences characterizing
the relationships between parents and carers in our sample (see Chapter 6). The
Daycare Trust (2004a) has recently published a booklet on parents' forums,
with suggestions for including parents in childcare services. Such initiatives
may be difficult to imagine within a market setting. Even in the Daycare Trust
examples, parents are involved in intervention projects (around, for example,
healthy eating, supporting young fathers and so on, rather than decision-making around service provision).[12] The lack of dialogue describes not just the
relationships between individuals but also public policy. Moss and Penn (2003)
suggest this as a reason for the sharp distinction between acute parental concern over their children's well-being and their lack of awareness around the
nature of the care and education they receive with providers, when they note

> the lack of vision at a public and political level and the consequent low
> level of public discussion. When it comes to early childhood services,
> Britain suffers a poverty of expectation and a low level of awareness of
> issues arising from years of policy maker's neglect and indifference.
>
> (Moss and Penn 2003, p. 24)

Chapter 4

Middle-class families

> This is a view of class as relational, emergent, contextual, dynamic, localised and eventualized. Class is not the membership of a category or the simple possession of certain capitals or assets. It is an activation of resources and social identities or rather, the interplay of such identities, in specific locations for specific ends ... Such assets underpin the capacity to act, they do not direct or determine action
> (Ball 2003, pp. 175–6)

Introduction

The recent history of class analysis and class theory is fraught, disputatious and complicated, but not altogether unproductive (see Savage 2000 for an excellent overview). There has been a particular and growing attention paid to examination of the middle class, as, in the view of some theorists, 'the new collective subject on the historical stage' (Lockwood 1995, p. 10). The key debates around the middle class focus on the extent to which this is a unitary class or a set of distinct fractions marked off from one another by values, lifestyle and political preferences and social relations; whether, if these differences are significant, they relate back to occupational divisions – professionals and managers, state and private sector employees and so on. In this chapter we review the literature in this field, and argue that a focus on an individual's occupation alone is too blunt an instrument to provide a correlation with values, attitudes and lifestyles. Drawing on our earlier introduction to the work of Tim Butler and colleagues (see Chapter 2), we consider how a focus on locality can be productive in mapping nuances of difference and similarity between middle-class fractions. The following chapters (5–7) go on to consider the differences and similarities between the middle-class respondents of Battersea and Stoke Newington, focusing in particular on their choice of childcare and education, but also considering the gendered divisions of care responsibilities within households.

In particular here we are interested in the day-to-day processes of social reproduction of the middle classes, as these take place within families, and in and through educational and childcare settings. For the most part, in education research on social class and 'in conventional class analyses' families 'appear like phantoms, clearly implicated in the intergenerational transmission of social and economic advantage, and yet assuming a unitary status lacking in real social content' (Witz 1995, p. 45). We hope, to some extent, to give some social content to these processes of transmission and to differentiate among families in a variety of ways. Thus, we are interested in people rather than class positions, and as will become evident, our respondents do not belong to class categories in uncomplicated and straightforward ways. They cannot be 'read' as though their experiences were transparent concomitants of the social category to which they are allocated. The ontological status of the middle class is not 'ready-made in reality' (Wacquant 1991, p. 57).

We begin with a discussion of two aspects of social class. First, some problems involved in identifying the middle class and middle-class fractions. Second, the relationship between social class and locality.

Class fractions and class localities

The key debates around the middle class focus on: the extent to which, in Goldthorpe's terms, this is a 'well formed' class; concomitantly whether this is a unitary class or a set of distinct fractions marked off from one another by values, lifestyle, political preferences and social relations; whether, if these differences are significant, they relate back to occupational divisions – professionals and managers, state and private sector employees, senior and 'cadet' class members; the role of gender, domestic arrangements and the occupational inequalities within the middle class (Witz 1995); and the internal coherence of families as class settings (Roberts 2001). As this list suggests, there is more to be said here than could possibly be encompassed in a single chapter which also attempts to engage with data. Nonetheless, we do want to underline some of the difficulties attendant upon the identification of differences or fractions within the middle class which rely solely upon the sort of occupational divisions noted above.

Rosemary Crompton's (2001) work on bankers and general practitioners is one research study that does identify sectoral differences. She found that professional jobs allow for more autonomy and flexibility than managerial ones. She goes on to suggest that a tangible difference in culture is related to the different occupations – different approaches to work/life balance, for example.

> There is a systematic difference between professional and managerial occupations in that for both men and women professional jobs offer greater possibilities for meshing employment with caring responsibilities than do bureaucratic or managerial jobs ... Professionals who give priority to family life are likely to choose a specialty or a niche that enables them to put their priorities into practice
>
> (Crompton 2001, p. 179)

In particular Crompton suggests that there are cultural differences between professionals and managers 'in values, aspirations, and expectations' in respect of family organization (Crompton 2001, p. 179). However, as Crompton (1992) herself argues, given the highly gendered nature of caring relations, especially those involved in childcare, and the diverse nature of household types, unilateral distinctions of this kind are difficult to sustain.

There are three related points to be made here, all of which undermine any possibility of straightforwardly reading off values and lifestyles from occupations. First, there is the possibility that the substantive differences that mark out occupational divisions may be disappearing or at least reducing (see Savage 2000; Roberts 2001; Butler 1995). The possibilities to 'hide from capitalism', as Bagguley (1995, p. 298) puts it, may have greatly diminished in the professions generally and the public sector specifically. On this point, Hanlon (1998) describes a struggle between two competing understandings of professionalism, a 'social service' version and a 'commercialized' one. Professions are no longer homogeneous. Webb (1999) makes a similar argument, seeing public sector workers as increasingly divided between entrepreneurs and those who continue to espouse a public service ethic. Second, there is also the problem of those who do not 'fit' into these categories (public/private, professional/managerial). These include the small but growing number of self-employed service-class workers, working in a freelance capacity or running their own business (see Savage 2000). In addition, there is the problem of 'composite' families, where partners come from different sectors. We should note that contributors to the class debate differ in terms of whether they stress the individual or the family as the unit of class composition, and this has been the focus of heated debate (e.g. Witz 1995; Bottero 1998). Third, there is a question of primacy which is begged here, but often not addressed; that is, whether the identifiable values or lifestyle differences which may mark off these fractions arise from occupational differences, or from prior values, orientations, and influences that lead actors to choose certain sorts of jobs (Bagguley 1995).

Taken together these issues raise fundamental questions about whether values, practices and attitudes can be 'read off' from occupational categories in any simple way. Certainly the evidence suggests that we may have to come to terms with a more complex formulation of the social formation of the middle class. As Crompton (1995, p. 74) puts it, this is 'a very fluid and rapidly developing situation ... this does not mean we are witnessing the end of class analysis ... Rather ... the best way forward is to explore a more flexible approach' – which is what we are attempting here.

Savage *et al.* (1992) offer another way forward. They have explored two approaches to the question of middle-class diversity, one based upon 'assets', the other lifestyle. It is not clear whether the two relate together in any straightforward way but they do connect lifestyle categories to types of employment. Drawing generally on Weber and more specifically on both Eric Olin Wright and Bourdieu they identify three 'causal entities' which are deployed as assets within class formation – property, bureaucracy and culture. The first are economic assets which underpin the position of the petite bourgeoisie. The second, organizational assets, deriving from skills and positions within organizational careers, which are mostly non-transferable, except perhaps in the form of the CV. The third type of asset is cultural capital, particularly represented in the form of credentials, which can in effect be stored and transmitted through families and can be 'translated' through education into material rewards. To a great extent, but with considerable added sophistication, these divisions, leaving aside the petite bourgeoisie, reiterate the professional–managerial divide. The authors also note that different assets may be combined within one household, again adding to the complexity of a family unit-based analysis of class composition. More recently Savage has argued that class should be understood dynamically, as a longitudinal process rather than a cross-sectional one (2000, p. 69). The transition from dual-earning, childless couple to household with children is one aspect of this dynamism.

The second basis for middle-class divisions which is explored by Savage *et al.* (1992) is that of lifestyle. An analysis of data on patterns of income-related consumption generates three sub-groupings. *Liberal ascetics* are 'education, health and welfare professionals', a group reliant on cultural assets, rather than money, and employed by the state. In terms of lifestyle and patterns of consumption, members of this group score heavily on health and exercise and 'high' culture and display a slightly above average commitment to family relative to career, anticipating Crompton's (2001) findings. *Postmoderns* are private sector professionals (e.g. financial services, advertising, property). Their lifestyle and consumption is marked by hedonism; they are equally at home consuming both high and low culture. The third group is the *corporate undistinctives*, who are managers and government bureaucrats. They have undistinctive patterns of consumption and a commitment to career over family. Various other approaches to the identification of the middle class map onto these differences. For example, the 'postmoderns' might also be that group which Featherstone (1991, pp. 34–5) refers to as 'the intellectuals and specialists in symbolic production' or those Bourdieu (1986) calls the 'new cultural intermediaries' or the 'new intellectuals' – those in occupations involving presentation and representation, symbolic goods and services, and cultural production and organization, who manifest the ideal of a new social consciousness which is constituted equally by economic and cultural resources.

Thus we can accept (following Savage *et al.* 1992) that there are certainly variations in middle-class lifestyles, values and attitudes, and there is likely to be a link of some sort to occupational groups. But this link appears weak and tenuous, and nothing like as simple as a binary divide between public and private sectors of employment, professional and managerial careers or modernist and postmodern jobs. The links between occupation, social consciousness and lifestyle remain fuzzy, which could be interpreted to mean that social class fractions are of little importance and that the middle class is perhaps, overall, more coherent than not. Nonetheless, we suggest that internal differences of some importance remain, but the situation is fluid. Almost all of the contributors to the class debate emphasize the need to renew class analysis 'in the context of current social changes' (Butler 1995, p. 35).

We hope to contribute to the class debate in two related ways. First, in relation to class fractions, to make a case for a set of complex interrelations between occupations, place, social values and strategies of social reproduction – 'class processes', the ways in 'which groups attain, establish and retain their positions within the social order' (Crompton 1998, p. 166). Second, through the focus on pre-school care, to begin to demonstrate the ways in which middle-class strategies of intergenerational transmission are in play from a very early age. Here then we address both the differentiation of class fractional values and lifestyles within our middle-class samples, and the ways in which these differentiations are enacted to produce and reproduce boundaries within the middle class, and between this class and other classes. That is to say, following Bourdieu our analysis is relational: the class and class fractional identities and distinctions we describe involve a sense of belonging to a group and a sense of differentiation from others (cf. Savage 2000, p. 115). Members of these metropolitan families are very much social individuals embedded in social networks which appear, in the Battersea sample in particular, relatively tightly bounded.

Thus, in considering the coherence of the fractions we identify, we attend to both 'the relational aspects of class … the extent to which a class can be identified through its more or less exclusive patterns of informal social interaction' (Lockwood 1995, p. 6) and the normative aspects of class, those shared values and beliefs which demarcate class groups. Lockwood suggests that both aspects are currently neglected in class research and are 'an open field of investigation' (p. 6). As we shall see the two are thoroughly intertwined within the class practices explored here.

The service class exists in a nexus of contradictions of identity, values and social relationships. It is a class betwixt and between, an 'intermediate zone' within which 'the indeterminacy and the fuzziness of the relationship between practices and positions are the greatest' (Bourdieu 1987, p. 12). We want to hold on to and explore both the distinctions and the fuzziness that characterize the middle class 'to capture this essential ambiguity … rather than dispose of it' (Wacquant 1991, p. 57). Writing about the class in this way, trying to be clear and subtle at the same time, is not easy.

We would note in passing that in contrast to the respondents described by Savage et al. (2001, p. 875), the individuals represented here were neither ambivalent nor defensive about their class identity and certainly did not see themselves 'outside' of class, as Savage et al. reported. Nor indeed did they regard themselves as 'ordinary', although, in the nuances of fractioning which we outline below, there were some respondents who positioned themselves over and against the 'unordinary' lifestyles which they saw as defining 'others' in the middle class. Overall, these parents seem to have little problem in seeing themselves as middle-class and as sharing a set of class traits with other families 'like them' – albeit different versions of being middle-class. As one mother straightforwardly puts it, her child's nursery is full of 'children like our children, so children of middle-class parents who can afford to spend nearly nine hundred pounds a month sending their kids to childcare'. We offer further examples below.

The data do indicate ways in which childcare and educational settings are sought and used by particular middle-class fractions to maintain and ensure social homogamy. However, as Bourdieu (1987, p. 13) goes on to argue, 'In the reality of the social world, there are no more clear-cut boundaries, no more absolute breaks, than there are in the physical world'. Social boundaries, he suggests, can be thought of as 'imaginary planes' or a more appropriate image 'would be that of a flame whose edges are in constant movement, oscillating around a line or surface' (p. 13). This metaphor is certainly apposite as a way of thinking about the distinctions we outline below.

The grounding of our discussion of intra-class fractions is within small differences and nuances rather than significant rifts, and we must eventually ask questions about the overall significance of these small divisions. Where should primary emphasis be given, to these nuanced differences within the service class or to the systematic commonalities across it? How important in terms of normative and relational differences are these nuances? In some respects it might be argued that class fraction analysis is not class analysis at all, in as much that the primacy and independence of the economic bases of class are subverted by the focus upon divisions and differences of social significance based on status and values, and non-economic assets. On the other hand, a distinction of the economic from the social is itself difficult to maintain: 'the "economic" can only be understood as ... a set of embedded social assumptions, obligations and claims' (Bottero 1998, p. 482).

The problem of categorization especially in relation to class fractions remains as an ongoing concern in our work, we are using and troubling our categories at the same time. We are also acutely aware that 'it is not possible to construct a single measure which could successfully capture all the elements going to make up social class – or even structured social inequality' (Crompton 1998, p. 114). Thus, as outlined in Chapter 2, locality and educational history are employed here alongside occupational criteria to add some nuance and depth to the minimalism of work-based divisions.[1]

All of these aspects of the classed people we represent here are embedded in Skeggs's (2004) description of class as a 'mobile resource' that is 'an amalgam of features of a culture that are not just classification or social positions but ... read onto bodies as personal dispositions' (p. 1). These resources are limitations for some and possibilities for others; a whole complex of cultural history is condensed within them and they are subject to moral evaluation by others. They are realized in terms of 'different forms of personhood and individuality' (p. 6). And particular selfhoods 'can be seen as performative of class' (p. 152). In these terms we go on to identify some common resources and 'individualities' among our sample, as well as some differences. While all of these families use choice as a basis for their self-production, accruing and developing culture, the accumulation of value, their specific choices and lifestyles, and their performativities differ, as do their aestheticizations – the 'knowledge of new goods, their social and cultural values, and how to use them appropriately' (p. 136).

As a further dimension to our analysis it is the family, rather than individual class actors, that is our focus. However, we do not simply take it that 'the family acts as an homogenous unit in the class structure' (Leuifsrud and Woodward 1987, p. 313), although there is no space here to develop the problems and issues that arise from intra-familial differences (see below). Within the 'black box of intra-household negotiations' (Devine 1998, p. 36) the childcare arrangements with which we deal here are sometimes the outcome of ongoing tensions and fragile compromises and within these arrangements 'gender relations are everywhere' (Pollert 1996, p. 645; also Chapter 5).

The data are presented below, separated by area. This enables us to point up differences of various sorts between the areas and point to 'an urban middle class which is fractured along socio-spatial lines' (Butler and Robson 2003), although we should reiterate that the commonalities are pervasive (Vincent *et al.* 2004) and some of these are dealt with in other chapters (5, 6, and 7).

Stoke Newington

In what follows, a complex set of themes is interwoven, characterized by tensions of similarity and difference, and integration and separation *within* the middle class and *in relation to* working-class 'others'. Two quotations from Stoke Newington residents Madeleine and Judy will introduce these themes. Madeleine is talking here about possibly moving her child from a private to a local authority run nursery. This is a move between two very different social worlds or class worlds. It is also a move out of privilege and advantage, and as she explains this provokes a sense of guilt (see Ball 2003, Chapter 6). Madeleine was one of only four parents in our sample (all of them in Stoke Newington) to seriously consider state-provided childcare:

> We're the wrong kind of demographics for [private nursery], which is very much into full-time caring, quite a lot of City [workers], quite a lot of minor media celebrities … which is why she's coming out of there … I think we're gonna have to because it's just too expensive for us … it's like paying half our mortgage every month for three days [a week]. At this moment what I'm going to do is take her away from there and take her to a state nursery with [adult–child] ratios of 1 to 13.[2] I'm just kind of riddled with guilt about it at the moment because I don't know if she's ready and I don't know if I can do that to her … In the [state] nursery there are about six or seven other white kids. There's 60 kids and I'd say at least half of them English is their second language and that's very different from

obviously paying through the nose … where she is now is not necessarily white but they're middle-class. They're professional parents … [But] this is why we live in London, I think to have this other experience, the shock and the kind of extremity of it…

There are a number of pertinent issues embedded in this extract. Primarily Madeleine points us to the fault line that exists between private and state provision, both in terms of the nature of provision and the demographics of access. The class boundaries here are sharp and relate directly to the ability to pay. Madeleine also indicates something of the complex interplay of class and race and the ways in which one or other may be to the fore in different contexts. Also here we see the contradictions, for some of our respondents, of being *in* but not *of* London – the frissons of spatial proximity and social and cultural distance, the shocks of extremity, of stark differences between classes, as against the celebration of multiculturalism. But Madeleine's account also points to 'softer' divisions within her class, the way that she differentiates herself, by income and identity from middle-class 'others' – those of the 'City' and 'minor media celebrities'. She is a translator and has a commission to write a screenplay; her partner is a theatre director and playwright. All of this seems to suggest that she sees herself as neither one thing nor the other: neither working-class nor entirely a part of the same middle-class fractions as families at the private nursery. She experiences some discomfort in each of the class spaces represented by the two nurseries.

Judy describes a move in the opposite direction, from a relatively cheap and socially diverse community playgroup to an expensive and exclusive private nursery, which offered the longer hours of care that she needed, and the costs of which were borne by her 'in-laws':

> The only problem with [private nursery] is that it's not inclusive, it's one of those places that if you're on a high income, so the only people who use it are City lawyers … the peer group is pretty much white and pretty much moneyed … and when they found out my [older] daughter's at the local comprehensive they all freak out, the peer group are all going on to the private sector … [younger daughter's] peer group at [community playgroup] are all going on the local [state] school. I am very community minded and my choices would be around the community and things that are inclusive. And this [private nursery] is one kind of blip.

Again there are several significant issues evident here. There is a sense, again, of a child moving across a boundary of values and income. Judy is 'giving up' on her values commitment to inclusivity in this instance, and her child is experiencing an exclusive class and ethnic setting as a result. The values and income differences are pointed up further by the reactions to her elder daughter's schooling. To the other parents Judy's choice of state schooling is alien and dangerous: it is outside of the moral boundaries of good parenting, as far as they are concerned. Judy's awareness of this, of her differences from them, is what we want to emphasize here, but there are also ever-present ambivalences: she goes on to say about the move that 'actually it's worked out really well'. There is a tension and duality embedded in the social and moral lives of some members of the middle class – like Madeleine and Judy, a tension between sociality and values commitments, an orientation towards a collective social good, as against individualism and the press of social reproduction. Such tension, as Nagel (1991) puts it, is between the personal and impersonal standpoints (see Ball 2003, pp. 111–18). Again we will return to this.

Two other Stoke Newington mothers expressed some dislike of the image projected by private nurseries that they had visited. Ann expressed a fairly strong sense of distancing herself from the class values of private nursery schools, and tried and failed to find a state nursery place for her child. Nurseries in nearby Islington were 'really expensive and not really the kind of – it's a bit presumptuous of me – not the kind of care I particularly wanted somehow'. She went on, hesitantly, to describe this both as an aversion to something as a 'business rather than educational' and as 'an inverted snobby thing. Because, well they're very expensive [and] too precious somehow, it's probably my hang-up …', but admitted seeing one such setting and being 'impressed by it'. Again values and advantage, aversion and responsibility, are juxtaposed. And Elsa also found herself responding negatively to an expensive private nursery, as 'a bit too twee, and they had French lessons and things … very nice but not particularly for us'. In these and the earlier examples the mothers are expressing again a sense of being out of place in certain kinds of middle-class settings, that are 'not us', a sense of discomfort among others ostensibly of their class.

As noted four mothers in our Stoke Newington sample did consider or apply for places in state, council-run nurseries; Hannah did get a 'marketed' place in such a nursery[3] and saw this as a positive thing for her children, the nursery in question being 'quite ethnically and you know, social class-wise quite mixed'. Mix comes about from the presence of both 'people like us' and 'others'. But when mix and its constituents is addressed there is often a hesitancy of tone in describing these, in naming 'others'. 'You get people like us, who are paying market fees and then, obviously, there's a lot of assisted places as well'. Hannah wanted her child to be somewhere 'where, you know, it was, sort of, you know different kind of colours and, you know accents and all the rest of it'. But she explained later that 'there's mixed and mixed'. She did not want her children exposed at an early age to aggressive behaviour; although 'not everybody who comes from, you know, a disadvantaged background is abusive … doesn't have any kind of respect for the community they live in, I mean, quite the opposite'. In other words, there are limits to the value of and tolerance of social mix. Caroline also looked at some state nurseries 'which were mainly African, African-Caribbean … there were no white children in some of them, and then in others there were a few … so I thought whether I wanted his name down in a nursery where the majority culture was not his'. Nonetheless, the private 'alternative' nursery she chose eventually 'is very ethnically diverse' and 'you couldn't wish for a better place ... in the sense the cultural mix makes it a vibrant place'. But this ethnic mix is also 'middle-class, middle-class professional, only because of the cost'. In contrast, and exceptionally, Elsa was happy for her daughter to attend two community nurseries with a majority of African-Caribbean children. One was 'quite friendly, very, very mixed, sort of ethnically mixed. In fact it was more Afro-Caribbean than white ... all of the staff were Afro-Caribbean'. Note the 'very very'! There is mixed, very mixed and very, very mixed. In the other nursery, her daughter 'was the only white child in that class. Which was nice really. You know, it's just probably if she hadn't been to nursery, she wouldn't have had that'. The last comments suggest the clear positivity of such 'mixing' which was commonly expressed by the Stoke Newington respondents but was the exception in Battersea. Emily, also in Stoke Newington, and herself part of a dual-heritage relationship, with dual-heritage children, explained 'what was driving us was having a nice mix of children, I felt that was so important, I didn't want him to be somewhere where socially it was all exactly the same children and racially as well, like most of the more expensive nurseries did tend to be predominantly white, I really noticed that'. Even so the nursery chosen is 'predominantly middle-class, middle-class working families ... but there's quite a few mixed-race and black children'. Despite the positive value attached to social mixing within childcare, the degree to which families interact, taking their liaison beyond the confines of the children's relationships in such 'mixed' nurseries, is an open question. Butler and Robson's (2001, p. 2157) notion of 'tectonic' social relations as 'social groups or "plates" which overlap or run parallel to one another without much in the way of integrated experience' might be apposite here.

It is not simply individual choice at work here. New Labour's National Childcare Strategy, which encourages a mix of private, subsidized and free places, embeds and reproduces class divisions, even where parents wanted to make choices differently: 'We were actually turned down at [council nursery] ... which is the state-run one, it's much cheaper, but obviously you have to be extremely poor to get into it ... unless you're willing to go private, you're not going to get a nursery place' (Jessica). The structure and economy of childcare is very directly related to social class divisions – within and between classes. In Stoke Newington then a nuanced awareness of inter and intra-class divisions seemed well established. Let us now consider Battersea.

Battersea

In Battersea the themes of mix and difference are played out again, but somewhat differently. The awareness of an 'us' and 'them', within the middle classes, was again evident from some of the respondents. In some ways, given the demography of the area, this was even more forcefully expressed. Some of the mothers were clear that they did not want their children exposed to settings in which social values with which they were uncomfortable predominated. There are distinct 'circuits' (Ball *et al.* 1995) of care and education in play here which are distinguished relationally (in terms of mix) and normatively (in terms of values) within the middle class. Again, mix here is a very relative term but in comparison to Stoke Newington there is a strong class and ethnic insularity in this locality. Very few of the Battersea respondents talked about mix or gave it a positive value. In this respect, for the Battersea 'dissenters', those who did value social diversity, mix is much more subtle, and not a matter of crossing stark boundaries of class or ethnicity. In order to pursue the theme of intra-class differences, most of the examples below are taken from those Battersea parents who found themselves 'out of affinity' or in disharmony with the local habitus and the self-evidencies of 'good' parenting.

Juliet draws firm lines between herself and other middle-class parents who are not like her, who have different values and higher incomes. She plans to send her child to a state school, as a private school is not a setting she feels comfortable about – either in respect of its particularity or its exclusivity. However, not any state school will do. For her, as for many Stoke Newington parents, 'mix' is good, but some 'mixes' are intolerable. For Juliet, both those schools which are too working-class and those which are too middle-class, or at least the 'wrong kind' of middle-class, are unacceptable. Juliet is thinking of nursery schooling, in part at least, in relation to where her daughter will go to primary school and whether she can get her into Goldwater, a Battersea state primary school, which is highly regarded, and where

> there's lots of well heeled middle-class parents but there's also a council estate on the doorstep so there's a kind of mixture which is nice. It's not all people driving four-wheel drives like the school across the road [a private school] where you see the kind of procession of armoured cars to collect these children. It's a fantastic school, they are interviewing children at three … [daughter'd] probably do really well but I don't like the whole deal really, plus you have to cough up a large amount of money not just for the school but for the uniform

Sally also pointed to some subtle differences between her child and what she described as the 'very well dressed class' that attends her daughter's nursery. She 'got an idea of who she [her daughter] was going to school with' from attending children's birthday parties; 'she's going to school with quite a few, sort of, million pound house type children'. Nonetheless, Sally also sees a value in social mixing, and is, unusually amongst Battersea parents, keen to find a 'more racially mixed' primary school for her daughter, 'that would be one of the main criteria'. Despite her view that the parents of other children in her daughter's current nursery are 'lovely people' she is not entirely comfortable with the social exclusivity of her current nursery, and while she is 'quite OK about sending [child] to private school', her husband is not. 'He hates the whole public schoolboy thing' and 'we don't want her to grow up with a bunch of snobs … like [nearby private school], which is walking distance, and the grounds are lovely, and the teachers are nice, and the classes are small, but they, you know, they're a bunch of little snots basically'. Once more there is a rejection of middle-class 'others', the middle-class which is 'not us', the carriers of values into which these parents do not want their child socialized. Once more, however, there is a second tension between normative differences and structural advantage. Because, 'then again, if we got into Goldwater [the local state school], she'd be thrown into a class of thirty kids … so I don't know, we are tending toward private at the moment'. Here, a school that is very acceptable to one mother, Juliet, is regarded with considerable suspicion by another, Sally, despite their ostensible sharing of the same class position.

In the case of parents like Sally we could say that private education is preferred both for and despite its effects of social closure, which is not always the case in our sample. It is a structural and rational choice, a way of ensuring particular kinds of opportunities which are not available to others, and is 'intelligible' (Goldthorpe 2000, p. 165) in this way, 'in relation to the class position they hold'. This is an example of what Jordan *et al.* (1994) refer to as 'putting the family first', that is the overriding responsibility felt by middle-class parents to try to achieve competitive social advantage for their children, despite a possible cost to their personal principles. And, as in the other instances, economic assets underpin the possibilities of these opportunities. However, these are not simply rational or utilitarian choices: the importance of 'class values, norms, "forms of consciousness"' (Goldthorpe 1996, p. 487) cannot be 'avoided' as Goldthorpe would prefer. As Hatcher (1998, p. 17) demonstrates (using a range of educational choice research evidence), and as indicated throughout our data, 'agents do not simply weigh courses of action in terms of their efficacy in achieving a desired goal; they evaluate the desired goals themselves in relation to a framework of values that is not reducible to personal utility'. In some families, principles over-ride the logic of utility and interest maximization (see also Ball 2003).

The interplay of calculative rationality and values is evident in Phillipa's choices: she, like Sally, although again intending to send her children to private school, contrasts herself and her family with the sorts of middle-class parents to be found in some of the private schools she has visited. They are 'sort of very City men and sort of flowery women, and we didn't feel comfortable with that either for the children or for ourselves'. Again differences in values are alluded to. This is made clearer in Phillipa's preferred private school Hill View, which she describes as 'sort of laid back and apparently more liberal and not quite so traditional sort of style', as opposed to those where 'you can get incredibly traditional minds and where there's a massive focus on looking right, shaking hands, wearing the right clothes'. Hill View is viewed as 'a much more broad-based school' and it has, 'for example quite a few Black or Asian people in it which you often won't see in other private schools' and 'it's got some sort of special needs type children', whereas 'some of the other schools we started to call Christian master race schools'. Again a *degree* of 'mix' is valued but again 'mix' is relative. There are a variety of boundaries and distinctions embedded here, drawn in different places by different families. Phillipa and her partner 'wanted a good education for our children but we didn't want to be kind of excluding our children from the vast proportion of society'. She is 'more confident I feel that my values and Hill View's values are fairly similar'. Here then instrumental and expressive choice coincide, a happy solution where exclusivity and (limited) mix are achieved in one move.

Alice, like others, is clear that the social mix of her child's private nursery is 'pretty limited … middle-class'. Again she does not see herself as the same in all respects as other parents, as part of this mix 'every one, except me I think, drives these wretched four-wheel drive things which I hate, but that's the one trouble, for this area's all very homogeneous really, so, I mean I don't think there's any coloured children here'. Again we see minor differences within what is 'homogenous', and major divisions between this class setting and other classes and ethnicities 'elsewhere'. Alice wanted the local middle-class state primary school [Goldwater] for her son: 'I'm very keen that he should go state … I think it's a really good start rather than imagining that the whole world exists of Volvos and four-wheel drives'. Again, by allusion, Alice points to and wants to avoid for her child the possibility of a life–world view constructed within and limited to a particular sort of middle-class social environment, different from her own – divisions are drawn on both sides.

Goldwater Primary has an interesting role in these accounts; some attention to this school points up further complexity and subtlety in middle-class tactics and strategies of social reproduction, and further complications in relation to the notion of social mix. Like the example of Hill View private school, Goldwater offers a happy solution for many parents to personal and familial dilemmas. It offers a degree of social mix, but not too much. It is within the state sector, while at the same time offering a good likelihood of high levels of achievement in a setting in which others 'like me' are in a majority. For many of the parents we interviewed in this area of Battersea, it was Goldwater or nothing as far as state sector schooling was concerned. Effectively Goldwater has been 'captured' and colonized by the local middle class. As such it is a focus of classed social networks and social interaction, especially among mothers, many of whom are involved in the school, in representative or supportive roles. Butler and Robson's (2001, p. 2150) comments about a primary school in one of their London research areas, Telegraph Hill, would apply equally well to Goldwater: 'the school has been nurtured by middle class parents and it is the focal point of social interaction and friendship networks', although for the families whose children attend Goldwater these networks are often already well established through participation in National Childbirth Trust groups, various local playgroups and local commercial children's activities. These integrated 'circuits' of care are a foundation for and focus of class interactions and normativities. The other point about these networks that Butler and Robson omit to mention is that they are gendered: the relationships are forged and maintained almost exclusively by mothers. In this respect class formation is very much women's work. The invisible work of mothers, as 'status maintainers' (Brantlinger *et al.* 1996, p. 589) is crucial to the knitting together and activation of different forms of family capital.

The relational and normative distinctions of class are thoroughly interwoven here. Some families' view of class relations and the responsibilities of advantage and social reproduction leads to choices which produce absolute relational separations – exclusivity and closure – some kinds of settings are sought and others avoided. For others such responsibilities are offset against a commitment to the importance of diverse social relations, a balance between the personal and impersonal standpoints (Nagel 1991) which rests on class ambivalences and produces much fuzzier separations.

Conclusion

Childcare may not, at first sight, seem to be a key arena of class reproduction, but we suggest that that is exactly what it is. Childcare opportunities and choices are strongly stratified and very closely tied to family assets. There are sharp and distinct class boundaries established and maintained within the socially segmented childcare market. The combination of cost and choice ensures that classes and class fractions are separated from one another in different and well bounded 'circuits of care' which are more or less tightly related to 'circuits of [primary] schooling' – state or private (see Chapter 7). Social and normative expectations and social patterns of attraction and rejection work to produce very different childcare cultures and environments. Nonetheless, throughout our analysis, we are trying to hold on to and convey the significance of the divisions both between and within classes. The relative rigidity of these divisions produces variations in the degree of social mix to which children are exposed. Childcare 'options' range from home-based childcare involving nannies and the more exclusive private day nurseries, both giving rise to defended, carefully crafted social relations and social networks, through a variety of less expensive and less socially exclusive nursery school settings, some of which are inflected with 'integrationist' and 'alternative' values. In this middle ground there are also childminders and a limited number of community nurseries with 'mix' policies based on a combination of free and funded places. And at the other extreme of class exclusivity, there is the state nursery sector, parts of which are primarily available to families deemed as being in social need. Childcare choices made by middle-class families, in combination with government policies of provision, both generate and maintain class divisions and work to reproduce differential educational opportunities. These choices have implications for educational identities, and as 'ability' markers are linked to access to, and preparation for, different and differently privileged long-term educational trajectories (we return to this argument in Chapter 7).

However, both the patterns of childcare choice and the values related to social mix differed between the localities in this study, reflecting both the local geographies of childcare and the differently prevailing values of childrearing and sociality in each locality. Some of these differences are indicated in Table 4.1 which shows the childcare choices of the respondent families.

We want to suggest that these differences in social values, as related to childcare, are indicative of more significant social differences, that is, that these different middle-class factions are engaged in distinct forms of local social relations (see Table 4.2 below). These forms can be characterized in a number of ways, capturing their different aspects, by drawing upon a variety of sociological vocabularies.

As Table 4.2 suggests, *inclusivist, community* values seem more embedded and more widespread in Stoke Newington, and *exclusivist, individualist* values more embedded and widespread in Battersea, but there were some *inclusivist* parents in the Battersea sample and a few *exclusivists* in Stoke Newington. In Stoke Newington, exclusivity was more evident as children neared secondary school age. In Stoke Newington social boundaries were more relaxed (Bernstein 1996) and more references were made to impersonal values (Nagel 1991) and the public goods. In Battersea social boundaries were relatively closed and personal values predominated. In these respects we can again reinforce Butler and

Table 4.1 Types of childcare used at the time of first interview

Type of care	Battersea families using care	Stoke Newington families using care	Total families using this type of care
Private day nursery	11	10	21
State day nursery	0	1	1
Community nursery	0	2	2
Private nursery school	5	2	7
Not-for-profit playgroup	0	5	5
Parent-run co-operative crèche	0	5	5
State school nursery class	2	2	4
Private school nursery class	7	3	10
Nanny, sole charge in employer's home	11	7*	18
Childminder, sole charge in carer's home	3 (2 unregistered, 1 registered)	4 (all registered)	7

* Only one of these is a professional full-time nanny. All others are informal arrangements. Some of the 59 families had children in different types of care (e.g. an older child in nursery, a younger with a nanny or childminder). Sometimes one child had more than one type of care (e.g. part-time nursery and childminder. Hence the total shown here for types of care used adds up to more than 59.

Table 4.2 Forms of local social relations

Stoke Newington	Battersea
symbolic mutuality	instrumentalism
vertical social capital	horizontal social capital
impersonal values	personal values
community	individualism – market-based
inclusivist	exclusivist
relaxed boundaries	common ideology – strong boundaries

Robson's (2001, p. 2159) comment that 'the common good in Battersea is established through market-based commonalities of interest based on households acting atomistically'. The social relations in each case may thus constitute different forms of social capital: vertical in Stoke Newington and horizontal in Battersea. In both localities values differences were related to perceptions of class fractional differences and to childcare choices, and thus to patterns of social interaction. However, like most other binaries these divisions obscure as much as they reveal. The analysis here which stresses differences between the localities has to be set alongside the commonalities in gender relations and educational aspirations which we discuss later (Chapters 5 and 7).

In small scale, this is a prima facie case here for the existence of relational and normative differences and differentiations within the middle class – generated by separations and boundaries that repel and attract. These separations are by no means absolute but there is a seeking out of spaces of differentiation – in nurseries, schools and through other childcare arrangements, by some families (Chapter 7). While, in contrast, others look for particular, but 'tolerable' kinds of social mix. Nonetheless, in many cases, 'social mix' is what might be termed 'designer mix': diversity, vibrancy, and safety, based on a 'commonality within difference', shared values around childrearing across ethnic or cultural variations but mainly within the limits of social class. Negotiating differences in values is, after all, demanding, and not something that many adults do, many of us preferring to mix socially with 'people like us'.

Through these normative and relational patterns and their attendant processes of social advantage, we can see ways in which class fractional differences are instantiated in everyday aspects of social reproduction, and are also embedded in and reproduced within social institutions. They rest upon and are revealed within the power of allusions, asides, avoidances and aversion – the work of loose-fitting but practical classifications, senses 'of place' and of 'being out of place'. There is a dual element then to these small acts of closure. On the one hand, there is recognition of others 'like us', a 'class-attributive judgement' (Bourdieu 1986, p. 473). On the other, is a sense of alienation, of difference, from 'others' not 'like us' – 'aliens among their own species' (Charlesworth 2000, p. 9). The existence of nuanced but serious differences in values-based views of and attitudes toward social mix is also related to lifestyle differences, consumption decisions and class performativities (cars, clothes, housing, etc.). These differences in lifestyle are obliquely glimpsed in these data: for the families they underpin 'reasonably genteel battles to assert their own identities, social positions and worth' (Savage *et al.* 1992, p. 100).

The other side of this is a much more distinct seal between the middle class as a whole and the working class. Strategies of closure are evident. While the divisions and classifications which demarcate fractions *within* classes are articulated in subtle terms, those which demarcate boundaries *between* classes are stark. In one particular form, what is evident here is what Wacquant (1991, p. 52) refers to as the 'self production of class collectivities' achieved 'through struggles which simultaneously involve relationships between and within classes and determine the actual demarcation of new frontiers'. In a sense what we are glimpsing here is the extent to which the middle class, as a 'theoretical class', is also a 'real class' and its fractions are 'real' fractions (Bourdieu 1987). That is to say, as well as socioeconomic categories, 'a class on paper', they appear as categories which agents use in relation to the social world and 'their place in it' (1987, p. 8). The distinctions 'on paper' have a basis in practice. These service-class families are aware of themselves as sharing certain dispositions, and are aware of the variation of these dispositions among themselves, and thus distinguish themselves from others within and outside of their social space.

What we suggest then, following Butler and Robson (2001), are two different but not necessarily distinct, localized, middle-class habituses, which are rooted in different combinations of capital and forms of social relationships. Battersea is more homogeneous, more 'self-contained' as Butler and Robson (2001) put it. They go as far as to suggest that there is a 'one-dimensional and rather stifling atmosphere of conformity' (p. 2153) and a 'very strong sense of "people like us" gathering together' (p. 2153). This commonality, and the concomitant sense of safety and convenience of schools and services, is important to many of the inhabitants. Social capital rests almost exclusively on horizontal social relations. Mutuality is interpersonal and primarily instrumental. In contrast, in Stoke Newington, diversity is generally a positive value, and social, particularly ethnic mixing, is actively sought by many parents as part of the experience of growing up for their child – a different kind of social capital. This is a sort of symbolic mutuality. Alongside this, in contrast to Battersea, there are various ways, in relation to childcare, in which 'active mutuality' is valued e.g. co-operative, community and 'alternative' nurseries (Vincent *et al.* 2004). Only in Stoke Newington do we find our respondents considering sending their children to council nurseries, or attending and participating in the running of community nurseries, or organizing and running co-operative nurseries (see Table 4.1). There is more evidence here of 'vertical' social capital. Stoke Newington parents are also much more likely to consider childminders. In contrast, in Battersea qualified nannies are widely used and there are a growing number of nanny agencies in the locality. In their study of six London localities

Butler with Robson (2003) found nannies to be the most popular choice of childcare in only two – Battersea and Barnsbury in North London – and they make the point that employing a nanny 'kept control by ensuring that all socialization occurred within the home' (2003, p. 114). In Stoke Newington, parents who did employ nannies tended to rely on unqualified, often young women from overseas. Indeed the 'grey economy' in childcare was much more in evidence in Stoke Newington. Nor were there any local secular private schools available to the Stoke Newington parents. A different or complementary way of thinking about the childcare arrangements in Stoke Newington is that they involve the use of social and cultural capitals, of which the families have considerable amounts, as an alternative to economic capital with which they are relatively less well endowed. And that, in part, the differences between Stoke Newington and Battersea inhere in 'different proclivities to prioritize particular capital stocks in order to meet the primary goal of social reproduction and the enhancement of their children's cultural capital' (Butler with Robson 2003, p. 73).

There are no heroes and villains here; things are not as simple as that, although the account is difficult to write without setting the emphasis on social values in Stoke Newington against the emphasis on family interests in Battersea within the choice of childcare. Both sets of parents are committed to doing their best for their children. They construe 'the best' and how to achieve it in slightly different ways, based on differently inflected local social values. They both accrue class resources for their families but in different ways, in different forms, producing potentially different individualities (Skeggs 2004). The moral geographies (Holloway 1998) differ and what is 'good parenting' thus differs, at least in these respects. Therefore, another way of thinking about these different socialities is that there are perhaps two different sets of interests at work – grounded in different work and career environments which in turn inform particular conceptions of social development and social life. One 'fits' the child for a socially exclusive world and socially homogeneous occupations (the world of finance capital and big business) and the other 'fits' the child for a more socially diverse world (the world of public and liberal professionalism, and the arts). Perhaps in both cases parents are making choices in relation to the 'imagined futures' of their children; for the Stoke Newington parents and the Battersea 'dissenters' social mix is important to them for their children's understanding of and being in the world. For these children, different views of the social mix are reconstituted through early social experiences, and different forms of cultural capital are acquired, leaving 'their more or less visible marks' (Bourdieu 2004, p. 18).

All of the above follows Bernstein's outline of the alignments between class fractions and educational codes. Indeed he suggests 'that location, hierarchical position in the field of symbolic control or in the economic field would regulate distinct forms of consciousness and ideology *within* the middle class' (1996, p. 113) and that agents of symbolic control (Bernstein 1990, pp. 138–40), the new middle class (as in Stoke Newington), with 'no necessarily shared ideology' (p. 135) appear more comfortable with 'relaxed' boundaries and relative social mix or are at least more willing to postpone the necessities of exclusivity (we return to this issue in Chapter 7). As noted earlier it was Stoke Newington's vibrancy, 'difference' and multiculturalism that attracted many of the respondents. This was something they wanted to be part of and have their children share but equally they have an ambiguous and ambivalent relationship with 'the urban' of Hackney. These parents were also more likely to participate in the public sphere, in organizing or contributing to childcare arrangements. They are also in some respects less sure of themselves and their values, more ambivalent. By contrast the traditional middle class, agents of control in the economic field as in Battersea, who are 'likely to share common interests and common ideology' (Bernstein 1990, p. 135), are more concerned to establish firm boundaries and relative social exclusivity from the earliest stages of their children's care and education (see also van Zanten and Veleda 2001). At face value the lives of these families seem more inward-looking and privatized. Many of the Battersea children move from nannies at home to private nurseries to private school, privileged and 'secure sites' (Teese 2000) insulated from the frissons of social mix and social diversity. To a great extent they avoid the ambiguities of the urban. The 'good life' is located firmly within the family. These families are sure of themselves and their values, they are confident and convey a sense of entitlement and yet also seem more wary of the risks and insecurities of social life in London.

What we have sought to do here is to establish a plausible case and a set of possibilities for further research which seeks to ground class in the practical principles of division and the actual systems of aversion and affinity which structure the social relations of particular social spaces – social structures in the head. That is to move beyond the 'theoreticist illusion' (Bourdieu 1987, p. 7) of 'class on paper' to take seriously how class 'gets done'. Childcare is a critically pertinent focus for such an endeavour. In several respects it is the heartland of the formation of classed subjects.

Chapter 5

Inside the 'black box' of the family

Gender relations and childcare

Anyone who talks about the family must also discuss work and money

(Beck 1992, p. 103)

Introduction

Over 60 per cent of mothers in the UK are now in paid employment (the government's Ten Year Strategy for Childcare cites a 2002 figure of 64 per cent of mothers in employment, HMT 2004). Between 1988 and 1998 the employment rate for women with children under five rose from 36 per cent to 50 per cent with full-time employment accounting for nearly half of this amount (Mooney *et al.* 2001). Clearly such an increase constitutes considerable social change, and brings to the fore a set of dilemmas and tensions for those mothers in paid work. One tension may be that traditional attitudes concerning children and mothering remain powerful and widespread. Such attitudes invest the mother with the primary responsibility for the care and development of her children. One recent study by Bradley *et al.* (2003) reported that a quarter of the young women interviewed in Bristol said their ideal was 'father working, mother not' whilst a further 38 per cent said it was 'father working [full time], mother part time'. In this chapter we consider whether the respondents in our research, a highly educated group of middle-class women in their thirties and forties, share the views expressed by the younger women (from a range of social class backgrounds) in Bradley *et al.*'s broader study. We also consider paternal involvement with their children, focusing on the views and practices of the small number of fathers who took part in our research. Other research on fathers (e.g. see O'Brien's 2005 review of research for the Equal Opportunities Commission (EOC)) suggests that traditional divisions of responsibility are changing – but very slowly. O'Brien notes, for instance, that whilst the amount of time men spend with their children is increasing, it is less than the time women spend. In dual full-time earner couples, men spend about 75 per cent of women's absolute time with their children. Additionally, whilst flexible working and paternity leave is endorsed by men, take-up of both remains low (O'Brien 2005, pp. 7–8). Another EOC survey reported that 79 per cent of men interviewed said that they would be happy to stay at home and care for their children on their own (Thompson *et al.* 2005, p. 10). However, only 20 per cent had made some adjustments to their working pattern when they had a baby and only 10 per cent had made a permanent change (ibid. p. 11).

Against this background, we explore in this chapter how the professional middle-class mothers in our research responded to the emotional and physical labour required of them by their role as both worker and mother, how they negotiate the tensions between the two, how fathers understand their role, and how couples adapt to managing employment, childcare and a household. Arguably, it is this social group of men and women who, by virtue of their relative affluence, are in a position to create new forms of and approaches to combining paid work, and motherhood and fatherhood. However, we suggest that 'traditional' responses, whereby the mother slows down or gives up her career and takes on the prime responsibility for caring for children and organizing care by others, are predominant amongst our respondent group.

Our research cohort is a very particular, highly educated one, as we noted in Chapter 2. These are women who have been educated to have careers, rather than jobs, careers for which they had trained and studied and which they enjoyed for their own sake. Catherine Hakim, in her study of mothers' attitudes towards paid work, argues that 'graduate women ... do not automatically prefer a career over family life' (2000, p. 94), but that higher education does give women access to and the expectations of a 'reasonably interesting and well-paid job' if they are in employment (2000, p. 96), an apt description of our respondents. Like the middle-class respondents in McMahon's (1995) study of American working mothers, they made the choice of 'adding children to their lives: work was taken for granted ... [they made] personal and financial investments in work and career that they found rewarding' (1995, p. 227). When they have children, our respondents, like McMahon's, have to work to reconcile a newly acquired identity as 'mother' with other existing identities as 'worker' (which are well established), because of the different demands of the roles. For some the task of reconciliation is impossible, for others it is not even attempted. For others, such as Felicity, finding some sort of balance between the two roles is vital:

> I loved going to work and I've always been a huge feminist. I went to one of those kind of girls' grammar schools that was incredibly correct in terms of getting people out doing maths and sciences. I just picked up this whole culture about women being able to do anything ... I like the fact that I earn more money than my husband does. I found it very good to be able to go back to work [after having a child]. I'd find it incredibly economically marginal. I found I hated being marginalized, just being seen as a mother ... So it was nice to get back to work but I kind of wanted the balance, I wanted to be able to have my cake and eat it, as in spend some time

with him [son] and some time working ... I wasn't ever going to be a very
good full-time mother and I think I would have got quite unhappy if I had
been

(Felicity (B), self-employed consultant and
writer, also lectures, works part-time)

Felicity would seem to present a stereotype of the successful middle-class, professional woman. She and her husband between them earn enough to cover an
estimated £35–40,000 per year in childcare costs (they have a nanny and her
son also attends some sessions at a private nursery). She travels abroad; she
works from home free from institutional constraints; she does not feel guilty
about not caring full-time for her son; she wants, as that infamous phrase goes,
'to have it all'. Indeed she generally manages the balancing act that requires, but
running alongside her acknowledgement of privilege is another narrative
revealing stress and distress:

If you had spoken to me last December I'd be completely, 'this is awful, this
is terrible, working with children and childcare and it's really dreadful'.
Well it is really hard work and it is really dreadful anyway, but I'm just
more positive about recent experiences. Last December I was completely
in despair about the whole thing ... How on earth do you keep all those
things going? How do you juggle it all? ... There was one occasion with
our old nanny where I had to go to a big meeting and I couldn't go and
literally people turned up at Kings Cross expecting me to be on the train
and I wasn't there which was one of the most dreadful experiences of my
life and they never paid their bill ... even though they were paying for
other things too. I let them down on a really big occasion ... I was in
floods of tears. I just sat on the floor and howled because there wasn't
much else to do really

If anyone could be expected to manage childcare and work, then one would
expect it to be Felicity with all her advantages and, not least, her certainties.
Yet when things go wrong – and we recognise that what seems 'dreadful' to
her may not compare to the crises experienced by some families – it is still she
who is left to pick up the pieces. However, we are not intending to make the
point that even affluent middle-class mothers cannot 'have it all' – the tabloid
press often appears to rejoice in tales of 'career women' who have given up
their lucrative and high status positions and returned home to look after their
children (Benn 1998) – this re-statement of traditional role models is, needless
to say, not a stance we share. It is rather an attempt to understand and document two interrelated features of the relationship between motherhood and
paid work. The first and easiest of these tasks is to identify the various practical and tangible settlements that mothers have made between employment
and mothering, and to describe the constraints under which they operate. The

second task is to reveal more nebulous settlements, how these highly educated women resolve the tensions between two competing discourses, one which values paid employment, especially in high status professional and managerial posts, and another set of disparate discourses around contemporary mothering which both value and devalue the work of caring for young children. We suggest this discursive tension is indicative of a fundamental confusion in society about the status of caring for young children, and the role of mothers, fathers and others in that task. As Grace (1998) argues,

> On the one hand, mothers are ascribed an almost holy status, providing some recognition of their contribution, but locking them into expectations of extreme self-sacrifice. On the other hand their work is considered non-work, is not economically rewarded and is not generally respected
>
> (p. 401) (also Hondagneu-Sotelo 2003)

It is not the norm for this group of highly educated, middle-class women to stay at home and not to go out to work. For this reason caring work is not necessarily central to their self-image in the way that it is for the group of working-class women assembled by Bev Skeggs (1997). Her respondents, students on further education 'caring' courses, frequently set their practical experience of caring (for children or the elderly) over the academic component of the course, and saw their practical abilities as innate: they were 'naturals'.

The women in our study who work do not hesitate to pay for care. Their attitudes also contrast somewhat with those expressed by women in Jordan *et al.'s* (1992) study of the inhabitants of a working-class council estate in Exeter. Bill Jordan and his colleagues comment that interviews with the mothers revealed that 'the obligation to put the children's needs first is binding' (p. 135), often over and above the needs of paid work and almost always above the needs of the mothers themselves. This attitude was also voiced by 'peripheral working class' women in a study of mothers conducted by Simon Duncan and colleagues (Duncan 2005). Together with Hays (1996), we recognize that the need to construct a morally adequate account of oneself as mother requires women of *all* classes to present their prioritization of their children's needs, as becomes apparent below. The class-specific differences between the working-class mothers in the Exeter study and also those in a study by Edwards and Duncan (1996; Duncan 2005), and the middle-class women in our study, are revealed in the different practical and discursive ways in which these moral accounts are produced within different 'local moral geographies of mothering' (Holloway 1998). Similarly Duncan (2005) analyses how women's choices around paid work and children are 'socially and culturally created' through various factors such as the extent to which work is, and is perceived to be, a career rather than a job, the extent to which partners share domestic labour and through the development of normative views in social networks. 'In this way [choices]

become social moralities. In turn these moralities are geographically and his-
torically articulated'[1] (p. 73). For these working-class respondents, paid care is
seen as inappropriate and unaffordable, and care by family members and close
friends is almost always preferable. By contrast our middle-class respondents
engage largely with the formal market in childcare (qualified nannies, registered childminders, private day nurseries), but also, in some cases, with the
informal market (unqualified carers, often recent immigrants) out of which are
made complex patchworks of care, which include the mothers themselves (see
Table 4.1 in Chapter 4).

These patchworks differ from one another. It is possible to identify a variety
of responses amongst our respondents as they sought to resolve what Hays
(1996) calls the 'cultural contradictions of motherhood' arising from two
opposing logics, that of the private family sphere and that of the public market
place. Duncan (2005) also noted intra-class divisions between the working-
class and middle-class mothers in his study with regard to their attitude to
work. In the middle-class groups (overwhelmingly composed of graduates who
had current or recent careers and were 'incomers' to their suburban and rural
areas – our metropolitan mothers after leaving the metropolis perhaps), the
'suburban wives' in an upmarket Leeds suburb had 'deliberately placed career to
one side' whilst the gentrifying group of Hebden Bridge in Yorkshire had
'brought career to the fore'. This division can also be seen reflected in our
respondents, although as will become clear, we have conceptualized the differing positions and investments as a continuum, as in some cases the women's
attitudes changed as circumstances altered (children grew, a new baby arrived,
their partner made a career change, etc.).

Some of the women in our study had chosen to give up paid work, others
shortened their hours and slowed the pace of their careers. The vast majority
had adapted their careers in some lasting way. Out of 59 respondents 29
worked part-time, 20 were at home full-time, 10 worked full-time at the time
of the interview, or were on maternity leave and planning to return full-time.
As Table 5.1 shows, this was one issue on which there was little difference
between the two areas of Battersea and Stoke Newington.

However, these numbers do not convey the range of different resolutions,
the variations in attitudes and circumstances. Working part-time for instance
varies between four days a week and ten days a month. Some gave up work
when their first child was born and have no plans to return, others gave up

Table 5.1 Mothers' working patterns

	Home	Part-time	Full-time	Total
Battersea	10	14	4	28
Stoke Newington	10	15	6	31
Total	20	29	10	59

more reluctantly as working and mothering became too stressful, or childcare too expensive. Others have moved between full-time, part-time, and no paid work as circumstances changed (usually the arrival of a new baby). Hays (1996) talks of the 'mommy wars' between two stereotypes, a stay-at-home baker of cookies and a superwoman effortlessly juggling home and career. For many of our London respondents the reality is more fluid as their work and care scenarios change as the children grow and circumstances alter. The difficulties of finding a balance between paid work and caring for children is apparent in the high number of women who now work part-time. They '"live a contradiction" by juggling options, possibilities and disappointments' in a context in which a 'socially organised' system for women to combine satisfactory 'work and family' does not exist (Padfield and Proctor 1998, p. 249, cited in McKie *et al.* 2001, p. 244; also Grace 1998, p. 407). Hakim (2000) understands this diversity as evidence of women making different kinds of positive choices, and with regard only to our relatively privileged sample we mostly agree (our respondents often noted their 'luck' in being in/out of paid employment as they chose). However, Hakim continues by saying that 'preference theory suggests that a change of emphasis is needed in sociological research, away from structural factors … towards the values and preferences that will shape behaviour in the twenty first century' (2000, p. 278). This stance, and Hakim's emphasis on 'individualised preference' (Duncan *et al.* 2003, p. 325) concerns us because we are acutely aware that many members of our respondent group are privileged in having employment that allows them a high degree of autonomy, flexibility and control, which is not available to many other working women (see Reynolds *et al.* 2003 on the importance of this for mothers' perceptions of paid work). Furthermore, as Hakim acknowledges, our study and many others (e.g. Hochschild 1989; Hays 1996; McMahon 1995; Duncan 2005; Gatrell 2005) illustrate how deeply embedded women remain within gendered divisions of domestic labour which pre-empt the possibilities of choice.

The rationales for the decisions mothers took vary considerably (see also Hakim 2000). We can place the respondents on what we have called an *investment continuum* ranging from investment in full-time mothering to investment in full-time paid work. Some gave up because they found it impossible to continue to do their paid work, because of the demands of long hours, or the difficulty in finding childcare with which they were happy. A few had no clear career plan. Others had no desire to continue in paid work once they had children. Some are in part-time work because they made a clear choice to do so, wanting a balance between work and being with their children, others because they found full-time work too difficult to manage, as they struggled to meet the demands of inflexible jobs and employers. A consideration of different women at different points in the continuum illustrates individual settlements, often temporary or fragile, between the demands of motherhood and paid work, settlements made at both practical and ideological levels. Let us look at some of these.

Working women

Staying at home

Generally the justifications given by mothers for staying at home, especially those who said they had made a clear choice to do so, were less detailed than justifications which women put forward to explain their paid work. In this sense, being a full-time carer of one's own children is understood as 'natural', 'normal' and needing little explanation, still less justification. Mothers spoke of their emotional commitment to being at home with children ('I was completely changed by having a baby … it just occurred to me I didn't have to go back, it was like a revelation' (Jackie, SN)), and their desire to care for their children themselves. However, in making the decision to stop paid work, the women exchange their high-status careers for a caring role, doing so in a society which devalues caring jobs (taken in the most part by poorly paid, working-class young women). Certainly some of our providers spoke about the way in which caring for children is not perceived as skilled work, but rather as something 'any old person from the street' can do (Garden nursery manager, SN). One childminder commented similarly:

> I think [people] think childminders are quite thick and quite stupid, and you're only doing this [job] because you couldn't do anything else. And it's like when [parents] find out that I've got a degree and stuff, they're kind of 'why are you doing this if you've got a degree? You could work'
>
> (Marcia, childminder, SN)

Many respondents were aware of the low status of caring roles, and were quickly frustrated by the implications of this. In this climate, where caring is casually disconnected from 'proper' work, mothers have to remake those connections for themselves and others, emphasizing that mothering is an important and valuable job, or even a 'vocation' as one refers to it. It is a maternal responsibility, almost a moral obligation to care for your own children. 'Own' is the keyword here; it serves to differentiate these mothers from low-paid, low-status carers:

> Whilst I palm him off on someone else [a nursery] for two days a week I didn't actually have him for someone else to bring him up … Some people think should I give up work or shouldn't I? I didn't have that dilemma, I knew what I wanted to do
>
> (Sandra, used to be in PR)

> When I put her in [one nursery] I cried every time I left her. She cried too … it was awful … And I did have slight feelings of guilt obviously because I wasn't working and it was my job to look after [her]. [Now] she doesn't want to hang around with me all day … so I don't have any guilt any more

about dropping her off. But I do still want to be there, you know, even when she's at school. I don't want her to be a latchkey kid

(Sally, B, used to be in PR)

I didn't really [ever consider getting help] ... 15 months apart is quite close together, [but] I thought they'll just have to learn ... there were days when it was absolutely awful and I really could have used some help, but I think it's a learning process ... that's all part of being in a family ... I've got a lady who comes and helps clean but the childcare I think, I wanted to do ... I value what I do ... I think that it is a worthwhile thing ... he's [husband] really lovely and he often tells me he couldn't do it and that I'm doing a good job and that I've got patience and all that sort of stuff that he doesn't have, which is nice ... When it's really horrible there's not a lot you can [do]. You know some days aren't good, like any other job.

(Suzannah, SN, used to be recruitment consultant)

In the back of my mind I knew I wanted to slip out of the working world for a while ... I felt my role as a mother is to bring up my children myself, and that's, you know, my vocation, I've chosen to do it and I should jolly well get on and do it, er, but as we're expecting a third and I was shouting at my children more and more, they were two boisterous little boys and I just thought I'm not, why am I fighting it, do you know what I mean? It's just things like [the proposed au pair] can help me just be nicer to my children because I've got to try, I found I was always ignoring them because you're trying to get on with tasks, the house tasks and the phoning, or you're sticking them in front of the video for hours because you're trying to organize something, or cook, or whatever ... I just felt I wanted to enjoy my children, I suddenly – looked at [oldest son], and although he's three, he seems so grown up, and I thought 'well where has it gone?' It's gone in me trying to stuff the washing machine and shouting at him because he's ripping something off the wall, and I thought I really want to enjoy this third one, I don't want to miss it

(Eleanor, B, used to be in PR)

There is a clear distinction in the women's words (if not perhaps in their practice) between staying at home to be with the children and staying at home to be a housewife. Eleanor's transcript is unusual in our sample for the extent to which domestic chores appear, unprompted by us. Walkerdine and Lucey (1989) argue that housework for middle-class mothers goes underground, transformed from dullness into a site of pedagogy for their children, offering opportunities to pair the socks as they come out of the washing machine, and so on! This is quite a difficult task for mothers to achieve particularly if their children do not want to co-operate. In any case, as Eleanor and Suzannah realize, au pairs and cleaners make the demands of domestic labour less pressing. The working-class mothers in Walkerdine and Lucey's study are clear that housework is their job, and must often be prioritized over playing with their children. For the mothers in our sample, housework is a job from which they can extract themselves by buying in others. Housework interferes with the primary focus on the child. Childcare and the mother–child relationship is represented as special in all this – special for the mother as well as the child, an opportunity to be enjoyed. However, such enjoyment requires particular conditions of care.

As indicated already, there are also risks attached to staying at home: a risk of loss of self and identity, well expressed by Jackie:

> I'm not always entirely happy with the situation [not working]. I can't quite relax about it. I'm a bit nervous about letting go completely of work and losing my confidence, and I also have days of complete frustration with [the children], so I feel I ought to do something probably … basically in the next year I want to make some kind of decision about what I want to do, I can't just leave it
>
> (Jackie, SN, was in publishing/translation)

> If I do go into another world, for example if I go with [partner] to a function or something like that, I do feel a little bit like I am completely out of touch with what is going on in the business world … It's taken me a while to realize that actually I do probably have to justify my brain or my existence, because they don't know me. They just see me as somebody's partner who is a stay-at-home mother. And perhaps I have to try a little harder to appear a bit more intelligent … In the last three years if people say, what do you do? I am more likely to say that I am a mother. But I would also probably say I edit this magazine [voluntary work]. To give myself some credibility. That I do something else
>
> (Sally, B, used to be in PR)

There is the perception that society pays only lip service to the value of mothering, whereas in the world of work, by contrast you 'are valued for what you can contribute' (Margaret, B, also Gatrell 2005). As Felicity points out above, to be a mother is to be marginalized in many situations. Similarly Eleanor talks of 'slipping out of the working world'. To be a mother is to be outside of 'society' and wholly inside 'family'. And being inside family is a risky place to be. Mothering is hard work. Whilst Beck and Beck-Gernsheim (1995) argue that motherhood can be a refuge from the soberly, impersonal working world, where emotion is largely frowned upon, seen as a distraction, the emotion derived from a home with small children can be raw. One mother talks of 'being consumed' by her children (Tina); another of the 'emotional rollercoaster' of having a baby (Anjali), and another about the utmost importance of having other mothers as support (Sandra). There is guilt about buying in care to give time for themselves rather than 'having' to buy care because of work, guilt about wanting to be away from your children, and fear (see Jackie above) of losing one's ability to engage with the 'outside' world (also Vincent 2000). The risks of staying at home are starkly summarized by Hays: 'In short, the world presents, and mothers experience, the image of the lazy, mindless, dull housewife – and no mother wants to be included in that image' (1996, p. 138).

In the labour market

Those of our respondents who remained involved in the labour market spoke of the liberation of working. This was meant both in the financial sense and also in terms of maintaining a particular and socially valued sense of self and a series of relationships separate and distanced from their children:

> With [oldest child] someone had said to me 'oh you're gonna find the first day you give over your child really difficult, it's really tough'. And I was in the car singing along to the radio, my own music rather than bloody *Wheels on the Bus*, just thinking this is absolutely fantastic
>
> (Kathryn, B, part-time speech therapist)

McMahon points here to the influence of 'cultural rhetorics of individualism' (1995, p. 2). For the middle classes in particular, she argues, a good mother demonstrates 'commitment without engulfment', and employs 'strategies of separation' (ibid. p. 153, p. 15). For middle-class women 'employment is constructed as an opportunity for the expression of self'. Concomitantly, Jordan *et al.* (1994) point to the moral imperative operating amongst the middle classes to 'make something of yourself', and Gatrell (2005) highlights the commitment of the middle-class mothers in her research to their paid work. In these circumstances, pregnancy and having children constitute a challenge to their working identity (Bailey 1999, p. 341). Returning to work, particularly to part-time work, can lead to a new resolution, a new alignment between different facets of identity. As Linda and Debra say:

> I positively want to work and I know I'm a better person for working, a happier person for working.
>
> (Linda, B, charity consultant)

> It was quite straightforward [returning to work] because I work for a big organization which has ... flexible working plans I think they're called. What I did was I met my immediate boss about a month before [I was due to return] just in a coffee bar, just you know 'let's meet up with the baby' and she said 'what would you like to do?' and I said 'I'd like to work three days' and that was it ... I actually like going to work, [working part-time] I think has really improved the quality of my life, not being in the office all week.
>
> (Debra, producer, BBC)

Debra refers here to the way in which motherhood can also be a positive inter-ruption of the damaging effects of 'engulfment' by one's employment.

A few respondents also spoke about performing socially useful work. Bailey notes that some types of work and mothering have important discursive simi-larities – redolent of responsibility, service, stability, interest and value (rather than status or money). Some jobs have a moral worth in the same way mother-ing does, but on a larger and more public stage (Bailey 1999, p. 342). Even so, within families there is always the possibility that the worth of work and the worth of the worker are reduced to a financial calculation:

> He [partner] and I have very different perceptions as to why one works. His is very definitely you work to bring money in to support the family. And the more money you get, the better you are at fulfilling that role, and therefore the more valuable your job is. My view is … what do I want to do that's interesting and useful? And so he cannot understand why I should want to go to work when I'm paid so crap and it sort of takes over … he can't see why when I've got the option of staying at home and looking after the children, and meeting friends for lunch and playing tennis why I don't do that. Because it doesn't bring any money in so why do I choose to put myself under pressures that I put myself under by going to work … I'm writing up a PhD, … so I have to work, I work most evenings and I'm getting up sometimes in the morning as well before the children wake up so that I can do a couple of hours before they get up … He will tolerate the intrusion of it as long as it doesn't intrude in any way … But to me working is fundamental to how you see yourself and how you see your role in society and your role with other people.
>
> (Kathryn, B; she is a part-time speech therapist, he is a lawyer)

Work here is central to identity and helps in the development of a sense of self-esteem, via one's contribution to society, not indirectly through the private sphere of family, but directly working in the public arena (also Gatrell 2005). We also glimpse here another aspect of the calculus of balance for these women – the absence of fathers in the discourse of care, but the need nonetheless to take partners into account in arriving at some kind of balance or resolution of identity and responsibility.

Furthermore, several women appeared to offer justifications for continu-ing to work. They resisted or rejected a key aspect of the dominant understanding of 'feminine' by asserting that they were not 'natural' mothers and contrasting themselves with an ideal 'natural' mother who consistently enjoyed being with her children, was skilled at stimulating them, was never in a bad mood, and was fulfilled by her role. Therefore, as they saw it, their working was to their children's advantage. Others, trained and professional, could do a better job:

By the time I'd started to work full-time again I was desperate not to be, I'm not a natural stay-at-home, raising kids and not doing anything else, I was climbing the walls

(Mia, SN, works now for NGO, used to work as arts administrator)

I do not believe my children would be better off if I was staying at home looking after them ... I think they'd have all the vagaries of me as an individual ... if I'm in a ratty mood for whatever reasons, that's going to be difficult. And I don't think I've got the skills to ... I can spot some of the stuff eventually, but I think I'm probably less ambitious for them, perhaps than the nursery is. So I tend to see them playing with something at the nursery and then think 'oh that would be a good idea to get at home' ... or I can be surprised by what they're doing. And I don't think I have a natural, a sort of, that doesn't that doesn't all come naturally to me.

(Monica, B, public sector accountant)[2]

Work/childcare tensions: 'the politics of time' (Benn 1998)

Stephens' (1999) study of female hospital doctors who work part-time and have children is an example of the workings of the 'politics of time'. For the women, time is 'earned' (she gives examples of women attempting to plan the conception of their children to allow them to start work part-time and still progress with their careers), or 'bought' (by paying for childcare or domestic help). Time for themselves has to be 'stolen' and their own leisure time was often subsumed by the supervision of their children's activities (see also Gatrell 2005).

Stephens' general point about the gendered nature of time applies to all our respondents given that in all our families, it is women who take responsibility for finding and managing childcare. However, the specific focus of her study – hospital doctors – points to the possibility of variations between occupations in terms of the flexibility which they offer. This argument – the importance of the organizational ethos and culture for how mothers experience paid work – is also made by Crompton (2001) in her study of GPs and bankers, and Reynolds et al. (2003), in their study of mothers who work for two contrasting employers, a public sector hospital and a private accountancy firm. Sometimes, as with Margot (from our study and quoted below), a particular individual in an organization can make a difference. Some jobs combine well with childcare, better than others, allowing mothers (it usually is mothers) to work part-time (see Debra above). Other careers, particularly those in the private sector, often the financial sector of the City of London, emphasize presenteeism and long hours, where the ethos demands that one submits to the 'male model of work often at considerable personal cost' (Phoenix 1991, p. 203; see also Pearson's 2002 fictional account of a middle-class City mother). Here the ideal employee is what is termed in the USA a 'zero-load' worker (the term deriving from Silicon

Valley), one who has no domestic commitments, can be flexible and mobile.[3] Justine and Margot both work in the City, and discuss how they address the contradiction between the demands of their children and their employment.

> Realistically it is hard to allow people with children just to work 9–5 so one way or another those people find other hours to work so when I went back to work the last time I used, after my son had gone to bed, I used to do a couple of hours at home … I'd say 10 hours a day isn't unusual, and the bank that we've just merged with I would say 12 hours was quite common there … I was still very determined to have a career, because with one [child] I think you can do it. I think with two you have to face up to the fact that you probably have to take more of a back seat … but given that my husband earns more than I do, it means inevitably that my career has to be kind of put on hold because one of us has to go and pick the children up from nursery
>
> (Justine, B, City accountant, husband also accountant)

Margot, who has three young children, talks of the new chairman of her bank, as responsible for creating some policy change in an organization previously unsympathetic to flexible or part-time working patterns. Even so the emotional tensions remain:

> He's been the first one since the bank's creation who's very much for what he calls the 'work/life balance scheme' … Until now you got part-time if your boss wanted to give you part-time. If your immediate boss didn't want to give you part-time, nobody cared. You didn't get it, that was it … Now [they] have to come up with something, because they have no option … I leave work at 6 p.m. … But what I've done is I've worked every evening on average, you know two or three hours after the children are asleep. When you are pregnant and everything it made the whole thing a little bit stressful [When I came back to work after our first child I felt] very guilty, felt unsafe a little bit, was not quite sure what was happening at home. Physically missed the baby in my arms. It was really very much a physical feeling. And that was for the first six weeks and then you know, I slowly got over it … Still the guilt of not being at home, that's something that never goes away I think for most mothers
>
> (Margot, B, lawyer in bank)

Margot's words illustrate the tensions embodied in the phrase 'working mother' as she struggles to manage her maternal feelings in what remains, despite the recent focus on 'work/life balance', as an impersonal and demanding workplace.

Occupations expecting long hours and participation in office politics are not confined to the City. Gaby is an architect and talks of the difficulty of being on the periphery of 'two worlds'. She does not want to immerse herself in either to the exclusion of the other, but the two do not easily segue. Neither does she feel there is any viable alternative to working four days a week:

> The only sad thing, and this is just, you know, it'd be really nice, it feels she [carer] gets to raise [son] and I don't. You know it's just, you know, you're giving your baby to a complete stranger, but as complete strangers go, I feel quite, quite good that it's her ... I don't think I would have wanted to take five years off but I certainly would be quite happy if I could have taken his whole first year off ... Meanwhile at work I feel it's so much this kind of work culture, and they all go out for drinks or whatever ... If I were to go out of it for five years it'd be harder to come back in ... [if I worked three days rather than four] I'd feel so out of the loop and I wouldn't be able to attend meetings and therefore it'd be all second-hand information and that's a power thing.
>
> (Gaby, SN)

Gaby seems to be caught acutely between the two worlds of which she speaks. She talks with intensity about not seeing her children enough, her awareness that they are growing and that she is not there to act as a constant witness. Neither is she a full-time participant in the culture of employment. She seems to lose out in both spheres, experiencing a dual dissatisfaction. Her ambivalence about full-time motherhood is revealed in the way she talks about her thought processes adapting to her return to work: 'I also feel it's very hard to come out of being off and your brain just kind of turns to mush. Or it's not turned to mush, but is concentrating other things'. Although she quickly denies that motherhood turns your brain to 'mush', she then continues by saying 'it's kind of like reverse senility. I, kind of, started and couldn't remember anything, my head was in a cloud' (or 'fog', elsewhere) (also McMahon 1995, p. 226). Motherhood is clearly not seen as intellectually demanding. Rather motherhood embodies a different relationship between self and others, a relationship that is traditionally expressed in physical and emotional terms, rather than through the more abstract intellectual challenge of professional paid employment. It seems that Enlightenment dichotomies of nature and body versus the mind and culture are still in play here. Although women now participate very markedly in the public sphere, the pull of nurturing is still strong. This is problematic only insofar as nurturing is understood as a 'timeless and unalterable activity, guided by natural laws and associated with the natural attributes of women' (Everingham 1994, p. 6).

Thus organizing participation in two worlds with contrasting rhythms and values remains a process fraught with ideological and practical difficulties. However this is understood in the UK solely as a problem of management for individual women (Grace 1998). As McMahon comments, 'the political, organisational and ideological contradictions between those spheres [caring at home and paid work] are reduced to the private problem of organising and scheduling, a private problem of balancing' (1995, p. 206). We consider below the ideology of 'intensive mothering' which appears to address the tensions between the demands of children and paid employment, although with considerable costs to the mother. Another way forward is indicated by Duncan *et al.* (2003; Duncan 2005) in their study of mothers' attitudes towards paid work. They identify three stances, practical/discursive resolutions which they term 'gendered moral rationalities' and which the mothers adopted. These bear some similarity to positions on our investment continuum. They are 'primarily mother', 'primarily worker' and 'mother/worker integral'. The latter position was held mainly by respondents of African-Caribbean origin and involved understanding full-time employment as *part* of good mothering (2003, p. 313). Duncan *et al.* comment that 'mothers' gendered moral rationalities still involve their primary responsibility for their children [but] how mothers exercise that responsibility varies' (2003, p. 327). The 'mother/worker integral' rationality appears to have the potential to resolve the tension between Hays' (1996) 'opposing logics' of the private family sphere and public market place:

> It is those with mother/worker integral views who seem to lie on the cutting edge of changing gender divisions in that they conceived providing for their children through paid work as part of mothering.
>
> (Duncan *et al.* 2003, p. 325)

But as our discussion and the data above indicate, such resolutions can be fragile and costly to maintain, both financially and emotionally. Clearly more work needs to be done in exploring the attitudes towards work/life balance, and the settlements made by mothers from a range of social classes and ethnic groups.

Intensive mothering, professional mothers

'The anxiety that one is not doing enough for the child' (Furedi 2001, p. 65) persists for most whether working or not. Hays' (1996) research with middle- and working-class American women and Windebank's (1999) work with French women argue that even those who work adopt 'intensive' styles of mothering. Hays and others point to the conflation of 'good' mothering with intensive mothering, what Walkerdine and Lucey (1989) refer to as 'sensitive mothering', or Manicom (1984) calls 'total mothering'. This describes the heavy investment of the mother's time, energy, money and emotional commitment into enhancing the child's intellectual, physical, social and emotional development. The toll upon the mother is considerable; 'having it all' becomes 'doing it all' (Benn 1998).

> One might argue that employed mothers in the middle class have more to gain from reconstructing ideas about appropriate child rearing than any

other group – not only because their higher salaries mean that more money is at stake but also because intensive mothering potentially interferes with their career trajectory ... But as I have suggested, middle class women are in some respects those who go about the task of child rearing with the greatest intensity

(Hays 1996, p. 151)

Yet for all they [working mothers] do to meet the needs of their children, they still express some ambivalence about working outside the home. And they still resolve this ambivalence by returning to the logic of intensive mothering and reminding the observer that ultimately they are most interested in what is best for their kids. This is striking

(Hays 1996, p. 149)

This ambivalence is, in good part, a consequence of our confusion over the status of motherhood. Women who have children stand at the nexus of two competing policy discourses. One, rooted in economic policy, de-genders a woman (officially at least), portraying her as a skilled and valued worker, contributing to the economy and capable of professional fulfilment and satisfaction. The other discourse, rooted in social policy, we could say almost excessively genders her, and celebrates her 'natural' abilities. It understands 'good' mothering as the key to a child's successful development, placing the responsibility and onus on the mother. As a result, as Hays comments, many middle-class mothers – like those in our research – whether in paid work or not, practise a kind of professional motherhood. They take their children to a range of carefully planned activities. They agonize over their development, their care, their future schooling. They read parenting books and magazines but treat expertise cautiously, engaging in 'reflexive encounters with expert systems' (Giddens 1991). And they do all this whether they work outside the home or not. Indeed, as far as we can judge from the data, all our respondents – whether engaged in paid work or not – could be described as 'professional mothers', practising 'intensive mothering'. Even those mothers who work for long hours and are in Hakim's (2000) terms career-oriented and 'work centred', would not, we feel, view their children, as Hakim suggests, as a 'weekend hobby' (Hakim 2000, p. 164). 'Being a mother [is] a constant social and emotional position' (Duncan 2005, p. 65). The women experience tension between their deep, intense love for their children and a sense of responsibility for all aspects of a child's development – an acceptance of intensive mothering, which acts as the dominant 'cultural script' (McMahon 1995) – versus the grind, boredom, and lack of autonomy and status inherent in looking after small children. Here they reflect a fundamental societal ambivalence about the status of caring for and by extension the status of children themselves (Brannen and Moss 2003). This dilemma between love and tedium, responsibility and marginalization is experienced for the most part by women – not their partners.

The 'second shift' (Hochschild 1989)

Along with other writers, researchers and commentators in this area, we have already noted the placing of childcare as the woman's responsibility. In a majority of cases it is the woman who makes the choice, having done all the research, and her salary pays for the care (Vincent and Ball 2001; Vincent et al. 2004; Himmelweit and Sigala 2002). Indeed this situation seems unchanged from that found by Brannen and Moss in their study of dual-career families in the late 1980s (Brannen and Moss 1991).

Writing in an American context, Hochschild also noted that in middle-class dual career families, women still bear the brunt of the childcare and domestic responsibilities. Rather than men increasing their contribution, the 'solution' is more often for the care responsibilities to be pushed 'down' to, particularly in the US context, lower paid, often immigrant workers (Hochschild 2003; Wrigley 1995). Ehrenreich makes the same point in relation to housework, contending that 'in the chore wars of the 1970s and 1980s, women gained a little ground, but overall ... men won. Enter the cleaning lady as dea ex machina' (Ehrenreich 2003, p. 89).

This is not the situation we expected to find amongst our respondents; with the 'new man' emerging in the 1990s in the UK as an icon of considerable cultural power (Benn 1998), surely research on childcare in the 2000s would show the new man's role was now a mature and established one? Apparently not. Our respondents suggested that in two-career families the pace of one partner had to slow somewhat in order to encompass caring responsibilities. It was the women who moved to part-time work, gave up work, or in a few cases stayed full-time but worked more 'limited' hours. Although we heard rumours of several, we found only one temporary 'stay-at-home' father in our research settings. As McKie et al. note, 'the ideological connection between women and caring (additionally located in the household) continues to underpin public, social and employment policies and notions of "the family"' (2001, p. 234; see also Himmelweit 2002a):

> When he's here he's very involved indeed. He's – I can completely – I mean not that I do – but I can completely just walk out of the door and he would know what to do without me giving any sort of instructions or leaving anything to sort out ... But he's not here very much. He works very long hours so he sees them ten, fifteen minutes in the morning and then that's it for the week, usually apart from the weekend ... I find it really interesting because ... we're both high achieving people, we're both successful in our field, and then you become a mother and suddenly, it's not for any reason other than because you want to be there for your children, and because you have to have some way of coping with the situation, suddenly your roles changed completely ... And you suddenly look at yourself and think 'blimey, I'm in these really traditional roles, and how the

hell did we get here?' ... I think these are things which are so fundamental that they're very deep rooted and you don't know that they exist until you're actually in that situation.

(Kathryn, B, she is a part-time speech therapist, he is a lawyer)

He doesn't see – he adores the children – he probably sees them two or three nights a week, just because they're both in bed at 7 o'clock

(Nancy, B, at home) (see also Justine above)

These extracts contains a number of interesting points. There is the implied assertion that Kathryn's partner is a 'good' carer, because he knows what to do with the children without any instruction from her. It is still difficult to imagine a father talking like this about a mother. Other research in this area also reveals women talking about partners who share in childcare and other domestic responsibilities in similar terms: as 'good' men whom they are 'lucky' to have (Hays 1996; McMahon 1995; Jordan et al. 1992). Men's absence from the home is understood as the reason why they can't be more involved, but the existence of any element of choice about how family responsibilities are organized tends not to be recognized (but see below). Of course, such choice is not open to all, but some of these professional, successful men have earned a degree of financial and working autonomy, and have perhaps more opportunities to choose in favour of time with their children than is commonly recognized. This is in no way to suggest that these men are simply reneging on their responsibilities to their children or that they do not love them sufficiently, rather to assert that motherhood and fatherhood are socially constructed: as different roles, conducted in different ways with different requirements. Thus male careers and working patterns still appear to retain priority even in dual-career households (see also Hatten et al. 2002; Warin et al. 1999; Gregson and Lowe 1994). Bringing up children remains, for the overwhelming majority, the work of women, whether mothers or other women carers. Many women in the study went to considerable lengths to explain and justify the impossibilities – practical and dispositional – of their partner taking on a more significant role in childcare:

Well, he just – well, he's conventional in the sense that he's a man who goes to work and ... I wouldn't want to call him a chauvinist because I wouldn't want to be married to a chauvinist. But he is, he's very male, you know, he's very – he can't do any more than he's doing. And, basically, what he'd – so he can – we have a life where he can leave for work at half past eight ... so he sees us in the morning. And then he comes – he can come back at 6. But after, after a half an hour he starts thinking: 'so when's the bath gonna be? So when are we gonna get them into bed because I've got work to do? And when are we gonna eat?' And there's a kind of – this kind of pressure ... because he comes home early and so he's got to do some work after supper.

And so we have – and I, you know, we've got to change this because I can't live with it … He does the bath while I, you know, tidy up the supper or make our supper, or … But, you know, I'm never, I'm never doing nothing … It's impossible, I think, for him to actually have that much involvement, just out of circumstance, not, not because he's not interested

(Connie, SN)

The traditional gender roles assume a naturalness and inevitability, which appears to at least complicate Hakim's (2000) notion of preferences. A frequent phrase used by female respondents when describing the reassertion of traditional divisions of labour after having children was that it 'just happened'. Another respondent, Linda, described how she and her husband both worked four days a week when their first child was a baby (they now have three children). She made the point that as the woman is seen by others as the main carer in the couple, slowly the woman *becomes* the main carer even if the situation started out differently. However, this is also her choice, whereas her partner chooses slightly differently:

There was an article on him [in an in-house magazine] because he was in the first man [in the organization] who was allowed to work a four-day week for parental responsibility … I always try and work a three-day week. Every time [partner] has moved jobs … he always tries to move towards a four-day week … and sometimes he's been successful and sometimes not … [He is self-employed now] and he's very much trying to work a three-day week … He does a lot more because he is around and he genuinely likes to do things with the children, but he doesn't any longer want to commit a day to that [childcare] and there's no need actually at the moment with the children … I think it happened over time. And I'm, I'm much more clear that I want to spend quite a lot and especially with [eldest son] starting a new [secondary] school, [youngest son] starting nursery, and [middle son] always finds it hard to move to a new teacher … So I wanted to be around much more and I feel that's my choice. But it's much more gender-stereotyped than we would have imagined when we were together before having children

(Linda, B, both self-employed, he is an education consultant, she a charity consultant)

The interesting point of course is why Linda feels the need to spend regular time looking after the children whilst her partner does not. Her comment about choice should not be overlooked; although there were some hints of resentment from women (see Connie above and below) these were rare. Whilst it is indeed possible, as Hays suggests, that mothers are involved in 'strategies to downplay gender inequities', not wanting others or themselves to realize the extent of the imbalance in domestic duties (1996, p. 105), there is also the possibility that in relation to their children, women wish to respond wholeheartedly to what Melissa Benn (1998, p. 233) calls the 'extraordinary pull, joyful and burdensome, of motherhood'. The women in our study did feel they had a choice and they made that choice in favour of their children, rather than their careers or their own time. But of course it was a choice that works within a 'dominant cultural script' (and is therefore simpler to make), a cultural script that posits men's involvement as laudatory but still voluntary (Hochschild 2003; McMahon 1995; also Jordan *et al.* 1992). Fathers are simply not understood to be so central to the emotional and physical well-being of their children as mothers are.

Fathering at a distance or 'the new man'?

Our analysis of the words of the mothers in our study leads us to emphasize the peripherality of the fathers. Many of the fathers were physically absent through work commitments, but even when they were present they were apparently not managing the care of their children to the same extent as their female partners. The perception of greater sharing of domestic and childcare responsibilities between mother and father is, Benn (1998) contends, just that, a perception, not a reality (although see O'Brien 2005 for indications of an increase in the amount of time fathers spend with their children). The commitment may often be qualitatively as well as quantitatively different as women may act as 'the organisational and emotional intelligence behind the scenes' (Benn 1998, p. 95; also Gatrell 2005). Our data offers support, therefore, to La Rossa's (1988) argument (quoted in Valentine 1997) that there is a gap between the *culture* of fatherhood – what is socially acceptable and appropriate for men to do as parents, and the *conduct* of fatherhood – what men actually do. La Rossa argues further that while the *conduct* of motherhood may have diversified in recent years (e.g. working mothers, single mothers), the *culture* of motherhood (the expectations of mothers and the romanticization of motherhood) has stayed largely the same. Similarly Caroline Gatrell (2005) notes the 'institutionalisation' of motherhood, a role about which society holds particular expectations and assumptions. Further, Sarah Riley's (2003) study of the way in which men talk about gender roles highlights the power of employment in constructing male identity and the persistence of the employment – (real) work coupling (also Hatten *et al.* 2002; Warin *et al.* 1999). She focused on the attitudes of a sample group (similar to ours) of 'professional white heterosexual men' (p. 99), to a range of vignettes, such as one where a man, made redundant, is asked to take on more domestic responsibilities by his employed partner. She notes that the men interviewed were aware of and often employed egalitarian discourses, but did so in a way that left the legitimacy of traditional gender divisions unchallenged. She concludes that, 'without alternative meanings associated with masculinity the loss of the provider role (which is coupled with masculinity) becomes equated with a loss of male-self' (2003, p. 111).

Taking up the issue of men's care being qualitatively different, the female respondents in Hays' (1996) study argue that when men do look after their children, their approach is different from their partners. When they liaise with the carer they may not ask the 'right' questions or remember names or get the children 'properly' equipped for the day (see also Hatten *et al.* 2002 on the practices of fatherhood). This was reiterated by the women in our study. Angie, for example, commented that despite the fact that her child's crèche took place in their home, her partner did not remember the other children's names. 'He's much more laid back than me, he doesn't get wound up like me … He doesn't know anyone's names [other parents], he doesn't remember names of children or anything like that …' (Angie, SN).

Hannah discusses the different ways her partner and herself relate to the children; the amount of time they spend respectively is also an issue here, but not the main one: Hannah is describing a difference in approach between the two adults. The strictures of 'intensive mothering' – responding quickly and sensitively to your children – have not had as much impact upon her partner as upon herself. In common with the women already cited, Hannah stresses both that these divisions appeared to 'just happen' without any planning, as couples 'fall' into apparently pre-assigned gender roles[4] and also, again, that the increased time she spends with and caring for the children is her choice:

> I think we have a very different way of caring for the children … It's diffi-cult, it's difficult to explain really. I think I take a lot more of the planning side of things on board … I sometimes get a bit frustrated if we're going out somewhere for a day trip, I'm *always* the one who gets everything ready. I mean he will do it, but I will say 'we need to take some milk for [toddler]'. That's what I mean by planning or thinking ahead to what's next. He will be much more 'oh, they'll make do' … He is very good at certain ways of playing, but it's like bursts of activity. He's also quite good about detaching himself. I find it really hard to, like if I'm in the room with the children, I mean he would manage to sit there and read a book or a newspaper. But I would never manage that. It's like the way you set up your interaction with the children I suppose and what they expect of you. And they always expect me to respond immediately, I think, and I do … I wouldn't say [the division of domestic chores] is necessarily uneven, but with the children, sometimes I do feel I take more of the burden, but I think it's partly just because, the kind of the things which I think are important to do, you know, are the things that I want to do … It's funny, isn't it, how you, like, you don't necessarily *discuss* the divisions, it just sort of happens somehow.
>
> (Hannah, SN; she is HE lecturer, he is IT manager)

However, we were very aware that our 'story' of the gendered divisions of labour around childcare was premised on the women's accounts. Thus during the time allowed in our research design for re-interviews, we increased our efforts to reach male partners, in order to try to understand their choices and the constraints upon them.

All together we spoke to fourteen men, four of them alone and the remaining ten with their partners.[5] The sample is small, a reflection of the difficulty we had in reaching men, and therefore the conclusions we draw must be read with some circumspection. As the details of the respondents below reveal, we spoke to a high proportion of non-traditional men. This might give the impression that more non-traditional men existed than is suggested by the previous analysis focusing on the women. However, it is unsurprising that the men interested enough and available enough to agree to speak to us would include a high proportion of those men more involved in childcare than some of their counterparts. We did not reach Nancy's partner for instance, to whom we referred earlier, who 'sees [the children] two or three nights a week' or Kathryn's who sees his children 'ten, fifteen minutes in the morning'.

Before considering our sample group in detail, we wish to give some background in which we can place the fathers, and identify some ideas which can help us to understand their perceptions of agency and constraint. Popular and policy discourses on fathers are not flattering. Whilst the popular portrayals of dads as bumbling incompetents may no longer be a comedy staple, fathers are still seen as somewhat fragile, helpless beings, unknowing and/or uncommitted, and in need of guidance. A recent survey of 2,100 British men suggested that they were depressed and pessimistic about their parenting skills, and keen to escape the demands of family life by staying at work (Hill 2004). (Similar surveys also note working women's distress, e.g. a survey for BUPA/Top Santé reported in the *Guardian*, 9 March 1999.) Policy in relation to fathers in the UK and elsewhere (especially the USA) focuses on the 'crisis of fatherhood', 'feckless fathers' and (in the US) 'deadbeat dads' (Hobson and Morgan 2002; Lewis 2002). Lewis suggests that fathers were largely absent from policy making discourses until the late 1980s, and then the focus was on absent fathers, and the need to tie men into families, to remind them of their responsibilities and to ensure behaviour consistent with fulfilling those responsibilities (hence the introduction of the Child Support Agency in the UK in the 1990s). In this policy context, men are often presented as capable of only fragile attachments to their children which may well weaken after a divorce (Hatten *et al.* 2002). There is also a considerable strand of literature, comparable to that directed at mothers, but perhaps more basic and less sophisticated in its approach, which judges fathers, and finds them lacking and in need of education (e.g. Ballantine 1999; Seibold 1995). Ballantine, for example, an American professor of sociology, in a brief article in *Childhood Education*'s column 'For parents particularly', exhorts fathers to 'Be there! Accept your own child! Use positive parenting! Share parenting! See fathering as worthwhile and satisfying!' (1999, pp. 104–5). Similarly, Lawhorn (1996) cites a twenty question checklist, 'Am I ready to become a responsible father?' developed to help men decide if they are ready to have a child. Discussions of childrearing, mothering in particular, are commonly couched in moral tones (Vincent 2000), so it is unsurprising to find that there has always been a 'strong but implicit undercurrent of value advocacy in fathering research and ... [that] there has always been a moral undertone to the focus on fathers' deficits' (Doherty *et al.* 1998, pp. 278–9). However, if mothers are commonly invested with responsibility for all aspects of the child's (physical, emotional, social and intellectual) development, then the particular contribution of fathers is constantly in doubt; fathering is understood as less clear-cut, more subject to negotiation between the father and others (e.g. the mother, extended family, employers):

> Fathering is uniquely sensitive to contextual influences, both interpersonal and environmental. Fathering is a multilateral relationship, in addition to a one to one relationship. A range of influences – including mothers' expectations and behaviours, the quality of co-parental relationship, economic factors, institutional practices and employment opportunities – all have potentially powerful effects on fathering
>
> (Doherty *et al.* 1998, p. 289)

Again, we see here intimations of the fragility of the father's identity, that it is so sensitive to a range of factors. Mothering is understood as being 'also contextually sensitive' but framed with 'cultural norms [which] are stricter on the centrality and endurance of the mother–child dyad, regardless of what is happening outside that relationship' (Doherty *et al.* 1998, p. 287). As fathers are located as inexpert, they are positioned on the periphery of caring. Doherty and colleagues quote feminist psychologist Vicky Phares (1996) to the effect that in much parenting research, 'mothers are considered the standard parent, and fathers are either ignored or studied for how they differ from mothers or how they neglect or abandon children' (1998, p. 284). Babycare books, even recent ones, still address themselves to mothers. For example, *What to Expect in the First Year* (Eisenberg *et al.* 1996) contains one chapter out of twenty-six directed towards fathers (see also Russell 1986; Fleming and Tobin 2005). The traditional, the familiar, the recognized role for fathers, particularly in the UK and the USA, countries with strong male breadwinner regimes (Lewis 1992), is as provider. The certainties of this role are not restricted to the USA and the UK however; as Hobson argues, there is no law or policy that penalizes non-resident fathers for not maintaining care; the penalties are based around financial support (2002, p. 3). Likewise we earlier cited Riley's study which drew attention to the identification with and adherence of her professional middle-class respondents to the traditional male role as provider, and the absence of a 'masculinity egalitarian coupling' (2003, p. 99) which would enable men to invest in an identity that encompasses a significant caring role. Additionally, Hearn summarizes the 'many studies that report alarmingly low amounts of time spent by fathers in personal family tasks and the relative rarity of fathers taking prime responsibility for them as opposed to "helping out"' (2002, p. 260, also Pleck 1997). An overview of the historical development of hegemonic masculinities, presented by Bob Connell (1998), emphasizes how masculinities came to be defined around economic activity, 'with both worker and entrepreneur increasingly adapted to market economies' (p. 14). Thus the proper concern for fathers in relation to the cash and care nexus is cash. One explanation, therefore, for the absence of many men from the detail of their children's daily lives is the insubstantial, unstable and often marginal nature of a fathering identity, except in relation to providing. This nebulous concept of fathering (outside of earning) sits uneasily with a historical legacy of patriarchal power (Hearn 2002), although Lewis and O'Brien (1987) attempt to reconcile the two through the concept of the 'paradox of patriarchy', whereby (some) men partly exert power and authority through their absence. One of the respondents in our study reflected on the difficulty of defining fatherhood, its meaning and practices. He lays aside providing for the family, and focuses on his interaction with his son. It is to traditional conceptions of discipline and physical play (particularly with boys) to which he refers. Beyond these is confusion:

> I think fatherhood's become more and more difficult to sort of delineate. And I, at times, really do get sort of confused by it. I mean, take discipline. Traditionally people talk about fathers having a disciplinary role. And I kind of see that … In terms of fatherhood sort of roles I think it's my job to roughhouse with him … I suppose, yeah you should be upright and honest … But I, if I start to think about it all, it all falls apart in my hands
> (John, B)

We have been talking to date of 'fathers', yet to conduct a debate in such general terms is less than revealing, obscuring as it does the (obvious but) important point that 'fathers' refers to a large and heterogeneous group of men of different ages, social classes, ethnicities, sexualities, living in resident and non-resident situations with their children. Hearn (2002) comments that 'the pluralizing of masculinity to masculinities … is not any kind of simple turn towards difference. On the contrary there has been a parallel concern with the analysis of both unities and differences between men and between masculinities,' (p. 248).[6] Clearly whilst the fragility of men's identity as fathers, their apparent bemusement about their role, and their ineptitude in enacting it are policy and popular discourses that are applied generally to all fathers, some fathers are more castigated than others (absent fathers who do not maintain their children for example). Also men are fathering in contexts very different from one another. Hearn argues that whilst fathers'/men's power exists and persists, it is neither 'solid nor unproblematic', but rather 'multi-faceted, diffuse, dispersed, composite, shifting' (2002, p. 271). This is a particularly interesting statement with regard to our respondents, who are what Hearn refers to as 'WHAFs' (white, heterosexual, able-bodied fathers). Our group of professional middle-class men are clearly succeeding on indicators of 'responsible' fatherhood. They are resident with their children and fulfilling their provider role with considerable success and relative ease. They appear as embodiments of hegemonic masculinity, and like Riley's respondents they 'may be understood as having the most to gain from maintaining the '"patriarchal dividend" (Connell 1998, p. 11) of traditional gender roles. However they are also the group most often associated with (although this is not always empirically supported) egalitarian family values' (Riley 2003, p. 100). Indeed on this last point, Grossman *et al.* (1988) report a consistent trend for men in higher status careers to spend less time with their children (p. 89, see also Pilcher 2000; Sullivan 2000). Connell (1998) suggests that some men from this social grouping, those who have careers in international business, occupy 'the hegemonic form of masculinity in the current world gender order', which he calls 'transnational business masculinity' (p. 16). He quotes a study of management texts on the particular construction which they present of the corporate executive, describing the image as one of 'a person with no permanent commitments, except (in effect) to the idea of accumulation itself' (1998, p. 16). Our respondents do not present such an extreme picture, although none of the men with whom we talked directly quite fitted the picture of the international corporate executive. Most however work full-time and for some this means very long days.

Our analysis of the transcripts suggested that the fathers to whom we spoke could be divided into two groups, and we expand upon this below. It is also important to view the men we interviewed in the context of the rest of the sample, where 20 out of 59 women were at home full-time, and had their households arranged on relatively traditional lines. Our analysis has two main strands, in accord with Morgan's (2002) argument that research needs to study the similarities and the differences between fathers and their practices. The first strand is the differences between the two groups of fathers, in terms of the level of involvement in the daily tasks associated with childrearing. This is closely connected to their employment patterns and their absence/presence in the home. The second strand is the difference between the men and the women (hence the similarities between the men), and we refer here primarily to differences between mothers, and fathers, approaches to caring (corroborating and expanding on the points made earlier) but we also reference the difference in the men's presentation of the families' interactions with the childcare market.

Corporate fathers[7]

We present first two different family organizations, both with corporate fathers. In the first, the mother, Monica, also works full-time and the care is delegated to others. In the second, the mother, Connie, works part-time and has some paid childcare, but otherwise looks after the children herself.

Steve is black British, born in the UK. He and Monica, who is white, have two children under five who attend a private day nursery full-time. Between the first interview and the second, the family had also employed an au pair to

Table 5.2 The fathers

Traditional (corporate fathers)	Non-traditional (juggling fathers)
Dennis (B) works as CEO of PR company; Sally was in PR, now at home.	*Gary* (SN) was in City recruitment, then became self-employed; Mary was a lecturer, currently running a children's art club part-time.
Steve (B) runs a public sector partnership investment company; Monica works full-time in local government finance.	*Ethan* (B) is a private sector lobbyist employed by a major corporation; Jill works part-time in the travel industry.
James (SN) is a hospital consultant; Connie works part-time as drama teacher.	*Mark* (SN) took voluntary redundancy from post in IT. When interviewed just about to start a management job in voluntary sector; Sarah works as part-time administrator from home.
Andrew (B) is a senior civil servant; Felicity is self-employed and works part-time as a consultant and lecturer in business studies.	*Tony* (B) moved from IT into freelance journalism, works at home; Annette teaches full-time.
Leo (B) is a private sector accountant; Lynn is a part-time civil servant.	*Paul* (SN) is an architect; Angie works part-time also as an architect.
	John (B) works from home as writer; Anjali teaches full-time.
	Jeff (B) is a journalist; Helen was in journalism, now full-time at home.
	Gustavo (SN) is a self-employed photographer; at the time of the interview, Alicia worked part-time in theatre.
	Matthew (SN) and Evelyn are both artists working from home.

help with childcare and domestic work. Steve is an interesting example here, because he and his partner diverge from the traditional pattern of male full-time worker, female partner at home. His partner works full-time too, and they are both committed to furthering their careers. They are both aware of and argue against what they perceive to be the common assumption that women cannot work full-time and raise children (it is Monica who voices the argument most forcefully, but comments from Steve in the full transcript show him to be in agreement):

> We also need to get to why, at this stage in the game, it is still women who are assumed to be the main carers. And we are still talking about … it's not possible to do a full-time job and have children. People say that … A whole heap of blokes manage it. A whole heap of men do it. And this comes up time after time. A woman who was elected as president of my professional institute … she said 'I don't think it's possible to have children

and do this job' ... And you think it's not possible to be a woman and do *that* job and have children – possibly. But why is that? And why is that still the case? And why are we not pointing that out on each and every occasion that that assumption is made? ... What [family friendly policies] tend to mean is family friendly policies for women ... I don't want to go along with the assumption that you are sorting this problem on women's behalf because you are not. You are sorting it out on behalf of people ... One person asked whether Steve was going to give up work when I was pregnant with my first child. One person. Out of all the people who asked [me] – what are you going to do afterwards?

(Monica, B)

Their views, as stated by Monica, emphasize a role equity discourse in relation to paid work, which resonates partly with a liberal discourse of equal opportunities and economic efficiency, aiming to allow women to operate in the workplace on equal terms with men (Ball and Charles 2003).

At the time of the second interview Monica had just accepted a new job which would entail a move out of London. Steve described the new post positively as 'challenging' and with potentially higher levels of satisfaction than her current position which she found relatively undemanding. He added 'I'm excited for Monica and I think that we as a family must support her'. He says relatively little about his own job other than to agree with Monica that it is 'very demanding'. He is however very forthcoming on the arrangements they have made to fulfil their responsibilities to their children and keep domestic tasks under control. The manner in which he presents the decision-making and choices is interesting. We comment elsewhere (Chapter 3) that the language women use to describe their childcare choices and interaction with the carers is 'saturated with emotion' (Lane 1991, p. 77). Steve however uses the more impersonal language of a rational consumer (a model which is understood to be masculine; see for example Kenway and Epstein 1996), gathering information, making appropriate and responsible decisions which are then subject to revision based on the evidence:

> [Childcare] is something you've got to keep under constant revision. We decided we needed some help and thought we'd try an au pair. Went through various agencies and found one where we thought you paid a little bit more but you perhaps got more. We were disappointed with the first au pair ... We took a decision to terminate that arrangement and try again. And second time around we're much happier with what we've got. [When we move] we'll have a sense of what we want, we'll research what's there, we'll pick the one we think most suitable ... and then we'll review. Because if it doesn't appear to be right, we are not just going to rub along and struggle. We'll say this isn't working – what else can we do?
>
> (Steve, B)[8]

Steve talks of establishing a 'very comprehensive support infrastructure' which allows Monica to return to work full-time and thereby 'be credible in the workplace environment'. Both parents describe how happy they and the children are with the nursery, but Steve rejects the interviewer's suggestion that they have been 'lucky' to have maintained stable and satisfying childcare arrangements, commenting that it was the result of an informed, considered interaction with the market:

> Well you say that. It might look like that on the surface, but it's important to recognize that we went through quite a bit of work before we selected [nursery], we put a lot of time and effort into getting something which we thought felt right for us.

Monica notes that they were fortunate that they could afford the nursery fees even though Steve had a short period without paid work. He responds,

> I think we are fortunate that we can meet the fees for the two of them, but it's kind of that's what we are doing ... at this stage in our life ... The children are our largest expense and ... we are OK with that. Because that's what we are doing now. Ten years ago we might have been on the back of a truck crossing Africa ... We are not doing that now. We are having children

Steve rejects the common refrain amongst the women respondents that their successful childcare arrangements are due to luck (see Chapter 3). From talking to the women in the sample we understood the childcare market to be unaccommodating and inflexible to their needs, to be a messy, confusing, and anxiety-inducing arena, a place where their considerable skills as consumers did not guarantee them an outcome with which they were happy. Steve however succeeds in reducing this emotionally laden 'peculiar' market to a manageable, controllable environment, subject to rational decision-making and action.

Work is important for both parents; neither wants to stay at home with the children:

> We discussed briefly whether Steve would give up work. That went like this – how about you giving up work? No! And the decision the other way went more or less the same way. Because I've never wanted to look after children full-time
>
> (Monica)

> I think we would just find it stifling that you [Monica] are not having some sort of discussion or intellectual challenge during the day.
>
> (Steve)

Steve and Monica both enact a traditional male role working full-time (although Monica's hours have some flexibility) and are highly supportive of each other's career development. Monica has slowed down the pace of her advancement since having children, but her new post marks a further stage in her career. There is however no evidence that Steve's career has been affected by the arrival of children, although the family's planned move from London will affect his working conditions. In the face of their dual-earning lifestyles, with both careers allowing limited time for childcare, they have delegated the care to others, firstly the nursery and then additionally, to relieve pressure points in the day (the mornings and early evenings) and to secure some time for themselves, an au pair. In accordance with their equal work commitments, they both say that the division of domestic labour is roughly equal and did not change with the arrival of the children. As we noted above, however, it is commonly the woman who undergoes the mental labour associated with running the family:

> She's doing the intellectual work to make sure that things are in order, whereas I'm waiting to be told and directed, and then I'll do it. So you can divide it up and say – he's doing x per cent. But I think you [Monica] are carrying the load because you are thinking through the stuff.
>
> (Steve)

James (SN) is a consultant, a researcher as well as a clinician. He is very successful and has a highly pressurized job which he finds rewarding. He travels often. Connie has a background in drama, and now teaches drama part-time. She has also started training in an alternative therapy. They have three children (two of whom are at school) and are well established in Stoke Newington.

Asked about the balance between work and family life, James responds:

> It's overwhelmingly towards my work. But I have a very intense, busy job and I enjoy my work enormously. So in a way I don't want to give anything up. I'd like to do more with my family, but I don't want to give up my job satisfaction as well because I have a wonderful job.

He is candid about the effects on Connie's career of his investment in his work:

> She has made the major sacrifice as far as the career is concerned. And I haven't made any sacrifices career-wise. But as a result she's not very happy with her professional life and she has poor self-esteem from a professional point of view which in a sense is, I suppose, my success is at her expense. So I don't think it's a comfortable mix but on the other hand I earn a lot of money now which is something that enables us to have a very nice house and lifestyle and travel whenever we want to. And so

there are many material benefits and the kind of income I have now, she could not, obviously sustain, irrespective of what she did now ... So there's a kind of evenness built in because of that

Whilst acknowledging the deleterious effect of his career success upon his partner's working life and identity as worker, James draws upon his undoubted success as a breadwinner, seeing this as not only justifying the inequities but also going some way towards cancelling them out. They have different approaches to managing the children's behaviour, which can cause difficulties as James is, in his own words, 'constantly coming in and out of the family unit'. Like Hannah's partner (Hannah is cited above), he is also unaffected by the ideology of 'intensive' or 'sensitive mothering' which as we suggested earlier demands near-immediate response to and constant interaction with the children:

> I don't feel that to be a good parent you have to totally subsume your own wishes and desires. So on a weekend I love to read the paper. So I'll certainly do something with the kids, but then I'll also have time out when I read the paper and they can, you know, do something quietly by themselves. I don't feel in order to be a good parent you have to be constantly doing things with them or stimulating them.
>
> (James)

However, he views Connie's endeavours to meet the demands of 'sensitive' mothering, with approval:

> I think we do much of the teaching or facilitating of learning as parents, so my expectations of the [primary] school are rather low or of any [childcare] help that we get ... Connie is incredibly creative with them, ... they're all playing musical instruments and you know, they are constantly painting and doing crafts, and that's the role of the home

Given the hours that James works and his resulting absence from the home, his ability to contribute to the children's daily activities is limited. This is Connie's responsibility which she undertakes with commitment but at a cost to her own sense of identity and well-being. We are not suggesting of course that all the mothers who are primary carers are unhappy with that role – that clearly is not the case with others in the sample, and not necessarily with Connie – although we would suggest that the demands of being at home with young children, or working part-time yet still having the main responsibility for the children, receive a rather vague and insubstantial recognition from those not carrying out these tasks. The immediacy and enormity of the demands upon Connie are acknowledged by her husband but not apparently recognized to the degree that she herself feels them. Here she contrasts the consuming emotion of a home with small children, juggling the demands of work and children, which are overlaid with the need to be a good mother (of which she talks earlier in the interview, 'most of the time I feel as though I'm completely crap at being a mother'), with the rationality of her husband's scientific work. To do this, she calls on a well established and ultimately oppressive (to women) binary linking the rational male actor operating in the public sphere, with the irrational emotional woman located (and best kept in) the private sphere. However she also seeks to undermine this binary, by insisting – as do other women in our study – on the emotional dimensions of childcare choice:

> It's quite difficult sometimes when you feel, you know, you've been here for weeks, days, and they've been fighting – you feel you've been trapped and … And then he comes back and says, 'God, I'm so tired.' Well, actually, he's been eating in posh restaurants – not that I want to do that – but, you know. He's actually, there's compensations for his life that is impossible to find when you've got children … He says, 'if it's what you want, if it's [what] you need, [in terms of childcare]' you know, he said, 'you need someone who can do this, so get rid of that person'. But he's very clear, and it's one thing to be clear about things on paper, and statistics and, you know, figures, but it's different to be clear about lifestyle and what you can tolerate and what you can't, and, you know, you're at home.

The themes in the interviews with James and Steve, particularly of male embeddedness in the workplace, reoccur in the others with 'corporate fathers'. Andrew's (B) work/life balance is also tilted, apparently irretrievably towards work, which his partner describes as a 'disaster'. Andrew does have options to change his working hours, and some motivation to do so, but at the same time he does not. He is caught in his current situation by his 'love' of his job, his investment of himself in it, which means that he does not want to be seen as failing in his contribution to the workplace, and the ever-present demands of the workload:

> In principle there is no reason why I shouldn't [change the balance], so I could now work four days or something like that. There [pause] I think there is still a tension between the formal policy and the options … and the reality. It is seen to some extent as a lack of engagement. And it is unlikely that my work would reduce by 20 per cent … It might even be easier than I'm imagining it to be if I made the effort. But there is still some kind of cultural expectation that … that's something women do [go part-time], but not men.

Leo (B) notes with some relief that he works fewer hours now than he used to ('we're still talking probably about 50 hour weeks') and like many of the women (see Margot above) notes the importance of a sympathetic boss ('my current boss is a very committed family man who tries to work, given the level that he is at, sensible hours and at least try and get back at some stage') and fellow workers who are also parents. He does feel he has made some degree of choice in favour of his family, and to protect his role as father:

> I've chosen a balance. I want to have my cake and eat it … I still want to progress, but I'm not going to, sort of sacrifice everything for that … Because there's no point in being successful in one part of your life only to see other aspects of it sort of disintegrate, which is where I felt it was going.

Andrew too has decided to limit his working commitments, saying he would not be prepared to take a post such as he had in the past, 'where the normal working day was 9 in the morning until 9 at night'. Dennis (B), on the other hand, is out of the house 'a straight twelve hours every weekday. At least.' He too mentions later nights, more weekend work and more travel in the past, but when asked if he actively sought a change away from these demands, he replies 'no, the job changed'.

The workplace is so vociferous, so demanding of these men, that 'slowing down' (Leo) means working only a 50-hour week and trying to avoid roles which apparently require 12- or 13-hour days. The corporate world has leaked into (at least some areas of) the public sector, with an ethos that demands commitment to the workplace above commitment to any relationship external to it. It demands 'zero-load' workers, an identity which none of these men have. Therefore they seek to find some sort of resolution or balance between the demands of having young children and demanding careers. These compromises are made with their female partners, and in some cases, to some small extent (e.g. Leo) with their workplaces. If their partner is not willing to give up a career (but all the women do make some modifications to their working life) then their employment allows them to interact with the market from a position of relative advantage and to employ comprehensive care. It is extremely difficult in the case of these successful career-focused men to disentangle the features of their employment which they do not wish to change from those they cannot change. It is possible that they themselves do not know (Andrew talks of things being perhaps easier to change than he imagines). We are not concerned here to establish an idealized model of 'fathering' behaviour against which to measure our respondent's practices, but rather to seek to understand the way in which the relationship with their children is set within and linked to other relationships and wider social structures (Morgan 2002). The references made by all the fathers to their children revealed love and concern, but 'intimate fathering' (Dermott 2003) is not understood by all as being defined by spending large chunks of time with the child. Thus these men are conforming to notions of hegemonic masculinity by being good providers, but also working to maintain a close connection with their children. Whilst physically they may be 'distant dads', they do not wish that to be the case emotionally.

Juggling fathers

The majority of the small number of men we spoke to fell into a category which took a contrasting approach to the corporate fathers, and here they bear some resemblance to the middle-class professional fathers in Caroline Gatrell's (2005) sample of 20 families, all of whom had female partners involved in paid work. With the exception of two fathers, she states the remainder 'did all share a significant proportion of the practical and emotional responsibilities for child-drearing' (2005, p. 134). Some of our sample could almost be called 'born again fathers' in that they had made specific career changes in order to spend more time with the children (they are not, however, full-time carers). Tony, who has three children, two of whom are at school, falls into this category. He presents a classic case of downsizing, giving up his career in IT for freelance journalism. Here he emphasizes the choice that he had and the different choices that other men make:

> We've both worked very hard I think to get to the point that we're happy with the arrangement that we have more time with the kids … we have less money then we had but it's less important … than having that time with our children … I've worked in IT for a long time and the hours are really long and a lot of people I know work in that industry – they don't see much of their kids and they're very stressed when they're at home … I really don't see the point of being a father if you can't be there for your kids. I understand sometimes it is financially difficult, and you have to take what jobs come along, but equally I know a lot of men – when I worked on consultancy – who couldn't wait to work on weekends … I think I was seen as some sort of weirdo because I actually enjoy time with my family
>
> (Tony, B, now freelance journalist)

Gary too is in the process of changing his working life, because 'he felt he was away from the children too much' (he has two children, one of whom is under five). He was also unhappy in his job and did not gain the same sort of pleasure from his work as the corporate fathers:

> I would probably deny that I'd ever made a career choice in my life any-way. It's always been a case of doing what I'm able to do. And if it pays me well enough I'll carry on doing it … I'm more interested and motivated by my children than I am by my job … in that I can never envisage a day when I'd wake up one morning and think – 'God, I'd love to go to work today. I can't wait to get into work today'. Work for me is purely a mecha-nism for paying the bills … A lot of my job could have been about entertaining clients and so on, going out in the evening. But generally speaking five days a week I was home by six thirty because I wanted to see my children. This was a specific decision rather than happenstance

His decision to leave work was influenced by several reasons, however

> I think perhaps it's a bit me passing the buck if I was to say it's entirely about the children, it's partly to do with my midlife crisis, perhaps in terms of me being fed up working ... so it is partly a justification that it is righteous of me to be ... not necessarily looking after [the children] but being around them. And it's partly I'm just fed up with a 9 to 5 existence
>
> (Gary, SN) (His actual hours were longer than 9 to 5.)

He feels that the extra time he now spends with the children (he looks after them for a day as well as being in the house more) *is* important in his relationship with them, and this is corroborated by his partner.

> Being home earlier you get to see them when they are actually themselves rather than these sort of mad deranged people [because of tiredness] running around. And I think it's brought me closer to them. I don't know whether they've appreciated it in any way or feel it in any way, but I do have a better understanding of them as people rather than the two days of the weekend I used to have.

However his income has dropped, thus affecting his provider role. ('One obviously has a need to earn an income and that's perhaps where I am falling down at the moment, that I'm not really making enough to make it a viable proposition at the moment'. The use of the phrase 'falling down' is interesting, illustrating the powerful provider discourse at work.) The family is addressing this in immediate terms by planning to move out of London (although the move is also part of their reappraisal of the family's quality of life).

Although Gary is spending more time with the children, his practices of fathering remain dependent on his partner's mothering. He refers to Mary as the 'primary carer'. By this he explains that his role with the children is to be the 'entertainer', rather than the 'comforter' (see Hatten *et al.* 2002): 'I'm probably more of a child than a parent in many ways, in that I'm quite good at entertaining them, but I'm not necessarily very good at either disciplining them or getting the functional routine items done'. He states that she has made the choices around childcare, and that she has 'trained' (his word) him domestically. Mary 'knows more of the children's routines' and 'takes on more responsibility' domestically. Similarly we have already quoted Paul's partner Angie (SN), who commented that Paul does not know as well as she does the names of other children who attend the crèche, nor those of the parents. Matthew (SN) also comments on the gendered way in which he and his partner interact with their son:

There's a certain sort of sterotyping going on. Evelyn will do one kind of activity with him and I'll do another. I mean Evelyn will do more cooking with him, I will do more climbing trees … If he wants a fight he comes to me

Returning to the issue of domestic labour, Jeff (B) comments:

I suppose I look at my role much more as, I don't know, trying to interact with them mentally rather than, I don't know, making sure that they've got the right number of jumpers on or … clean socks. I wouldn't necessarily notice that … I think I'm quite good at [sharing other domestic tasks]. [laughter from Helen]

Helen goes on,

I do delegate quite a lot, don't I? [J: yeah] And you're very good at doing it. But in the same way you wouldn't think 'oh the laundry basket's full, I'll just put a load of washing in'. You know, I have to say, 'could you just put this in the washer please?' or whatever. [J: Yeah]

It is interesting to note that even these involved fathers position themselves/are positioned as incompetent and not responsible in terms of domestic tasks. Gattrell's study (2005) also confirms these distinctions. The fathers in her research were – in pursuit of 'intimate fathering' – concerned with their emotional bonds with their children. They were rather less interested in the domestic support work needed to keep a family functioning.

One exception in our study as regards domesticity was Mark (SN). As we noted earlier we did not originally find any stay-at-home fathers, although the re-interviews revealed we had missed a temporary one, between the first and second interview. Mark, like Gary, was not enthusiastic about the work he was doing and took voluntary redundancy. Again career and family motivations are mixed.

In taking voluntary redundancy I was influenced by the fact that I would be able to spend more time at home with my son … I had this plan to get out of IT … it's all part of a long-term strategy to change my career.

In the nine months he was not in paid work, Mark took over all the domestic responsibilities to the extent that Rachel 'doesn't know where things are in the kitchen any more, he's moved everything around to suit him … I've lived like a man and he's lived like a woman. Traditionally in the traditional sense of things …' (Rachel works part-time and does voluntary work). Mark commented 'I quite enjoy domesticity, I have to say I do enjoy it. I find it quite rewarding to get everything … Because it's an important part of life you can't just live in a pigsty … and you can't just starve'. This enjoyment of caring (their son also attended a school nursery, so again, Mark was not a full-time carer) and home-making was such that, 'I suppose the ideal would have been if I could have earned as much money as Mark then we would have reversed roles (Rachel). However Mark is about to start a new job, so 'we'll go back to how we were before' (Rachel). Mark is interesting because of the ease with which he appears to switch roles between breadwinner and stay-at-home father (his particular domestic interest is in cooking, a role which several of the men – James, Leo, Jeff – claimed to enjoy). It is possible that taking voluntary redundancy as part of a career plan means that he approaches his new and temporary role in the home without the blow to his sense of self that redundancy or dismissal can deliver. Here are partners who would swap roles, but are prevented from doing so (despite Rachel's high level of qualifications) by the inequities of a gendered labour market which results in women receiving earnings below those of their male counterparts.

While Gary and Tony left their jobs in order to have a lifestyle which they considered more enjoyable with regard to both work and family, Ethan (B) is unusual in that he works for a private corporation, yet works reasonably manageable hours. His partner works three days a week. When asked about his role in childcare he initially says 'well first and foremost the financial provision of it', but he also drops the children off at nursery on the days his partner works and if a child's illness coincides with her working days he takes time off, allowing her to gain some semblance of what Steve referred to as 'credibility in the work environment'. He leaves home at 9 a.m. and gets back around 6 p.m. – relatively short hours compared with the corporate fathers. He has flexible working hours and can work from home. These benefits, although not ubiquitous, are not unique to his company, but, unusually, he appears willing to take advantage of them (see Camp 2005). By the time of the second interview, the couple had had another baby, giving them three children under five, and thus making their home life quite high on demands (they split domestic responsibilities evenly). Both feel that they manage because neither have very pressurized jobs, and neither wishes to look for a more 'challenging' position, which would disrupt their fragile balance. Ethan notes that the flexibility which both employers offer, and which allows them to juggle work and children, is contingent on a strong economy:

> It's just down to my employer and the nature of the job, that I don't have a pressurized job. But in a sense I don't earn as much money as maybe other fathers do. But I earn enough to provide childcare and a comfortable lifestyle … We've got a fairly good life/work balance right now, I think ultimately. Because of the location [of care and work], because of the travel, because we've got flexible employers and also because the job market is quite buoyant. I'm not quite sure what would happen if the job market went pear shaped

Six of our juggling fathers are self-employed which would seem to offer them flexibility in 'being around' their children (Gary). However, having neither the clear, overt demands of an employer to satisfy, nor an assured, fixed pay cheque, can generate anxiety. In some senses, this is an issue which also goes beyond employment status. Just as some of the women we interviewed spoke of feeling anxious that they were not juggling successfully, that one element or both, work or home, was suffering, the men in this category were also feeling their way towards some kind of balance. In a culture where the female homemaker/male breadwinner model is accepted without question, doing things differently generates tension and anxiety. Whereas with the women the focus of anxiety tended to be with the children, with Paul and John below, both working from home, their anxiety derives from their perceptions of their progress with work. Paul looks after the children half a day a week and is around the house at other times:

> I've got very mixed feelings about it. In some ways I don't want to miss out on spending time with the children and losing touch with them … But I also feel very anxious about not doing enough work or getting enough work done. And certainly work is a kind of escape as well. You know, when they are being very demanding, it's very easy to shut the door in the office and concentrate on something less stressful in some ways. I kind of want to have a balance but I don't know what the right balance is … I don't know what I want out of it. So I'm just going to try and do everything not very well
>
> (Paul)

> Sometimes, to be honest, I get little fits of anxiety about the impact on my career of being involved strongly or regularly in his upbringing, because you see other fathers … when they do get into work struggles, their wives will possibly boast about how long they are away from home and so on and so forth. And then you begin to think … am I compromising my career by trying to do the right thing as it were? … It's difficult to do the right thing … I mean virtue, obviously, is supposed to be its own reward … I mean in terms of writing, I personally know a few men who devote their lives to writing. And are pretty bad at being parents as a result. But they produce, you can see the benefit as it were in their work. … Doing the right thing as a father now can be difficult is all I'm saying … I mean you constantly hear of these successful men, I mean, not that I'm even saying I'm unsuccessful, I mean, I'm successful within my own terms. But they are able to do things and are almost congratulated for them by society, because they've worked so hard for what they've done. What they mean is they've worked so hard for themselves, rather than say for their families or whatever.
>
> (John)

A range of contemporary discourses stress productivity as a key virtue: compromises and work/life balance do not sit easily with, and are maybe subordinate to, the constant demand to produce. John notes that whilst women spend a lot of time discussing these issues, men, in his experience do not, 'I mean you don't know when you talk to another man whether you should complain about your position or celebrate it'.

However, despite their anxiety and concern, John and Paul remain juggling fathers, concerned to find some balance between work and spending significant parcels of time with their children. Jeff presents a slightly different approach: he works full-time as a journalist, whilst his wife worked part-time and had at the time of the second interview decided not to return to work after her second maternity leave. The family is moving north and Jeff, in contrast to the other men, is very vague about his future career plans:

> Q: Are you still going to be working for the BBC [in the north]?
> Well it's funny you should say that. I don't know. There are a couple of opportunities … There's always the opportunity to go into print [journalism] [names a regional daily]. Apart from that, you know, I don't know. Might end up doing something completely different you know, researching a book or something. But I want get a job that gets a wage in and think about it, you know, take it from there

He did however initially see the move as detrimental to his career:

> I was obviously quite reluctant at the time because obviously I was thinking of my work, career pattern. But you know soon realized it was going to be the only thing to do for the family

Jeff and Helen may be unusual in that they both present a relaxed approach to work. ('Really Jeff and I don't know what planet we're on, didn't ever think about working [after university], sort of thing.') Both privately educated, they spent time travelling after university, and got into the BBC at relatively low points, moving up the hierarchy. The remaining two men, Gustavo and Matthew, who were friends, were similarly distanced from career talk, but this is owing to the artistic and decidedly non-corporate nature of their working lives. As Matthew, an artist, explains,

> I mean [amongst the people I know] hour for hour I think the women do more [childcare and domestic tasks] but it depends quite what you mean. I think that, the fathers, all the fathers I know, are very, very present with the kids. They take them out and do things … Most of them are self-employed or unemployed so they're not out at work all day long and that makes a difference … I suppose because of the nature of my job, I tend to know people who do similar things … It's not average, probably the group of people that we know, I don't know.

Gustavo, like his partner, Alicia, was born outside England and attended progressive schools. He helps out at a small co-operative nursery, established by his partner, in Stoke Newington. Like the women cited above, he emphasizes that it is his choice to be involved to the extent that he is:

> Being a freelance I'm able to do it; and as well as a proper belief – I want to do it. I don't know, I don't really know about the rest of the families but I see that perhaps I'm the father that more often works at [i.e. helps at] the nursery. I don't know if it's because I have more time, or because I really want to do it, or … And maybe one of the reasons that I don't want to be – work in a full-time job – is because I've always been very proud of this – myself being free to decide what I want to do. And this thing about having a child, to be involved, is one of my choices
>
> (Gustavo)

Conclusion

Morgan (2002) identifies a threefold division of opportunities for individualization and the construction of personal autobiographies amongst men. The first group contains those with high and stable incomes where ideas of individualization and choice might seem to be possible, and who live in a political environment where fathering is positively valued … We may also include here those who deliberately chose to opt for more conventional or established divisions of labour or more distant patterns of fathering' (2002, p. 285). The second group contains those whose life chances are less stable, who have aspirations around fathering, but who are vulnerable to, say, uncertain working conditions. The third group contains those whose 'economic or domestic circumstances may be the source of stigmatized fathering practices: absenteeism, economic under-provision and so on' (ibid). Our sample clearly falls into the first category. However our analysis shows the differences and variations in men's circumstances and beliefs, in relation to the nature of their employment, their enjoyment of it, their relationship with their partner and decisions around her involvement in paid work. Implicit in all of this is their varying understanding of how important it is for them as fathers to spend time with their children on a *daily* basis, and whether this involvement can be replaced by the more constant presence of the children's mother or another (usually female) carer.

The intensification of professional and managerial work and the 'presentee' culture of the 'corporate world' which has spread to affect other non-corporate workplaces, engender real constraints on men with children. They perceive strongly that they have little space in which to limit their hours and still be successful in their chosen careers, and in many areas of work they are probably correct in so thinking. Some react by leaving these areas of work, others by trying to establish some boundaries between home and work even, whilst they are aware that these are skewed in favour of the workplace. Others avoid these workplaces and forge careers in areas which give them a higher degree of autonomy and control over their working lives. What is not clear is the question of primacy. It is unlikely that any of the men chose their careers with having children in mind – certainly none of them suggest this (nor do their partners, and our participants were overwhelmingly in their thirties and forties when they had children). But it is possible that some of them chose careers, as Gustavo says, which would allow them to be 'free to decide what I want to do'. Those, like Mark, Gary and Tony who have changed career direction, have been clearly influenced by wanting to spend more time with their children, but that was not their sole motivator. They wanted to make changes in their lifestyle partly to enhance their satisfaction at work.

For those men who do decide to invest a significant part of their time in caring (and in none of the families in the sample was the father a full-time carer), the tensions and ambivalences they felt in negotiating work and care were, as several of them pointed out, similar to those experienced by mothers in the labour market, also juggling paid work and home life. Similar perhaps, but not identical. Arwen Raddon (2002) presents a study of academic mothers in which, using similar terms to those we used earlier, she talks about mothers having to engage with two competing discourses, that of the 'selfless mother' and the 'best of both worlds' working mother:

> Thus a mother might ask herself is a 'good mother' a selfless woman who puts her child first … or she is economically active, productive as well as reproductive, and forging some sense of identity outside of her mothering role: or can she be both?
>
> (2002, p. 395)

Women with children, we suggest, are discursively positioned as mothers first, and then the identity of worker is additional to that. Not necessarily optional – as many women have no option but to work, and some women, like some of our respondents, feel they would be unhappy without their paid work – but an addendum (also Himmelweit and Sigala 2002). Conversely, for men, the discursive imperative is the role of paid worker, and the 'involved father' identity is additional. Men may have to face the 'structural' constraints of balancing employment with family (e.g. the nature of available jobs), but they do not experience the same order of 'normative' constraints (McRae 2003, cited in Duncan 2005, p. 61). The latter includes women's own identity and sense of self as mother and worker, as well as gender relations inside the family. Mothers in professional occupations, Raddon notes, both position themselves and are positioned by contradictory discourses which privilege traditional or modern views of what mothers can and should do. Her biography of 'Susan', an academic mother, suggests simultaneous disempowerment by the discourse of the 'successful academic' and of the 'good mother': complete immersion is demanded in one role or the other. However, as Raddon notes, Susan appears to also feel empowered by the discourse of the 'successful academic', as she receives satisfaction (as well as stress) from her work, and it gives her potential access to a space in which she can construct new ways of being both an academic and a mother.

The fathers in our sample are positioned to some extent by the discourses of a successful worker and practices associated with that, as defined by various institutional environments, but they are also positioning, in that they have more space than mothers to define for themselves what is a 'good' father. A good father can be a successful breadwinner, a good father can be an 'intimate' father without being over-involved in the daily details of childcare and childrearing, and a good father can be one who makes some alterations to his working life to spend more time with his children. All of these discourses are culturally acceptable. The last is certainly seen as 'virtuous' and 'righteous' as John and Gary recognize. Yet women's modifications of their careers are taken for granted and expected by most, as Monica pointed out earlier.

The juggling that men perform in most cases is of a different order to that performed by women. First, because their experiencing of tensions between the demands of paid work and children locate them as 'good men', 'new men', whereas with women in paid work there is always the possibility of being seen as a 'bad' mother for leaving your children, or too much of a mother to be a committed worker, neither of these insufficient identities are likely to be generated for fathers. Second, because it is our respondent mothers who in large part do the planning, remembering and knowing around the children. Men have the socially acceptable possibility of being incompetent, or at least vague about the detail. In the vast majority of cases women take responsibility for organizing childcare, for planning changes to that care as circumstances change ('I've probably done most of the research and then when I've found something I think might be positive … we've had a conversation about it', Angie, SN): they are the ones who know the children's friends, their mothers, what day they go swimming, and what they need to take.

In our analysis of the lives of these 'metropolitan mothers', we concluded that despite the social and economic advantages of this group, despite the educational and labour market opportunities experienced by the women, these men and women are not presenting a serious challenge to a traditional understanding of family relationships, a tradition which focuses on the ties binding women and children together whilst locating men on the periphery. We recognized however the need to focus on men's perspectives. This we have been successful in doing to a certain extent – the number of men we spoke to is relatively small and the number we spoke to alone smaller still. The interviews do add important detail and nuance to our original, rather general picture of absentee men. Whilst there are those men who invest considerably in their careers and are absent from the home for long periods, these men also perceive and validate a need to spend time with their children, and use the spaces which they feel are available to them to accommodate that need. Other fathers, a majority in our small sample, give a greater precedence to time spent with the children, and have employment or have moved to such employment as allows them to spend time at home. The men do not all have the degree of investment in a career that previous research has suggested for this social grouping (e.g. Riley 2003), although that is not to say that acting as a provider does not remain an important part of their identities. However, in all cases but one (that of Mark and Rachel, and that is for a temporary period) the mother remains the primary carer, the one who spends most time with the children (even if most of the care is delegated to others), the one who plans, knows and remembers the daily details involved with the caring for children. It is thus the mothers who remain key figures through the heat and noise of early childhood, even if they themselves are also engaged in paid work. This has considerable implications for the orientation of women towards the labour market. In place of the full investment in their careers that most made before having children, those women who return to work inhabit a series of temporary settlements with which they are more or less satisfied. They continue to work with and around contradiction. As Beck says, 'the lives of women are pulled back and forth by the contradiction between liberation from and reconnection to the old ascribed role' (1992, pp. 111–12).

Chapter 6

Power, control and communication

The hidden logics of childcare relations?

On her dresser in our home the faces of Marta's two children were framed: her son standing in a colourful but shabby living room, her daughter in a blue satin dress posing for her Sweet Sixteen. They were both being brought up by sisters or aunts thousands of miles away in Belize, and Marta had not seen them in six years. I could not imagine the economic hardships that had compelled her to leave them, never mind the emotional ones she now had to shoulder ... Could I blame her if there was a transference of love from her children to mine? For she had become like a second mother to Celeste, responded to her with effusive affection ... What mother lets her children be raised by other people? And the answer is: mothers just like us ... Inevitably the time came: Celeste was rapidly approaching preschool age and soon, I would no longer need Marta's services ... she was already moving into that oneiric place where all Martas went – dark-skinned women and mothers who shepherd our children through some of the most pristine moments of their lives.

(Ollivier 2005)

Introduction

In this chapter, we focus on the relationships between the parents and their home-based carers. The original title of our research – 'A market in love? – highlights the ever-present possibility of tension between parents and providers in a market relationship requiring financial exchange, and involving the hotly emotional dimensions for parents of having others care for and develop a relationship with their young child. In this chapter we ask what kind of care parents are seeking. Is the possibility of 'co-ordinated care' (Uttal 1996), i.e. care that arises from practice underpinned by shared parent–carer values, likely to be realized? What sort of social relationships do parents and providers develop, and do sole home-based carers (e.g. nannies and childminders) take up a different position vis-à-vis the family from carers who work in a nursery? What are the opportunities for dialogue between parent and carer concerning the child? We concentrate here, to some extent, on a small number of parent–carer dyads, whilst also endeavouring to give a flavour of the issues raised across the sample group.

The concept of care

Julia Brannen and Peter Moss (2003; Moss 2003) argue that *care* and *childcare* are terms with a high exposure in current and recent policy documents, but that these same texts give little consideration to the fundamental elements underpinning the care of young children. High quality care is frequently evoked, but, beyond policy rhetoric, understandings of care as practice are contested.

The ability to care, at least where women are concerned, is often portrayed as 'natural', and it is primarily women who fulfil care roles. Caring is not understood as intellectually demanding, but rather as an unsophisticated activity of the body and the emotions. There is a sharp distinction here with education, deemed specialist and highly skilled in comparison to the intuitive processes of care. The capabilities of care are also often associated with specific groups of women. Hochschild (2003, p. 23) argues, in the US context, that women carers from developing countries are often seen romantically as 'naturally' loving, symbolizing the apparently strong family and community ties of 'poor but happy' countries (also Uttal 2002). A study by Pratt (1997) of nanny agencies in Vancouver uncovers similar stereotypes of Filipina nannies in Canada. Their perceived 'family oriented' culture and the fact that many nannies have children themselves is seen by the agencies as an asset, symbolizing love and devotion, but with 'the actual obligations of that [maternal] role resid[ing] halfway round the globe and serv[ing] only to tie nannies to employment' (1997, p. 166).

However, understanding care as a natural process or capability results in the silencing of the issues of power and control which are embedded in caring roles and relationships. Issues which are inherent in relationships between men and women (with the latter far more visible in both paid and unpaid care work), between classes (with the majority of the childcare workforce traditionally composed of low paid, working-class women) and between rich and poor countries (there is now a global market in carers, Hochschild 2000; Ehrenreich and Hochschild 2003). We wish to draw attention to the ways in which power and control shape the parent–carer relationships in our research, although we also suggest below that these patterns are not always as clear-cut as the examples outlined by Pratt and Hochschild.

Until recently, it was possible to agree with Tronto (1996, cited in Tuominen 2003) that care was seen either below the concerns of the public realm (as part of the emotional, subjective private realm) or above (of high moral worth, as the needs of others are set before one's own). 'In either case, care is cast outside the parameters of the public sphere, so those who engage in the work of care are at best revered and at worst invisible' (Tuominen 2003, p. 175). One result of Labour's 1998 National Childcare Strategy and subsequent policies is that public policy is now seeking to engage with care, to control how and where it is performed, and the skills and training of those that perform it (see for example the *Children's Workforce Strategy Consultation*, DfES 2005). However, developing processes of regulation in a climate of 'new managerialism' (see for example Clarke *et al.* 2000 on the spread of new managerialism) has resulted in the commodification of the caring process 'as a series of discrete activities which can be defined, regulated, packaged and priced, then traded as products in a market place' (Brannen and Moss 2003, p. 9). (It is worth noting here that different kinds of carers have different relationships with the commodification process, regulation impacting more heavily on group settings, and now child-minders.) One current aspect of this commodification is the proliferation of Quality Assurance schemes for early years settings (see Chapter 3). As Brannen and Moss (2003) go on to elucidate, these attempts portray care as a technical, neutral market-based procedure, again obscure relationships of power and control. Tuominen (2003) goes further, suggesting that 'paid care work is an oxymoron. Caring which involves relationship and attachment is antithetical to market notions of the dichotomy between work and care, reason and emotion' (2003, p. 49). We developed this point in the conclusion to Chapter 3.

Very few contemporary policy documents set out a developed and holistic pedagogy of care (see Chapter 3 and Moss 2004b), although the government framework, *Birth to Three Matters* (Sure Start 2003) may be a move in this direction, as it seeks to recognize the holistic nature of development and learning, and encourage reflective practice. However the proposals in the 2005 Childcare Bill to formalize and extend *Birth to Three Matters* as the Early Years Foundation Stage were seen by some commentators as an attempt to structure, to an inappropriate degree, young children's activities. Furthermore, the vocabulary of pedagogy seems at its most starkly absent in discussions with the nannies and childminders participating in the research. This is not in the least to suggest that the care offered by these individuals is lacking or that they are 'bad' carers as a result, but rather that the dominant understanding of care, particularly of the under threes, emphasizes certain standard and straightforward elements: affection, warmth, attention. Proponents of this view, such as several of the childminders and nannies in this study (see below and also Mooney *et al.* 2001) would argue that caring, as a 'nat-ural' ability, does not need to be taught, although lived experience is helpful. This attitude, we will suggest, leads to a devaluing of the occupation of care.

Given the limited availability of a vocabulary of care and the prevalence of a discourse of naturalness, how can parents act as (supposedly rational) choosers? What is it they are choosing? How do they judge and discriminate between carers and forms of care? Once the choice has been made, what form of com-munication best facilitates the care arrangement? If the silence, which we suggest is common between parent and carer, were to be filled, would the com-modification of care be an inevitable result? As the last question suggests, we also wish to raise questions about potential risks in the otherwise worthy desire to professionalize care, to develop a pedagogy, a vocabulary, and training and accreditation programmes to pass such skills and attitudes on to others. This process may invite commodification, to reduce parent–carer dialogue to information-giving, to lists of targets, boxes to be ticked when the child achieves a particular task. Neither of these two discourses – caring as natural, nor caring as professionalized and, we would argue, at risk of commodification, are adequate. Later in the chapter we suggest a slightly different theoretical framework in which to place the issue, as we see it: a tradition of under-developed, haphazard dialogue between parent and carer.

The key relationship here is between mothers and female carers. Although the male partners in our study took some part in delivering and picking up their children from care (unless the mother was at home full-time), their engagement, as reported by the women, tended to be somewhat superficial (see Chapter 5). Linda explains that childcarers expect a relationship with the mother but not with the father, reinforcing the apparent 'naturalness' of gender roles:

> When you have children that's the point [your relationship] gets unequal because nannies and au pairs and other mothers talk to you about child-care, ... also the nannies we employed, they relate to me. I mean we toyed with the idea of him being the person that they would relate to and real-ized they would actually feel very uncomfortable with it
>
> (Linda, B)

Not only were men marginal to all this, they were also, in the eyes of some respondents, not very competent. A manager of a Stoke Newington nursery commented that fathers get 'terribly upset' if staff members relay concern about a child's behaviour and so they try to talk to the mother first, feeling she will react more pragmatically. Another nursery manager said:

> Sometimes the dads are a bit wary of the whole thing [engagement with nursery] and if you ring them up, they say, oh I can't deal with that, I'll put you on to my wife, they think it's all a bit, I don't know what, ... some-thing they can't cope with, some of them
>
> (Rebecca, B, nursery 1)

In this chapter we want to take a close look at the richly detailed texture of care, and at how care by non-family members is experienced, at least by the adults involved. Accordingly, we root the remainder of this chapter in what par-ents and carers have to say about their choices, their practices and their contact with and perceptions of each other, and the endless intense adult activity revolving furiously around the seemingly passive central point of the child. We focus here on home-based carers – childminders and nannies – and briefly consider nursery pedagogies in Chapter 7.

Caring relationships

A useful starting point is to consider Lynet Uttal's (1996) three possible cate-gories for mother–carer relationships. Based on her study in California, Uttal suggests 'custodial care', 'surrogate care' and 'co-ordinated care', all of which can be understood as parent and carer having different degrees of control over the situation. The first, 'custodial care', is where the mothers remain the primary socializers. As in Uttal's research, several mothers amongst our respondents spoke of changing their work commitments so that they were able to retain this role (48 out of 59 mothers, or 81 per cent, limited or gave up their work commitments on having a child in order to spend more time with him/her, and the remaining mothers spoke of slowing down their career progression). For example, Linda and her husband both worked for four days a week when her oldest son was a baby, and thus remained the primary carers:

> Hours in a day he saw us more than a nanny. I think it gets difficult when your nanny sees your child a lot more than you do. But actually we've always structured it so that's not ever been the case
>
> (Linda, B)

In cases of 'surrogate care', the childcare provider has, seemingly, the primary relationship with the child. In Uttal's research, mothers cited in this category either had such long working hours that they saw little of their children, or felt persistently unconfident about their abilities as a mother. None of our respondents fitted into this category, although one mother did suggest that the provider's training and access to professional knowledge gave them more skills than she had.

> I think the standard of care [in the nursery] is brilliant. ... And they're not sort of backwards in coming forwards and telling you what the child needs. I remember going once and they said, 'this child needs a coat, mummy'. And I'm 'alright' ... They tell the parents where they're going wrong, which when you're a new parent and you don't have, necessarily, family backup, it's actually quite helpful for somebody else to give an opinion about your child ... And I don't think I've got the skills to ... I can spot some of the stuff eventually, but I think I'm probably less ambitious for them, perhaps, than the nursery is.
>
> (Monica, B)

But Monica certainly does not understand this as the nursery being the key carer; instead she identifies the relationship as a partnership: 'they're looking after our children, and it's a partnership, and [the communication between parent and carer is] to be consistent between the two sets of carers'. Partnerships, or what Uttal calls 'co-ordinated care', is posited by her as the preferable model for parent–carer relationships. She describes it thus: 'they [mothers] acknowledge the degree to which other people are caring for and influencing their children's social and moral development ... they perceive themselves as sharing mothering with their childcare providers' (Uttal 1996, p. 303).

Uttal's categories do not 'fit' neatly alongside our data, and we suggest that although her three categories are useful starting points in understanding differentiated mother–carer relationships, they cannot encompass some of the nuances found in our data, nor do they encompass changes in relationships over time. Many of the London mothers talked about the experiences the carer and care setting could offer the child that were different from those offered by themselves, a form of care we could perhaps term 'supplementary care'. These differences encompassed increased opportunities for social interaction, a wider range of activities than was possible at home, and, in relation to nurseries, a more structured environment. For a small number of mothers (four, all in Stoke Newington) 'supplementary care' involved widening the child's immediate peer group to include those from a different class or ethnic background from themselves (see Chapter 4). For many parents, a limited degree of difference between the home and care settings is acceptable, even valuable, and this is an issue we discuss further below. However, we found limited evidence of 'synchronizing philosophies, values and practices' which Uttal sees as characteristic of 'co-ordinated care' (Uttal 1996, p. 305). This is partly because there appears to be limited dialogue between parents and carers that extends beyond the physical needs of the children (what they have eaten, when did they sleep, important issues of course, particularly with babies). In Chapter 3, we suggest that the London childcare market is producer-driven. Therefore, in many cases, the power in the care relationship lies with the provider and the parent has to take or leave what is on offer. Uttal also asserts that co-ordinated care relationships suggest that mothers are 'redefining child rearing from a privatized activity to a social one' (1996, p. 309). It is possible that the focus middle-class families place on the household unit and their use of individualist strategies to sustain and promote their position acts against collective, co-ordinated strategies of this sort (Jordan et al. 1994). However, in Stoke Newington, there are at least three examples of parents coming together to provide co-operative care arrangements (see Chapters 3 and 7).

Love and money: home-based carers and parents

It is in discourses around home-based care that the influence of 'attachment pedagogy' can be seen as most strongly represented. This refers to the normative expectation that care by their mother in their own home is most appropriate for the optimum development of young children (Gregson and Lowe 1995; Mooney 2003). The persistence of this view (although with variations between and within social groups: Duncan 2005) appears all the more remarkable when the number of women who work but also have young children is rising steeply. However, this increase is fairly recent, and deeply entrenched social attitudes are slow to change (Bradley et al. 2003). Modifications have been made: if the mother is not available then the next best thing is a replica; one-to-one interaction with a female carer (the mother/mother substitute–child bond is one that also works to marginalize fathers or other men). Another modification concerns the age of the child: the majority of our respondents identified one-to-one care as the most appropriate for children under two. In fact some of the most emotive comments were made concerning day nurseries as some mothers spoke of their perceptions of 'warehousing', 'institutionalization', inflexibility and unnaturalness.[1] Nurseries became more popular as children reached two-and-a-half or three years of age. Children of this age were understood as needing and benefiting from social interaction with their peers, a wider variety of activities than most individual carers could offer, and some degree of 'structured' environment. This 'readiness' was understood as part of the 'natural' development of the child:

> But by two she was really really ready to go, just to have something more, stimulation from other larger groups of children ... you know, role play and sand, and all those things that the childminder doesn't exactly have to offer
>
> (Gaby, SN)

Indeed the discourse around the most appropriate care for pre-school children over two has changed radically over the last 40 years. Non-family care, recently seen as necessary only for those with the most incompetent mothers, is now officially a 'good thing' for this age group, promoted by a government that increasingly sees early years learning as key to achievement at later stages, and also wishes women to return to the workforce. However, Moss's description of this policy change suggests that a degree of ambivalence remains:

> In the old discourse, exemplified by the Plowden Report, mothers with young children who also worked were to be deplored (CACE 1967). In the new public discourse, the 'good parent' is socially constructed as a user of childcare services – or at the very least it is possible to use childcare services and still consider yourself a good parent
>
> (Moss 2003, p. 34)

Whilst home-based relationships are preferred by most of our sample for babies and toddlers (54 per cent in Battersea and 70 per cent in Stoke Newington of under threes are cared for at home, meaning either their home or at a childminder's home), individual care relationships are the ones that throw the tension between love and money into the sharpest relief. Nelson's (1989) study of family daycare providers, as they are termed in the USA, notes that women working in their own homes, with years of socialization orienting them towards caring, often had difficulties in asserting themselves. Furthermore, as Mooney et al. (2001) argue from their study of childminders, it is in these relationships where children are cared for by a sole carer in their own or the carer's home that the boundaries between the public arena of work and the private sphere of home are most blurred. We suggest that these tensions are of three sorts: class-based and around class-inflected approaches to childrearing and care, emotional tensions around the child's affections, and exchange-based tensions around payment, punctuality, reliability and so on. One example of the latter is the negotiation over fees that takes place with individual carers, but not with nurseries. In our study, the childminders especially described their difficulty over putting up their rates or their accommodation of late payers (also Mooney *et al.* 2001; Nelson 1989), and refer to parents 'haggling' over money:

> Honestly, what they ask me most is how much I cost … I don't think apart from one – [the parents of] the girl I have now – I've never ever had anybody either who I've taken or I haven't who said, 'what are your rates?' And I've told them and they've gone 'oh cool,' … They've all tried to haggle … . [One prospective client] said 'I want you to do thirty-five hours a week', All right, you know. 'How much are you going to charge me?' And I said well at the moment it's three fifty an hour. 'That's an awful lot of money for what you do. It's money for old rope isn't it?' … So she didn't get much further
>
> (Marcia, childminder, SN)

One of Marcia's current families had been involved in the type of negotiation which she describes, although in the mother's interview this is presented as Marcia voluntarily dropping her rates:

> When I was meeting with her, we didn't talk about the money at first, and I was thinking, 'oh I just won't be able to afford her' because she had said it was thirty-five pounds [a day], three fifty an hour. And I know it's ten hour days as far as what I need goes … And I think she really liked me, and [son] as well. And I think she just decided 'oh, actually I really like them,' and so she was more accommodating and she just dropped her rate
>
> (Gaby, SN)

Carers understood this reluctance to pay as parents not seeing the job as a demanding one. Research on childminders or family daycare providers has noted the tensions for these providers between love and money. Childminders are in fact running small businesses, but this cannot be to the fore in their relationships with parents, or even it seems, their thinking about their job, because it is essential – to both carers and parents – that carers are looking after children because they enjoy doing so, and are affectionately attached to or capable of building such an attachment to particular children (Nelson 1989; Mooney *et al.* 2001). Bringing business to the fore would 'spoil' the carers' 'preferred' identity. Childcare work is a version of the sort of emotional labour that Himmelweit (2002a) and particularly Hochschild (1979) wrote about: 'the commodification of feeling'. Both sides act as if they are not really part of the cash nexus. They play out a drama of surrogate love, which is part of what is being 'sold'. In line with this, both the childminders interviewed in our study emphasized the advantages of small-scale family-based care which they offer: 'That's what parents want, they want a home from home' (Audrey, childminder, SN). Part of the appeal of home-based care is that it offers a (partial) re-creation of the mother–child relationship; the warmth and privacy of the home are set against the cold, public arena of a nursery. From the surrounding conversation it is clear Audrey is contrasting 'homeliness' with the more routinized, standardized care of a nursery environment where they 'all sleep at the same time, eat at the same time'. However, finding that 'home from home' is harder than it may seem, with middle-class parents being very aware of the visible and invisible differences in environment between their homes and those of working-class childminders. Additionally, childminders operate from their own homes, and are not subject to the control of parents in the way that nannies working within their employers' home may appear to be.

Choosing difference, choosing similarity?

Julia Wrigley's (1995) study of middle-class parents and home carers in the USA identifies two groups of parents: those who choose difference (i.e. carers who are from different social and often ethnic groups from themselves, mostly immigrant women) and those who choose similarity (carers from more similar social groups, often European nannies or young Americans). Pratt's (1997) Vancouver study displays a similar binary in perceptions (of nanny agencies this time, rather than employers) between Filipina domestic 'servants' and European 'professional' nannies. The supply of carers in the UK is currently more homogeneous than that in North America (although migrant carers, especially from Eastern Europe, are common in the au pair and unqualified nanny sectors of the market). However, childminders usually lived in very different social environments compared with the middle-class parents in our sample, and the parents were keenly aware of the differences:

> I got the childminder list from the local council and I was ringing up a number of childminders and I was finding it a totally depressing experience … You used to have people saying 'oh well I don't like having [children] when they're too old because they're too hard to train' … Or just not being particularly enthusiastic or didn't sound like home people … Didn't sound like caring people or people that I just thought they lived in tower blocks and things like that and I had quite a clear image in my mind of the kind of person that I wanted … I wanted a home from home.
>
> (Isabel, B)

> Q: So somebody with a house like yours?
> Not necessarily like mine … but somebody with my attitude … I'd have to say if I hadn't found [chosen childminder], I don't know. None of the other childminders appealed to me in anything like the way she did and a lot of them were very depressing
>
> (Isabel, B)

Another mother said that her current childminder's home 'was so much nicer than anywhere else I looked. Clean, bright, not too clean, not damp. Normal family ...' (Jessica, SN). A third and fourth commented on the 'fairly grim estates that I didn't even particularly want to go to', and 'rough estates' that were 'threatening environments'. We want to focus for a moment on one particular relationship, already referred to above, between Gaby, a Stoke Newington based architect who works part-time, and Marcia who looks after Gaby's son. When asked what she liked about Marcia, Gaby commented on her 'soft spoken' personality, the good relationship between the children Marcia was currently looking after, and also her surroundings:

> You hear lots of negative stories. Even [daughter's] old childminder said she knew lots of childminders that were not very good, ... it's getting money for not doing much work. They don't necessarily do anything but have the TV on all day ... [Marcia] just seemed like a person, she's travelled a lot ... she's just a little bit more worldly than a lot of other childminders. Her house, the way she did it up was much more like the way I would even choose to do it and saying that as an architect is a pretty high compliment. It sounds shallow and superficial, but it's not, it's where your child is going to be spending their time. It was very clean, bright cheerful colours, each room was a different colour, it was all maybe IKEA furnishings, but really very simple, nice pine, simple you know, it was uncluttered. Most of the ones are, you know, floral carpet differently textured walls. And it would just be cluttered and musty and dusty and just years of junk accumulated in tiny little – unfortunately because they're usually in council estates – tiny little dark rooms.
>
> (Gaby, SN)

Gaby describes Marcia's environment in some detail, perhaps owing to her professional interest in the use of space. However, the distinctions she brings to bear are of the same order as those we all make, a process of deploying loose-fitting but practical signifiers to help us 'place' people in the social world. As Bourdieu argues, 'Taste classifies and it classifies the classifier. Social subjects classified by the classification distinguish themselves by the distinctions they make, between the beautiful and the ugly, the distinguished and the vulgar' (1986, p. 6). For Gaby, Marcia was not entirely 'like me' but there were enough points of similarity both in Marcia's personality and environment for her to feel comfortable enough to leave her baby there. In the 'other' childminders' houses she feels 'out of place'.

However, in relationships between childminders and parents potential clashes between different class-based values and practices were never far away. Food is a case in point. Food, as Bourdieu points out, is another class marker: 'oppositions similar in structure to those found in cultural practices also appear in eating habits' (Bourdieu 1986, p. 6). 'Organic' food has come to symbolize a particular facet of 'good' parenting for the affluent middle classes, based on an awareness of 'bad' and 'good' foods and a desire to protect children from the former.[2] To return then, to Marcia, the childminder and Gaby's son. Aversions and alienation work both ways. Marcia says:

> I wouldn't give them anything I wouldn't give my child. He doesn't eat McDonalds and he doesn't eat chips so ... But some of the others are like, 'its got to be brown rice and its got to be organic'. And sometimes like [Gaby's son], [another child is] sitting there eating a nice little rich tea biscuit and [the] poor [boy] is munching his way through this organic ... And I feel really sorry, like this piece of cardboard that doesn't taste of anything ... But you know that's what I've been asked to give him so that's what I'm gonna, you know, I'm not gonna behind, I mean I could give him a biscuit, she wouldn't know, but I just think, well I've been asked not to so ... I wouldn't be able to look at [Gaby]
>
> (Marcia)

TV is another point of difference. A common reason for rejecting a childminder as an option for care was that the children might be 'bunged in front of a TV' (Emily). Parents displayed concern that a childminder would just 'mind' children, another kind of 'warehousing'. A common reason offered for moving a toddler from a childminder to a nursery was the latter's potential to better develop and stimulate the child. The other childminder interviewed in our study,[3] Audrey, remained firm in both her approach to TV and food, clearly finding some parents overly sensitive on these issues:

> We might have a problem, they might say, I mean once years ago I had the telly on, it was half term, and the mum come in late about ten o'clock that morning, and she went 'ohhh, the telly's on'. She was horrified that the telly was on ... And she went out in such a thing about it, she went and crashed her car outside the house. Because the telly was on, she was obsessed with not having the telly on ... And you'll get them telling you, 'don't let them watch the telly' and then the child will come in and say to you, 'can I watch Cartoon Network, I watch it at home'

And on the subject of food, Audrey commented:

> I tell [parents] if so and so is having, we'll say Skips [prawn cocktail flavour crisps], that one can't have without the other, so they'll all have them ... because you can't leave one out ... I think if you explain to them that you're not stuffing sweets down their throat all the day, and fizzy drinks ... I think if you're truthful with them and you explain ... occasionally they'll have them but not all the time. And they're quite pleased with that.

Since relatively few family–carer relationships in our study, particularly those involving childminders, were of class equals, class differences simmer away as a background to most relationships. Often they become visible only through particular flashpoints (TV or food) but unless that point is reached, one or both parties overlook them, although they may have played a part in some care scenarios being rejected or avoided altogether, as some of the earlier quotes about childminders suggest. However, sometimes different value perspectives are not made explicit at all, but nevertheless play some indirect part in shaping interactions. Marcia is clearly aware of the class differences between herself and some of her minded children's families. Although careful not to mention names she talks with a degree of antagonism about the perceptions and understandings of professional working mothers, and draws a distinction between those who *have* to work and those who *choose* to pursue careers:

> I think the women who have to work are much more appreciative and sympathetic towards me than the ones who have gone off and forged this fantastic career, and they're looking at me like this sad little person sitting in their council flat you know … And the ones I've had from Islington[4] have had much less high powered jobs than the Stoke Newington ones, and earn a lot less money. And are a lot more working because they have to. Stoke Newington ones seem much more career-minded and sort of money-orientated … Funnily enough the Stoke Newington ones who earn more are much less willing to pay me than the Islington ones who don't earn much more than I do. Which is, which is quite, quite strange

Marcia, who at one stage in her interview, points out that she took up childminding because she wanted to care for her son herself, has, at best, ambivalent feelings towards the notion of professional mothers pursuing a career. Although she has considerable sympathy for those mothers who have to work for financial reasons, there is an implication that the professional middle-class 'Stoke Newington' mothers are greedy, greedy in pursuit of their own careers and in not fully valuing and recompensing her for her work caring for their children. This may hint at the sort of class-related differences in values and approach to combining mothering and paid work that are discussed in Chapter 5. Despite the moments of tension, Marcia, like other childminders in our own and other studies (Mooney *et al.* 2001; Nelson 1989), commented that the job gave her a considerable amount of enjoyment and also autonomy. In contrast, carers who work in their employers' homes, particularly those who live in, may find themselves subject to more direct forms of control and surveillance.

All of this is compounded in those relationships where carer and mother come from different social groupings. Most of Wrigley's (1995) employers who 'choose difference' appeared to do so because they wanted cheap labour, to clean the home, and care for their young children physically – whilst they retained responsibility for more overt education and development. Our data suggest that, notwithstanding the haggling over payment the childminders experienced, it is mostly au pairs in the UK and young nannies who could be described as experiencing forms of exploitation. A Battersea au pair describing why she had left her first placement said:

> I worked a lot, I did everything in the house: washing, ironing, and clean-ing, had to drive them – everything … food for the children, and cooking for them, shopping
>
> (Lise)

> The first job I had was very … I felt quite alienated. I could eat with the kids, but I never ate with the parents. And it was sort of like, I just felt I had to go and sit in my room of an evening … I was a lot younger and I didn't have the confidence … to do anything about it … Even the nicest, nicest people sometimes take advantage of you, if you know, you offer to do something and before you know it, it's part of your everyday job. And if you don't do it you are in trouble so … But that hasn't happened to me for a long time. The last four or five jobs have, sort of, been really nice.
>
> (Tracy, nanny, B)

Au pairs and nannies are differently socially positioned in relation to the fam-ily, but all are susceptible to being 'taken advantage of'. As previous research (Gregson and Lowe 1994) has indicated, nannies and au pairs occupy an ambiguous and fragile role within the family life of the employer. Although several mothers expressed concern over the relative youth of many nannies, nannies are likely to be closer in class position, at least, to the families than childminders. Gregson and Lowe (1995) comment that the nannies in their study of domestic workers tend to be from intermediate class positions and therefore closer to their employers' status than the cleaners in the study who were clearly working–class.

Employing a nanny does also apparently allow a parent to retain closer con-trol over such issues as food, TV and activities: 'And it [the care given by a childminder] is not really within your control because it's not in your house, whereas a nanny can only be in your house' (Gaby, SN). 'You'd have much more say, wouldn't you, in their day? You could say "I want them to do this today"' (Helen, B). For some parents with sufficient financial capital this was their choice (the average rate for a central London full-time live-out nanny was £27,000 gross in 2004). Let us now look at one successful relationship, between Michelle, the nanny, and Angie and Paul, her employers, as a case study in choosing class similarity. Michelle was aware of the classed values of employer families and of the value of seeming to be 'people like us' to potential employers:

It's basically middle- and upper-class families that employ nannies. And a lot of it would just be to do with my voice, basically, just the fact that I speak properly, for some families I think would make a really big difference with them. And you know I can speak French and Spanish quite competently. So it's kind of a snob factor.

Michelle works part-time for Angie and Paul, taking care of their two daughters. The parents live in Stoke Newington and are both architects. They have had a variety of care arrangements, putting together a fragile mosaic of care for their two young children, which has included small nurseries and a parent-managed creche, as well as nannies. Some of the changes in these arrangements have occurred because current provision was 'not working out', others because circumstances changed. Within all this, Angie does seem to seek 'co-ordinated care', by choosing, when she can, someone to replicate their approach to the care and rearing of the children. In this she was somewhat unusual in her degree of clarity, both in emphasizing that she seeks similarity between their own behaviour and approach as parents and those of the carer, and also in being able to identify those elements of their ethos that she wants to find in a carer. She emphasizes the particularity, the specialness of each child. Here the possibility, at least, of responding to the particular is set over and against the 'warehousing', one-fits-all approach of nurseries. Also we see the emphasis on creativity as a key part of the child's experience:

> I guess in a sense I've always looked for something that appeals to me from the point of view of how we are as parents. We do like to sit down with them and cuddle them and read them stories and kind of carry them around. That's the way I am as a parent and even though [younger child] is different [in character] from [elder] I still would want those small-scale environments for her because I sort of feel that's more of a home environment ... We do look for a creative environment definitely

For a short period of time, the younger child was looked after by a nanny in a pre-existing nanny share. The other families involved were friends of Angie's which initially made her feel very positive about the arrangement (see Chapter 3 for the importance of 'hot knowledge'): 'it sounded perfect on paper'. However in practice it made her feel uncomfortable:

> And I guess I haven't gelled with [nanny] either as a person. I mean she's very nice and I completely trust her ... it's early days, but I haven't sort of, I don't quite know how to talk to her. Because I never interviewed her or anything ... We did meet up ... but it was kind of, I couldn't really ask her. In a way the relationship was a given relationship, so I couldn't really begin to question it at all ... I know [the other mothers] quite well, but somehow I felt I was getting into a bit of their lives that I didn't

understand in a way. It's not really on my terms, I guess that's the issue …
[The other mothers] obviously don't have much in common with
[nanny] either, but that doesn't matter to them, they obviously don't feel
like they can't communicate with her, but she's coming, she's a completely different person from them and they don't have an issue with that
at all … She's a different generation, she's an East End woman, she's intel-
ligent, but she's not highly educated. She's very good with them, but she's
not like we are with the children I suppose. And whereas our [former]
nanny, I've realized now, the reason, part of the reason I like her, she's our
age, she has a similar kind of background, she's interested in films and
theatre and interested in the same kind of things we are … She's not
somebody that would become a close friend, but she's someone I can sit
down and chat with about the world as well as the children and that's
important to me. Rather than [the other mothers] liked [nanny] because
she's more like their mother or something.

Angie finds the class- and age-related differences between herself and her
friends' nanny insurmountable, to the extent that she doesn't 'know how to talk
to her'. Somewhat baffled by her friends apparently being able to overlook the
differences between their lives and their nanny's, she comments that 'she's not
like we are with the children'. But it is not simply the nanny's approach to the
children that Angie finds so alienating (she does after all comment that she
trusts the nanny with her baby) – it is a gulf in lifestyle and background. This
nanny does not have the same sort of background or education, nor does she
indulge in the same sort of cultural pastimes; they do not, in short, have a
shared disposition on which to draw (Bourdieu 1986).

Angie and Paul agreed to be re-interviewed 18 months later. By this time,
their care arrangements were a mixture of a small informal nursery (for the
younger child), school and a new part-time nanny, Michelle. At first sight,
Angie was unsure about Michelle's appearance which she thought 'grungy' so

my immediate response wasn't positive. And she came in and sat down and
we just talked to her, and almost a second immediate response for both of
us, that we felt quite comfortable with her. We weren't asking her lots of
questions related to the job, we were just talking to her. And I felt at ease
with her. She felt like she could be a friend and she is a friend. And it
sounds a bit corny because she's not part of the family but she is familiar
with us … We kind of recognized that we could be friends with her, rather
than it be a business arrangement.

Angie's 'ease' and 'comfort' with Michelle indicate the social manifestations of
a shared habitus, a commonality of class dispositions. Michelle as we see below
does 'fit' with the family, developing close affectionate relationships with the
children and embarking on creative activities with them. She appears to be and

feels 'one of the family'. However this is a more unstable position than the term suggests (see below).

A contrasting set of relationships between nanny and employer is presented by Margot's family, who appears to see class differences between themselves and their nanny as expected and inevitable. Margot and her husband have three young children. They are both full-time workers in the City (although Margot was on maternity leave when we spoke to her). They have a live-in nanny who is Black British, and a cleaner who will help out with the children in the afternoons. Their nanny, who is qualified, has been with them three years and works from 7.30 a.m. to 7 p.m. Margot has a high opinion of her nanny's abilities with children:

> She's someone we trust immensely who is very, very good with children and when I go to work in the morning I know they're in safe hands and I know they're looked after by someone who really likes them, cares for them and really does the job very well
>
> (Margot, B)

However, when asked to comment on having her live in, Margot presents a relationship that is clearly not one of equals:

> She's extraordinarily discreet and quiet as a person. So the minute she's finished, let's say at 7 p.m., you would not even know there's someone living with you. I mean she goes to her room, although we've told her, you know, the house is hers and she should be free to walk around and go to the kitchen and whatever. But I don't know whether it's her character, but I think she's also she'd been extremely well trained by the family she worked for before … And obviously I rang the mother for references, and she said well [nanny] was superb, but she made me understand that they had actually trained her because she had never been with a family before [i.e. lived in as nanny]. And they've done a very good job. So this plus [nanny's] personality the end result is that it's very pleasant to have her here … She's like a little mouse in your house … The [nanny] agency had told me that [nanny] did not relate well to grown-ups and adults because she … was very, very shy, and it's true you know … She's someone who definitely talks to us now, obviously much more freely than she did the first day we met her, but also is someone who is not desperate for conversation which is quite nice, because you know when you come back from work at 7 p.m., I like someone who can tell me what has happened during the day in you know, ten, fifteen minutes … But I don't want someone who needs someone to talk to for another three hours. So she's part of the family, but she's not quite part of the family either.

The nanny did not want to be interviewed as part of the research and therefore we were unable to get her perspective on her employment. Margot's account presents it as an extraordinary throwback to the days of domestic servants coming from a different and inferior class background to their employers. The nanny is presented as a child–adult, clearly competent with the children but needing to be 'trained' as to how to act around the grown-ups.

'Love and love': the fallacy of kin relationships

In her writing about 'global care chains', Hochschild (2000) suggests that first-world families benefit from the displaced love their third-world employees, parted from their own children, lavish on their charges (see also opening quotation, and Pratt 1997). Although we did not find such care chains replicated in our London localities, it was clear that the issue of loving the children they looked after was a potentially fraught issue for home-based carers. The carers often voiced clear attachments to and affection for the children in their care; however carer relationships with young children are often not long-term, and carers had to decide how attached they could get to the children, thinking both about their own emotional well-being and that of the family.

Michelle differentiates herself from other 'career nannies', who work and then go off travelling, leaving the children in the process. 'Maybe I'm a bit different … but I would find it really hard to say, "right actually I'm gonna give up".' Both Marcia and Audrey, the childminders, mentioned attachments that had lasted, with older children now in secondary school, still coming to see them. They both said they treated their minded children as 'part of the family', as did Crystal, a Stoke Newington nanny with her own children:

> I always try and make sure their children are happy and I treat them like I treat my own. And if that's not right for you and you want them brought up a different way then I'm not the right nanny. And I think you probably couldn't work better than that anyway – treating someone like your own family, you know? Which I do right from the start. And I've kept in touch with every job, that I've done, every job. Because even when you leave it's important to carry on. I mean I'm still, I still go and visit a child I had when I was nineteen/twenty. And she's eighteen now, and she still gives me a big hug and kiss.

Audrey pretends a role as surrogate mother to her charges, although she is very careful to emphasize that she remains fully aware she is not the children's mother:

> I think the way it is with me, I know they're not mine, but I pretend in my mind they are. So I treat them the way I would my own children … I'm aware that their mum's not here so I'm her mum at the moment. Although I know I'm not … That's what parents want, they want a home from home
>
> (Audrey, SN)

As these accounts illustrate, references to 'family' are frequently used to denote closeness (or qualify it in Margot's case). The claim of kinship symbolizes close, warm and loving relationships, drawing on deeply rooted notions of the home and the mother. Gregson and Lowe (1994) comment that the symbolizing of the carer by the parent as 'kin' allows the parents to exploit the carers. Their work is not 'work' at all, but an acting out of their love for their charges. Thus conditions of employment (holidays, pay rises, hours of employment) become almost irrelevant. We also want to make an additional point here: these relationships, between carer and young child, are vulnerable to the parents' actions. Whilst most parents said they were pleased that their children were close to their carers, carers were aware that parental, particularly maternal jealousy was an issue of which they had to be aware. If the parent fell out with the carer, if the family moved, or if the parent felt the child was in need of a different type of care, then the relationship was dispensable, as Marcia had found:

> I've had another parent who when I finished and the child went off to nursery, she was just like 'bye' and off. And I'd had the child for like a year-and-a-half ... You know, I mean, it's not being big-headed but surely she's gonna miss me a little bit. She's gonna say 'why aren't I going round to Marcia's today?'

Such an abrupt departure reveals the basic market nature of the relationship, wherein care is a commodity exchanged for cash. From the carer's perspective, this gives the relationship a fragility which means that if they become very emotionally involved, they can be vulnerable. Again, Michelle provides an example. She talks about the 'mutual respect' and 'trust' that exists between herself and Angie and Paul:

> It is like another family basically ... My relationship with [the parents] is really amazing ... it's a bit like an aunt and uncle who are actually the same age as me, I can sort of talk to them about everything ... You know it's just really – it's just a proper, legitimate. It's a real – I don't know. I feel a bit gushy really.

Michelle clearly characterizes her relationships with the family as one in which the employer–employee strand is secondary to her affective response to them. This however makes her vulnerable. 'Two times, [Angie] has really upset me, but I don't think she realized that she was doing it ...'. On one occasion, Angie, asked by a teacher in Michelle's presence if anyone else had been involved in the child's growing up, said no. On the second occasion, 'Me and [elder girl] had been talking about poetry, and I was sort of explaining to her, you know, what a poem was and everything. And then she wrote this poem ...'. The poem won a competition,

And I was there when, you know, they got the phone call that she had won this competition. And I felt really like someone sort of should have said 'thank you' or 'you helped her do that'. And no-one did. And I felt really – and I just burst into tears because I just felt really sort of ... And I kind of left ... But they didn't really notice that I'd kind of left in this funny way ... and then they were really, you know this family, and I wasn't part of the family in that instant

(Michelle)

Despite Angie describing the relationship with Michelle as more friendship than business, it is difficult if not impossible to completely bury the financial transaction and its effects:

I mean there was a stage where I thought Michelle was too emotional with them and would be ... unhappy with a bit of behaviour that had gone on. And yes, stressed and I wondered at one stage if she was coping with them.

(Angie)

No more than you'd worry about the same things in yourself. You think – oh God I'm not coping with this very well today. Sometimes you think that about ...

(Paul)

There was just one point where I thought I'm paying her quite a lot of money and she seems not to be coping with a relatively normal day. And actually I think she was having a few problems herself. And that's fine. You have to kind of ... and it passed.

(Angie)

Angie is sympathetic and understanding towards her nanny, but she quite clearly, despite her partner's interjection, disassociates her own experience of stress from that of her nanny, who is paid to cope.

Louise, a nanny in South London with nearly 30 years' experience, has learnt the script. Unlike Michelle she does not develop intense relationships with individual children. She does not keep in touch with past children ('although I think it's a good idea at the time, it doesn't happen in practice'):

[Parents want] somebody who's going to be nice to their children. I think that must be the be-all and end-all. Someone that will do *nearly* as good a job as they do. Somebody that will get reasonably attached to their children, but not *totally* attached

(Louise, original emphasis)

She has, in fact, perfected what Nelson (1990) refers to as 'detached attach-ment', a careful blend of warmth and restraint. In effect, if they are to continue to work as professional carers over a long period, these women must learn to manage their emotions when 'at work'.

Talking it through?

We were struck, as we noted earlier, by the lack of reported communication between parents and carers concerning the child's development. Other research in this area points to the difficulties employers and domestic employees have discussing any problems (e.g. Wrigley 1995). Nelson's (1989, 1990) account of family daycare providers and mothers argues that both parties are hampered in their ability to talk freely – mothers by their emotional involvement with the children which makes them wish to preserve untroubled relationships with carers for the children's sake, and carers by their reluctance to risk being seen as uncaring and 'in it for the money'. Uttal (2002) found the mothers in her study worried about a whole range of concerns, and felt strongly the burden of 'responsibility without presence' (2002, p. 27). However, they were often pre-vented from speaking by the lack of immediate threat to the child and 'a sense that the provider's style was unchangeable' (2002, p. 75). Similarly Hondagneu-Sotelo (2003) concludes in her account of 'blow ups and other exits' that employers and domestic employees rarely manage to talk together and settle disputes, suggesting that personal engagement and employment do not easily sit together. Clearly dialogue is constrained in these examples by a concern not to offend, or if criticisms are made, then they are indeed experienced as very personal and hurtful.

We suggest there is also a problem of finding a suitable language and suitable 'space' in which to hold parent–carer conversations (also Uttal 2002). Although the developmental 'milestones' (when children walk, talk, etc.) of early child-hood may have become broadly familiar to the general public through their dissemination through the media and professionals such as health visitors, the professional vocabulary of child development has seemingly remained just that – an issue for professional carers where parental knowledge of the child is sec-ondary to professional expertise (Hughes and MacNaughton 2000). As a result, access to this professional vocabulary remains unevenly distributed across both the parental and home carer populations. This may be changing as parenting becomes more professionalized, as training for childminders and other child-care workers increases, becoming more widespread and formalized.

McLure and Walker (1999) identify a similar vagueness characterizing inter-actions between parents and teachers at parents' evenings. Parents may not know what questions to ask to elicit detailed information and teachers seem unsure as to how much to offer. Furthermore, any instance of probing parental questions may be met with professional defensiveness (Reay 1998; Crozier 2000). Since McLure and Walker's data were collected, detailed target setting has become a common strategy in schools, and it may be that the haphazard and ill-matching conversations which the researchers witnessed have been replaced by detailed references to the National Curriculum levels at which the children operate or are expected to operate. However, returning to our earlier fears about commodification, we would argue that knowing your child is likely to attain a 2A in Key Stage 1 numeracy tests, for example, gives you an insufficient and impoverished view of that child and his/her school life. These constructions of care and learning may be indicative of more generic trends towards the commodification of social relations (Ball 2004).

There are two interrelated issues here: one about finding a language, a vocabulary for a shared discussion, the other about professional control of the formal concepts of child development. With regard to the first, the desire of carers to establish a difference between themselves and parents based on their access to and awareness of a specialized body of knowledge around child development *may* be more of an issue with institution-based carers than those individuals based at home. The vagueness of the interactions applies, as far as we can tell from our data, to many of the parents and carers in our study, whether their children were at nursery or cared for at home. Developing a dialogue requires, we suggest, a willingness to construct a space (not necessarily a physical space, but a temporal, intellectual and emotional one) in which to engage a shared set of concerns. This is, of course, neither an easy nor straightforward task for parents or carers. Moyles (2001) talks of the difficulties for early years practitioners in

> resolving their multifaceted and affectively dominated role against the lack of clear perception in our society as to what kind of values, responsibility, funding or time young children's education and care should demand … Coupling a political mindedness to value for money and pin-pointing 'performance' as the basis of value compounds the difficulties faced by early years practitioners in clearly articulating their roles to less knowledgeable others
>
> (2001, p. 85)

We identify in the conclusion to this chapter some theoretical approaches which may help us take this forward.

In her later work Lynet Uttal (2002) identifies three kinds of relationships between mothers and providers: those who stayed business-like and had minimal contact with the provider, those who befriended a provider, where the adult friendship took over from the focus on the child, and, the most common (involving 35 out of 48 mothers), those who formed a childrearing partnership. However, these partnerships seemed to vary considerably in intensity and depth, from those mothers in brief but regular communication with their providers, to a few acting as advocates for their children and directly intervening in practice, to one mother developing multicultural training for staff at a nursery (2002, p. 147).

Our data contained no interventions of that degree. Indeed, our sample included only one carer, the experienced Louise, who had both clear ideas about childrearing and the confidence to state them firmly. In this she was re-negotiating the boundaries of power and control in her relationships with the children's mothers. Sometimes her attempts to do this worked and a dialogue took place (one of the very few examples in the data), sometimes not. Louise succeeded in one case in refusing to administer behaviour-controlling drugs personally to a child, 'We both had our say – end of story. I mean, they did respect what I did'. However, in another case when a different mother was present, the toddler had a 'temper tantrum' and the mother was unhappy with Louise's advice to put the child in her room until she calmed down. The family then called Louise to say 'don't come back'.[5] Louise's forthrightness was an exception. The other home-based carers in the study and the parents who needed their services muddled along with each other, both parties keen to preserve a good working relationship, even though this may have meant compromises and silences on either or both sides.

Conclusion

One issue that emerges very clearly from our data is the ever-present potential for antagonism between carer and parent. This is particularly noticeable in home-based care as labour market relationships invade the private sphere of the home, within which there is little capacity to formalize and distance employer–employee relationships. Antagonism as actual hostility is rarely overt or manifest in individual social relations. Rather what we mean by antagonism is more abstract: that mother and carer occupy opposing and rival standpoints, that while individuals may be able to build and sustain warm relationships, the possibility of fracture and dissension remains. In some cases, as with Marcia cited above, these differences between mother and carer are also class-inflected. Margaret Nelson (1989, 1990) suggests that it is in the interests of a working mother to have fairly instrumental relationships with family daycare providers. Nelson argues that a working mother needs care to be a flexible, convenient, and affordable commodity, and should have no reason to wish to become involved in a close relationship with the provider. Instead working mothers 'defined their obligations narrowly: to pay well, to come on time, and to keep the provider informed of changes in the household' (1989, p. 21). Whilst we think such a blanket assertion cannot be applied to our sample, and have indeed in this chapter attempted to set out some of the different tones and nuances of parent–carer relationships, we do concur with Nelson's main point about different, and at times opposing agendas, between parent and carer.

To give two examples of potential dissensions and fractures between parents and carers: first, both home-based carers in our research and those working in nurseries voiced opinions in favour of mothers staying at home with their children (also Nelson 1989, 1990; Tuominen 2003), thereby putting them at odds with working mothers:

I basically think if you have children you should look after them

(Louise, nanny, B)

It sounds really awful because I'm a childminder, but I didn't really want to leave him with somebody else … I thought well, he's mine, I chose to have him and I would rather look after him really

(Marcia, childminder, SN)

I mean I'm terrible with my children, the only people I leave them with are people that I know very, very well, and I know who know me very, very well

(Crystal, nanny, SN)

Things are moving towards, you have your child and six months later you don't have your child any more, except on Christmas Day sort of thing, and you wonder what the point is, sometimes you wonder why they bother to have children

(manager, Pigeon nursery, B)

Second, the occupation of care is devalued, something carers complain bitterly about (also Tuominen 2003; Moyles 2001). We cited Marcia on this topic in Chapter 5, but her words bear repeating.

I think [parents] think a lot of childminders are quite thick and quite stupid … and when they find out I've got a degree and stuff, they're kind of 'why are you doing this if you've got a degree? You could work'

(Marcia, childminder, SN)

If parents looked on nannies as professionals and used them in the right way, and not as housekeepers or skivvies basically, then they'd have a much better relationship with their nannies

(Crystal, nanny, SN)

Ringing up childminders and saying 'how much do you charge?', then saying 'would you consider charging less than that?', that's awful, but when you add it up it's over half of my salary towards childcare … I'm paying my cleaner more per hour than for my treasured possession

(Katy, mother, SN)

The nanny will go [be made redundant] before the cleaner goes

(Louise, nanny, B)

Carers themselves are not exempt from the devaluing of childcare. Home-based care roles in particular lack the badges of a 'proper' job: promotion, a career structure, for instance (although the National Childminding Association is working to change this). Whilst Michelle concurs with the other carers that 'There's a lack of respect for people who look after children because I think it's viewed as not very important,' she also states that she wants to move on from nannying. Otherwise,

> I'd feel like maybe I'd just been stuck in the same place for too long really, and not gone forward … It's quite funny like when I meet people from school and they've all set up publishing companies and I've been rolling around in the park.
>
> (Michelle, nanny, SN)

The underlying friction between opposing subject positions is unlikely to be addressed in situations where there is a lack of dialogue between parent and carer concerning all but the most basic circumstances of care. We suggest that such circumstances are not uncommon. Mothers were often vague when asked about the details of their child's day with the carer, echoing Mary (mother, SN), who said, 'What else does she [the nanny] do? I don't know really. They just play'. As we noted earlier, there is a lack of an appropriate vocabulary in which to have such a conversation or a tradition to support it. Time is limited for both parents and carers at the start and end of the day, and both parties share a desire not to criticize the other and thereby jeopardize a working relationship. Thus, what we find instead characterizing relationships between parents and carers is absences and silences. In-depth dialogue concerning the child, is, as we have suggested, an absence in many cases, making the development of the type of 'co-ordinated care' relationship as envisaged by Uttal largely illusory, in our sample at least. Silence surrounds issues of power and control shaping carer–family relationships. There is a tendency for each party to see itself as vulnerable and reliant on the other: carers on parents' behaviour as service users, their ultimate say in dictating the extent of the relationship with the child, and parents on carers' behaviour towards their children, their awareness of the lack of alternatives in a market that is (in London at least), producer-driven. Uttal refers to this phenomenon as 'dual powerlessness', locating it as a result of 'the political economy of the childcare market which privatizes care and devalues [childcare] labour' (2002, p. 110; also Nelson 1990).

We finish by making two points. The first is to concur with Nelson (1989), who argues that if this situation is to alter, structural change is necessary. An increase in the respect accorded to childcare, childcarers, and the experiences of young children, and a move towards flexible working practices for parents that would allow both mothers and fathers to work and spend time with their children would begin to impact on the barriers currently existing between families and carers.

The second point considers the nature of the dialogue that might go some way towards ameliorating the silences and absences we found characterizing many parent–carer relationships, whilst avoiding the filling of those silences with the language of commodified care. Such a shift in dialogue would also contribute towards the structural changes involved in re-evaluating care. The work of the American political philosopher, Iris Marion Young, perhaps offers an alternative way forward. Young has written extensively about deliberative democracy and the mechanisms, attitudes and values needed to expand the opportunities for participation and collective decision-making throughout society, but particularly where marginalized social groups are concerned (Young 1990). Becoming dissatisfied with the concept of deliberation which she saw as privileging a culturally specific and gendered form of speech – competitive, formal, dispassionate and disembodied – over all others, she developed the concept of 'communicative democracy', a wider definition of 'appropriate' speech which includes 'greeting, rhetoric and storytelling' (Young 1996). It is the last of these that we wish to explore briefly.

Ideas based on storytelling and communication are also developed by Hughes and MacNaughton (2000) in relation to nursery settings. They describe 'The binary opposition at the heart of the politics of professionalism in early childhood education: staff present their professional – scientific – knowledge of the child as the binary opposite of parents' anecdotal – narrative – knowledge' (2000, p. 252).

The validation of telling stories may go some way towards disrupting this professional–parental binary. Hughes and MacNaughton suggest an approach based on Lyotard's (1984) 'petit recits' or 'little narratives'. 'Little narratives' describe people's approaches to specific issues – a small slice of their world-view – that can be shared with others in dialogue and debate. Hughes and MacNaughton give an illustration of the approach in an early childhood centre in Australia as staff held a parents' meeting to discuss a proposed gender equity policy. After this discussion, Hughes and MacNaughton suggest that

> [staff] and parents could share their little narratives with other parents and staff via newsletters and notice-boards inviting others to express their views about gender. In doing so, these other people would add to the narrative and create a continuing dialogue about gender within the centre
>
> (2000, p. 255)

Hughes and MacNaughton relay Lyotard's comments about the inevitability of contradiction, disagreement and dissensus. They do not go on to suggest how staff charged with policy-making react to such disagreement,[6] but perhaps Young's (1990) notion of reaching temporary settlements, finding points of temporary consensus, is apposite here.

Hughes and MacNaughton's approach is suited to institutional policy-making. A version based more directly on Young's ideas of storytelling could take a more informal form, and therefore be suited to one-to-one carer–parent relationships. A dialogue between parent and carer based on telling stories about the child's actions and interactions would be valuable in at least two ways. First, there is of course the substance of the story, what it illustrates about the child and his/her development, his/her moods on that day, his/her likes and dislikes. Second, as Young argues (1996, pp. 131–2), the storytelling process can reveal much about the subjectivity, the values and the priorities of the storyteller, a step towards filling the silences and absences between parent and carer. Of course, this process goes on all the time, childminders, nannies, nursery staff and parents telling stories to each other, usually when the child does something amusing or noteworthy in some way. But the value of this currently haphazard and occasional interaction needs to be more widely recognized. Such narratives could be understood, not as little more than female gossip, but as a regular and valuable daily exchange – about the child's activities, interactions and moods – contributing to and developing a joint picture of the young child and his/her developing awareness, skills and abilities. As such, we suggest that it presents a basis for meaningful dialogue between parent and carer and a way of building bridges across opposed subject positions.

Chapter 7

'Making up' the middle-class child

'Parenting mania' ... That is not to say that everyone catches it. The profile of the target group is roughly as follows: highly susceptible are middle class women who are well educated city dwellers, expecting their first child at a fairly advanced age

(Beck and Beck-Gernsheim 1995, p. 117)

Introduction

The importance of education to the middle classes is commonly noted (e.g. Ball 2003; Power *et al.* 2003). Indeed Butler with Robson (2003) argue that one of the key determinants in shaping further gentrification in London is parental perceptions of the quality of the available schooling. This preoccupation with education which starts in babyhood, was apparent in our research when the children entered nursery at two-and-a-half or three years, and continues through primary and secondary education to choice of higher education (Reay *et al.* 2005). 'Education' does not, for our middle-class parents, only describe what goes on in nurseries, schools and universities. Instead, education is an all-encompassing engagement with the child. As part of this the children have access to a wide range of 'extra-curricular' activities, chosen from the options offered by burgeoning local markets.[1] In this chapter, therefore, we examine three areas. First, we discuss differences in style and ethos between some of the nurseries used by our parents, linking apparent differences in provision to the choices and priorities of different middle-class fractions. Second, we focus on the choice (or proposed choice) of compulsory education, made by parents in Battersea and Stoke Newington, paying particular attention to the private/state divide, and showing how choices within exclusive 'circuits of care' translate, for the most part, into similarly exclusive settings for compulsory schooling. Third, we focus on the roles and purposes of extra-curricular 'enrichment' activities.

Nursery education

We begin this section with a caveat. Our project was neither focused on peda-gogies of care nor 'good practice' in early years (unlike for example the Effective Provision of Pre-school Education (EPPE) project: Sylva *et al.* 2004), and we did not spend time observing carer and children in the care settings. Our sources of data are therefore the accounts of both nursery staff (usually the manager) and parents (we have already noted in Chapter 6 that parental accounts of how the children spent their time were often vague). This section is included despite these caveats because on analysing the data we realized that what information we did have suggests interesting differences between some of the Battersea and Stoke Newington nurseries, differences, that is, in nursery practices and parental preferences for care.

Unsurprisingly parents have a more diffuse and distant relationship with carers in nurseries than those who offer home-based care. Our respondents often talked about the ethos and character of the institution itself, and referred to staff by roles (headteacher, key worker, manager) rather than names. Their choices were based on locality, facilities, availability of places and their affective response to particular settings. Very few parents appeared to have a clear idea of what they wanted from nursery education. The same general themes were reiterated through the inter-views: 'structure' (of varying degrees, too much structure could be a disadvantage), 'stimulation', and 'socialization' (especially peer group contact) re-occur fre-quently. However, the vagueness of these concepts means that the same language can be used to describe quite different experiences. In some ways, this lack of focus on the goals of early years education and care – even from these highly edu-cated and education-minded families – is unsurprising. Moss and Penn note that

> Many parents of young children, quite understandably, do not have the time or inclination to become involved in theoretical debates about early childhood services. Demands on their time and attention are heavy and constant while needs are pressing and immediate.
>
> (2003, p. 18)

Additionally, we have already commented in Chapter 6 on the silences and absences that seemed to constitute many parent–carer relationships. As a result, many of the parents knew only the generalities of their child's nursery day: the children's accounts were spasmodic, often surreal; parents, working parents espe-cially, were rushing when they picked up and dropped off their children; furthermore, the settings themselves varied in how much and what kind of information was sent home to parents. Parents' prime indicator of a successful placement was the child's 'happiness', usually judged by their willingness to go to and stay in the setting, but the parents' own practical needs and constraints are also important in the choice of settings. Anjali, a teacher, describes her choice of a nursery, a private Montessori nursery school (Chaffinch nursery) for her son:

It suited our needs really well because of the location. So I didn't shop around an awful lot, because there were those factors … I liked it because it was – I had the flexibility of choosing a morning place or an afternoon place … And it was just a big room and it had lots of little activities going on – just seemed very calm and quite colourful and the headteacher, the person who ran the nursery seemed very accommodating and it just had a nice atmosphere. And the three children I know who had gone through the nursery had, you know, enjoyed it. And it had everything, I mean I wasn't looking for anything, you know, particularly … I wasn't looking for a sort of stimulating [formal] curriculum, I didn't want him to like, you know, learn to read or … you know, there was lots of creative activities and there was also those sorts of pre-school skills, preparation for school skills. You know, some work with letters … I really didn't have any particular strong views about his nursery education, other than it was more to do with suiting my needs

(Anjali, B)

Notice the importance of her affective response to the setting, the key role of 'hot' knowledge (Ball and Vincent 1998), and also her comment that she has few strong ideas about nursery education (despite being a primary school teacher). Although she suggests she wanted creative activities, rather than an emphasis on formal early learning, in fact she chooses a relatively formal setting (see below).

One emphasis that did run strongly through the interviews was that parents liked small, intimate settings. This was a strong motivation, displayed at its strongest by those parents choosing the co-operative crèches in Stoke Newington. The attraction is derived from the discursive appeal of 'family' settings and the consequent negative appeal of 'institutions' (see Chapters 3 and 6). Jackie's daughter started off at a playgroup, and when that closed, moved to a popular Stoke Newington day nursery, Garden nursery. Jackie felt initially concerned about Garden, when contrasted to the other settings:

I thought [the playgroup] was a little freer and easier and slightly less formal, and erm was a little bit cheaper … I had an idea that all these places [the playgroup and two parent run crèches] might be preferable to [Garden] because I just thought it was a bit more institutional, possibly, … [but] there might be all sorts of things about [Garden] that appear more institutional than some of the other arrangements, but they are very affectionate with the children, and that's what matters basically … They [the staff] are absolutely there concentrating on the children and that's what you want, and it's on our doorstep and it's got fantastic facilities.

(Jackie, SN)

As we noted in Chapter 3, Moss argues that the emphasis on the small and intimate disrupts the search for a pedagogy of care that is distinct to group settings. As a result of this lack of a coherent and distinctive pedagogy the potential benefits of group care are obscured by the understanding, culturally embedded in the UK, that any form of care should mimic that given by the mother; in other words that early years settings should create substitute mothering. As Moss (2004b) comments there are only the beginnings of a recognition that children can thrive in environments other than the home, and that those environments can and should be qualitatively different from the home. He argues for a holistic approach emphasizing pedagogy:

> The pedagogical approach is holistic. The pedagogue sets out to address the whole child, the child with body, mind, emotions, creativity, history and social identity. This is not the child only of emotions, the psycho-therapeutical approach; nor only of the body, the medical approach; nor only of the mind, the traditional teaching approach. For the pedagogue, learning, care and more generally upbringing ... are closely related (indeed inseparable) activities at the level of daily work.
>
> (2004b, p. 21)

Despite apparent limitations in the current philosophy of early years care, and a lack of public debate around the purposes of early childhood care and education, it is clear from other research that there is considerable variation in the ethos and pedagogy of existing settings (Siraj-Blatchford *et al.* 2003). Our settings too appeared to differ quite dramatically from one another, and to some extent, we suggest, this was spatially determined and related to class fractioning.

The parent respondents used a variety of different types of group care, the range of variation being particularly broad in Stoke Newington (see Table 4.1 in Chapter 4). We interviewed seven providers in Battersea, including staff in the nursery class at Goldwater, the state school. All the other providers were private day nurseries or private nursery schools. We were not granted access by any of the private prep schools. In Stoke Newington we interviewed providers at four nurseries (three private day nurseries and one state early years centre) and at two of the parent co-ops.

In general terms, and as noted in Chapter 4, there is more reliance on the private sector, including nursery classes in private schools in Battersea, compared with some reliance on the state sector and co-operative provision in Stoke Newington. The four nurseries and two parent crèches in Stoke Newington appeared to be less formal, with less emphasis upon developing formal learning, than four (out of the seven visited in total) of their Battersea counterparts.[2] The small numbers here mean that we cannot make general claims for this aspect of our analysis, but we argue that there were some significant differences in provision across the two localities. Although we focus on only four out of the total seven Battersea nurseries, the point is that it is difficult to imagine this group of Battersea nurseries in Stoke Newington and vice versa, such is the difference in ethos and presentation.

Table 7.1 Respondent providers in Battersea

Name	Type	Hours	Fees
Sparrow	Private nursery school	Sessional, mornings only	£850 per term
Chaffinch	Private nursery school	Sessional, mornings or afternoon	Morning session £850 per term, afternoon session £650 per term
Goldfinch	Private nursery school	Sessional, mornings only	£935 per term
Blue Tit Montessori	Private nursery school	Sessional, mornings only	£970 per term
Robin	Nursery school in college premises	All day 8.00–6.00	£42 per day
Pigeon Montessori	Private nursery school session	Sessional, mornings or afternoon	Morning session approximately £850 per term Afternoon session approximately £700 per term
Goldwater	State primary school nursery class	Sessional, morning or afternoon, some full-time places	free

We asked all the provider respondents about the organization of the setting and the structure of the day. These descriptions differ from one another quite radically, although the same sort of language reappears across settings. The ubiquitous 'learning through play', is constantly heard, as are 'stimulation', 'structure', and 'socialization'. We give two very different examples here: Bankside, an early years centre, actually slightly out of the area, but used by some Stoke Newington residents, and Chaffinch, a private nursery school, in Battersea.

The head of Bankside, which offers a third of its places as marketed places, states a clear pedagogical position:

> When parents first join us, we make it clear that we're not here to teach children, that we will not be teaching them their ABC, we will not be teaching them their numbers. What we will be doing is valuing play and everything we will do is through play ... There are facilities in every area for children to write and to explore numbers and to explore the language of maths. And if a child's really showing interest and becoming fascinated by lessons then we will follow that interest. And explore out, and do phonic work, and in terms of writing, getting them to write their names, write their mum's name, all the things that are interesting to them ... We used to have a parent who was very keen for their children to write, and

we said we weren't going to do it you know [i.e. specifically teach child]. And we said if they wanted to do that, then they needed to go to another nursery that could provide that sort of facility … I think what you have to show parents is, how does painting help my child to write.

(Radhika, head, Bankside)

Here the child is at the centre of activities; the classification of these activities is avoided. Play, number and writing are seamlessly interwoven in what the child wants to do. By this account there is little explicit sequencing or pacing of knowledge: rhythms are relaxed and acquisition unspecialized. But there is, of course, an implicit structured curriculum, hence phonic work and the language of maths.

Table 7.2 Respondent providers in Stoke Newington

Name	Type	Hours	Fees
Garden	Private day nursery	All day 8.00–6.00	£38 per day for full-time place
Rainbow	Private day nursery	All day 8.30–5.00	£90 per week for full-time place
Ladybird	Co-operative crèche operating from parents' houses	All day 9.00–6.00	£23.70 a week (parents are expected to help run the crèche)
Butterfly	Co-operative creche	Short day 9.15–4.00	Approximately £300 per month (parents are expected to help in the crèche if possible)
Bankside	State Early Years Centre	All day 7.45–5.20	Offers combination of marketed and subsidized places. Fees for marketed places vary between £160 and £110 per week depending on age
Dragonfly	Community nursery	Playgroup mornings or extended hours until 3.00	Playgroup morning sessions £75 per week, extended hours £110 per week. Nursery £125 per week

These tables are to give some indication of the range of hours offered and fees charged by the providers who participated in the research. It proved impossible with the data we had and the wide range of different arrangements – sessional care versus full time day care – to convert provider fees into a single measure (i.e. prices charged per day).

By contrast, Chaffinch, the private nursery school that Anjali mentions above and which sees many of its children go on into private schooling, has a very different approach. For 30–45 minutes, the children work in groups 'according to their age and ability'. The headteacher comments further:

> We have a set curriculum which we follow. So the very tiny children that start with us at two-and-a-half, they [are involved in] all the Montessori practical life exercises. So it's sort of pouring, spooning, threading – all hand–eye co-ordination and developing their concentration. And they're also introduced to colours and shapes. The next group they move on to, term two, which is pencil control worksheets. So again we're getting them used to holding their pencils, being able to follow dots going from left to right, up and down ... Then their third term, they're introduced to the first half of the alphabet and numbers one to five ... and then they progress onto the second half of the alphabet and numbers six to ten. And then again, until they – just preparing them for going on to full-time school. Then moving onto word building, three letter phonetic words, they're doing addition using Montessori beads.
>
> (Megan, headteacher, Chaffinch)

In contrast to the strong 'learning through play' ethos at Bankside, the head-teacher at Chaffinch talks about 'doing some work' with children, clearly differentiating that from 'arts and crafts' and 'free play'. We can see the beginnings of a 'classification' of activities here, the assertion of boundaries between education and play, the serious and the playful. The curriculum is visible and exists independently from the children's immediate interests. Control in terms of pace and sequencing appears to be by the teacher (although this would not be strict Montessori practice).

Differences between the settings that may seem relatively minor from parents' point of view can be sharply reflected in practices. One example of this is the degree of adult guidance given to art work, again a Battersea–Stoke Newington contrast:

> Basically, whatever goes home from nursery, it must be significant to the child in some way and they probably want to talk about it, and if they're interested in something, then that's something that can be worked on and developed ... But it doesn't necessarily mean you do the work for them so that it looks good for the parents
>
> (Eva, co-ordinator, Garden, SN)

Here again the emphasis is developmental; the child is at the centre of the process, as is his/her acquisition of metacapabilities. In contrast, at Goldfinch nursery the acquisition of specific skills and the 'quality' of the outcomes has been of greater significance.

We got criticized [by Ofsted] for not doing enough free art ... There wasn't enough of the children's work. So last year [we] spent a lot of time letting them really produce their own stuff with minimal guidance. And then we got complaints that the artwork wasn't good enough, up to a decent quality from the parents ... So you have to try and balance that out.

(Sylvia, staff member, Goldfinch, B)

One example of presumably adult-guided art work was reported on by Anjali, (although she does not raise the possibility of adult guidance).

One time he did a project on South America, because one of the teachers there was from South America, and he came back with a little pasta collage, and all the Andes were done in lentils. Yeah, that's quite impressive you know when you're two-and-a-half

(Anjali, parent at Chaffinch, B)

The Stoke Newington settings tended to stress their relational informality, as well as the loose structuring of their curriculum offerings:

I like working in here rather than going to Muswell Hill [a largely middle-class area of North London] and being told that we all wear uniforms and I don't know, just little bits and pieces that I find really pointless and restricting. So I do like, I think it's easy to have this kind of ethos in a place like Stoke Newington because it is quite progressive in terms of people's ideas and sort of liberal in the most kind of, I don't know, positive sense. I mean you can take that to extremes ... I mean I'm totally against sort of hippy ideas of, I don't know, drumming all day ... .

(Eva, co-ordinator, Garden, SN)

And the range of professional middle-class white families I've got. I'd say about seventy or eighty per cent of them don't want their children taught in any structured way. They actually want them to play ... people come to me for that purpose, because they know that I let the children play

(Ella, manager, Dragonfly Nursery, SN)

Dragonfly is an interesting case as it has developed a particular position emphasizing its relatively loose structure. Although a new facility, Ella, the manager, had previously run a playgroup in the area and is known by local parents. She comments on her preference for staff who have had life experiences other than childcare,

people who have been artists and writers and have done something else, and at the same time had their own children and then decided to go into childcare and do a course, it's like they bring a huge range into their work.

This is another form of weak classification, in two senses – as a move beyond the paradigms of childcare training, and as a way of bringing the world into the classroom. Recognizing that her setting appeals to a particular class fraction, she contrasts the parents of children at her nursery with

> City workers with their children in [daycare] at 8 o'clock, full day care, come back all fed and dried and changed and handed over. It's a different kind of background, different expectation, so the types I get tend to be quite often they're people working part-time or job sharing
>
> (Ella, Dragonfly, SN)

Bernstein's well known distinction between visible and invisible pedagogies to which our commentary here has alluded, describes the former as being one where the 'regulative and discursive' order of learning is explicit, and the latter where such rules are implicit.

> A visible pedagogy (and there are many modalities) will always place an emphasis on the performance of the child … the external product of the child … [The focus of invisible pedagogies] is not upon a 'gradable' performance of the acquirer but upon procedures internal to the acquirer (cognitive, linguistic, affective, motivational)
>
> (Bernstein 2004, p. 201)

Infant schools, and by extension, pre-schools, are normally understood as having invisible pedagogies – where hierarchical rules, sequencing rules and criteria for completion of a task are implicit. However, it appears that nurseries such as Pigeon, Goldfinch, Sparrow and Chaffinch display *some* characteristics of visible pedagogy, such as an emphasis on early reading (Bernstein 2004, p. 204), and the pedagogies are relatively more visible than those of their Stoke Newington counterparts.

> We're not a pushy – I wouldn't say we're a pushy school at all. But then, if we know a child is able to achieve a certain amount of work, we won't take, sort of, their sloppiness, we'll say, 'oh come on', you know, 'we can do better than that. Let's have another go and see if we can do it even better than that.' But just, sort of, you know, being fun about it, but pushing them on to that next step all the time … . So, I think every parent just says, when they come in, they just love the atmosphere, and like the balance of, sort of, work and play, that we don't, sort of, just, sort of, strictly teach direct all the time
>
> (Sheryl, manager, Sparrow nursery, B)

Again, work and play appear differentiated, and teaching at least some of the time is also explicit and direct. Similarly, a teacher at Goldfinch explained why the nursery school was not strictly Montessori, pointing to the nursery's links with the prep schools in the area.

> Montessori is all about free choice. ... And you do not sit them down [in a strict Montessori establishment] and say, 'right, we're all going to have a work session now'. If they spent their entire time doing exactly what they chose to do, when they went ... on to [named local private prep-schools], they would struggle *so* badly, because they're made to sit there. And that's why you really – we couldn't do it, could we?
>
> (Sylvia, Goldfinch, B)

As noted in Chapter 4, Bernstein argues that a preference for particular pedagogies is closely related to middle-class fractions.

> The assumptions of a visible pedagogy are more likely to be met by that fraction of the middle class whose employment has a direct relation to the economic field (production, distribution and circulation of capital). Whereas the assumptions of an invisible pedagogy are more likely to be met by that fraction of the middle class who have a direct relationship, not to the economic field, but to the field of symbolic control and who work in specialized agencies of symbolic control usually located in the public sector.
>
> (2004, p. 204)

We are not suggesting that the staff in the Stoke Newington nurseries do not value and engage in helping children to develop early literacy and numeracy skills, but they do not, *as far as we can judge from the data*, prioritize them or make them explicit *to the extent* that their Battersea counterparts do.

One day nursery in Stoke Newington, Rainbow, is owned by a humanist trust and places a great emphasis on yoga and meditation.

> At 9.30 it's circle time, at the beginning of the circle time it's movement ... which is exercise or yoga, there would be dance games, and that leads into more subtle [indecipherable] about the love inside us, and ends on a rhythmic chant which means love is all around us, and that can be sung to any tune, it has like a lullaby effect on their mind and they move from side to side, it calms their mind and then we ask the children to sit straight in a line, they sit straight and tall with their hands in their lap and close their eyes, and to feel the warm love inside them.
>
> (Uma, manager, Rainbow, SN)

Interestingly, here is a visible pedagogy with fixed temporal structures and a specific end point, but this end point is, in part, the child's knowledge of his/her self and unrelated to formal educational knowledge. In general, staff at the Stoke Newington nurseries were keen to avoid the trappings of an overt curriculum and fixed expectations of the children's development. The manager at Garden, for example, spoke of the presumption that children have to be fully occupied at all times during their day at nursery:

> And I know that in some nurseries the parents get a little booklet where it's written down, you know, 'Billy played with Lego' and it's [inaudible]. And then I think, 'well, what would happen if Billy didn't do anything?' You know, you can't write [that], you know, it's an expectation that that's what he does.

The Stoke Newington parent co-ops particularly stressed the virtue of their small size and the resulting intimacy, and again, at Butterfly in particular, the avoidance of explicit structures and fixed goals. Here the size and intimacy allow for the retention of particular familial qualities to interaction over and against institutional ones (see also Chapter 3):

> Because we're eight, or seven at the moment, so we can really sense that this person's good at this, and that person's, you know, and this individual attention is very rare, you really pick up things. So I think it comes, that was another thing that really encouraged us to do this, and a lot of the people that now joined, like [a] father today was saying 'I like this because it's not so regimental, and not so strict'. It's very relaxed, it's very family-orientated, and the kids thrive
>
> (Alicia, founder, Butterfly, SN)

Staff and parents at Butterfly also prioritized learning through play:

> We didn't want our children to be learning letters at two-and-a-half because they're not prepared yet, we believe their minds are not prepared to be learning letters at that time, they should be playing, you know, yeah, going and exploring life, and as well our choice of toys that we have here, we try not to clutter with toys, there are places which are cluttered with plastic toys and it's overloaded with nothing, plastic tack, that's not doing anything for the kids, you know, all they need is a bit of mud, dirty and messy play, that's what they like, they don't need all this plastic.
>
> (Alicia, Butterfly, SN)

The quotations that we have included give some small flavour, we hope, of the differences in tone and approach between the four settings in Battersea and their Stoke Newington counterparts. However, the argument for a distinction between settings is not clear-cut. This is partly because of the small number of settings we accessed, and partly because we are again indicating relatively nuanced differences, to set against commonalities in practice across pre-school settings. Nursery staff in both areas commented on the diversity of parental expectations, from those who were keen to see the children develop formal skills to those who wanted the child to play.

> You get certain [parents] who are 'push them, push them, push them' ... And then you have other parents who are 'I'm not interested in them knowing their letters and numbers, I just want them to come and play and enjoy themselves and have social skills'
>
> (Sheryl, Sparrow, B)

> There's constant, there's fantastic diversity – what do parents want? ... There used to be like two years back, there were more parents who were concerned about [early reading and writing] ... I think it must have been more debate on excessive scrutiny of children in the media. And perhaps parents have tuned into that a little bit. It may not be in their best interests, this observing and contrasting
>
> (Eva, Garden, SN)

Parental input is hard to trace at the nurseries; the emphasis at most is on keeping parents informed of the setting's aims and their own child's progress. Rainbow and the two parents co-ops in Stoke Newington, Ladybird and Butterfly, held regular meetings, and the manager at Rainbow gave us an example of developing the creative opportunities in the nursery at the suggestion of some parents. Rainbow and the parent co-operatives are, however, exceptions: there were otherwise few forums for dialogue. A general emphasis on educating parents is apparent in both areas. Whilst working-class parents are normally the target of professionals' educative attempts, staff in settings that attracted a homogeneous middle-class group also expressed a desire for parents 'to be a little bit more knowledgeable' (Sheryl, Sparrow nursery, B). In the parent-run crèches, one might expect parents to be more closely involved with issues of curriculum and pedagogy. However, even here the workers appeared to exercise considerable autonomy, certainly as they become established, although the co-ordinator at Ladybird also responded to parental suggestions:

> Even though the workers organize the day to day running of it and we decide, you know, we listen to their [parents] suggestions. You know, one said, 'oh look we'd love it if you did the jungle'. So we did a whole theme about the jungle.
>
> (Mia, co-ordinator, Ladybird, SN)

However, parental deference to professional expertise is also visible. When asked if her plans for the future are debated at parents' meetings, she responded:

No I tell them, I just tell them … We've had some parents visit and they've said, 'oh no' you know, 'God that's a bit educational'. And we're like 'well it's not, it's not really because it's like even though by the end of their time at [Ladybird] they know exactly where their name is on the board and they know what 2002 looks like and they know the days of the week, yes, but we don't force it upon them

(Mia, Ladybird, SN)

The differences between settings may be difficult for parents to 'read' given that they are likely to have only a quick visit and the setting's literature from which to judge. Nonetheless, we suggest that particular settings do appeal to particular parents, and this appeal is an indication of what they instinctively feel comfortable with. Particular strategies, practices and presentations by different nurseries meet particular parental ideas about what nurseries 'should' be like. This may be quite subtle, with neither pedagogies nor ethos strongly articulated by either provider or parent. We have pointed tentatively to class fractional differences. It is however impossible to determine from this data whether, as Bernstein suggests, there is a relationship between forms of instruction, regulation, and the organization of time and space inside the family and preferences for particular nursery or school pedagogies (although see Angie below and in Chapter 6).

In summary therefore we reiterate that it may be difficult for parents to read the differences between providers when they get only a snapshot visit, and the accompanying vocabulary shares similarities across the sector despite clear differences between individual providers. The providers' brochures across the sample do reveal those differences – to us, reading them in conjunction with the transcripts, but they may well be invisible to parents reading two or three from providers in one locality. Indeed, we were struck by how little information many providers give in their brochures about the structure of the day, and details of the curriculum. The most prolific in this respect was the humanist nursery, Rainbow, whose philosophy is carefully explained. There is therefore always the possibility with the other nurseries that parents may read incorrectly and end up with a situation which does not suit them and which they feel is inappropriate for the child. Angie (SN, see Chapter 6) describes a nursery (not part of the sample, as it closed during the research period) which turned out to be a complete mismatch with the family's expectations, one which appeared to her to give priority to order over creativity and formality over intimacy. The implication here is that there is a disjunction between the instructional and regulatory order of the home and those of the nursery.

I put [daughter] there as well [as her cousin] and she absolutely hated it and we hated it as well. And it was kind of the worst mistake we ever made with her care. You know it was dreadful … . It was a much bigger and more institutional environment [than previous parent-run crèche]. It was very uncreative. ... Everything was very ordered there. They would sit down and they would do an activity, which was really prescribed. They would count things into a box, up to ten and she could already count and do anything. ... They were very detached, they were teachers rather than carers sort of thing, they were very detached, very school environment. There was a lot of lining up, a lot of sitting cross-legged; there was no cuddles, no intimacy and suddenly this big scale, huge. ... She had nightmares, she cried all the time, she screamed, having been the most outgoing sort of settled child up until that point ... she was deeply unhappy.

(Angie, mother, SN)

Education

One of the possibilities we have been exploring in our research is the extent to which childcare is viewed as part of a longer process of 'making up the child' as an educational subject. That is, do parents see childcare as one stage in the production of a 'successful' student? We asked all our respondents whether they had thought at all about the transition from childcare to school. No-one, even those with young babies, dismissed the question as premature. On the contrary, most answered with reference to local 'circuits of schooling' (Ball et al. 1996), either state or private, and could discuss their preferences and the chances of being offered a place at particular establishments. This is unsurprising given the prime importance of education to the middle classes. Educational success plays a crucial role in the social reproduction of the middle classes as a whole, and offers individuals access to the 'right' universities, and particular points of entry into the labour market. What Prout (1999) calls 'futurity' and planning ahead surround the children with class-related hopes and expectations. Education is an investment against 'the fear of falling' (Ehrenreich 1989; Walkerdine et al. 2001; Ball 2003), a mechanism through which the middle classes can close themselves off from the working classes.

Mothers in our study did however differ in the degree of planning they had invested in school choice. Suzannah for example had devised a plan designed to fulfil her goal – getting her daughters (aged three years and two years) into one of two independent schools.

I was just getting over the childbirth thing and venturing out of the house and people said, 'so, what schools?' And I just thought, but she's a little baby, but you have to put them down. I sort of got panicky, then I researched it. I bought the books, *The Top 500 Schools* and you just read, and obviously area, and you just try and dwindle it down ... so I was ringing round when [daughter] was five months old for a school at four, and then I worked backwards ... What I did was speak to the admission secretary and said 'which [nursery] school do you find that seems to have a similar way of teaching?', and they give you a list. They can't recommend, all they can say is statistically speaking we get six from [child's current nursery school] and five from [competitor nursery]

(Suzannah, SN)

Suzannah then enrolled her daughter in one of the statistically promising nurseries in order to maximize her chances of gaining a place in one of the highly selective girls' schools. At the other end of the continuum, Debra (with a child approaching two), and also in Stoke Newington, was noticeably vague and unfocused about the specifics of school provision, but she is anticipating a family move to what she would see as a more favourable educational location. Asked if she had any plans yet, she replies:

Not really, although I've started to think about it, but I'm not that sure because of house prices that once she's in full-time education that we'll still be around here. But I know just from my own knowledge of the area that the schools aren't that fantastic, although a lot of schools are getting better. It's not a prospect I'm really looking forward to.

Debra is very clear about the importance of finding a suitable school for her daughter. Although she has not yet acted, she has drawn up several contingency plans – finding a church school, moving out of London – which she feels will help her find the 'right' school for her daughter.

I don't think he [her partner] realizes just how important it is to find the right kind of school. You know I'm not hugely bothered by results because I think she'll get a lot of support from home. I think it's more things like discipline and the kind of attitudes that children have within a school. Education is important. And it's not maybe something we'd get the best deal for her if we stay in London.

(Debra, SN)

All our respondents stressed the importance of finding a 'good' school, and understood it to be their moral obligation to find appropriate provision for their child (Ball 2003; Swift 2003). The possibilities of different options are, as we shall see, embedded in family histories and locally shared perceptions and assumptions about schooling. Many felt that things were different from when they went to school, for those considering the state sector, things they had taken for granted were now matters of doubt. As Monica said, '*Everybody* panics about school. It's difficult for my husband and I because we're of the generation where you just went to school around the corner. And you do have to lose all of that' (Monica, B, original emphasis).

The extent to which all the respondents would agree with Monica – that 'you do have to lose all of that' – does vary, and place is a factor here. There are more families in Battersea than Stoke Newington who will only consider private schooling (15 families in Battersea out of 28, with another six families hovering; however five of these 'hoverers' would consider only one state school, Goldwater). In Stoke Newington, only two families seriously considered private schooling, although one of these families later moved out of London and plans to use the state sector. In Battersea, unlike Stoke Newington, some families have a specific tradition of private schooling:

> My husband comes from completely the private system including boarding school. He's quite nervous about the whole thing. I mean he knows there are some very good [state] schools but it's like an unknown world to him, and unless they are highly recommended to him, I don't think he would touch them. Although [husband] is, I think, very open, his family have been at Harrow since the seventeenth century.
>
> (Margot, B)

Whilst parents' own educational experiences were an influence on the kind of education they wanted for their own children, their choices and priorities cannot be deduced entirely from their own education. Overall, out of 28 two-parent families in Battersea, 26 respondents had been to state secondary school themselves, 20 had been to private schools, while a further ten experienced a mix of state and private schools (usually state primary, followed by private secondary). Among the 31 Stoke Newington families, 34 had attended state schools, 19 private schools, and a further eight a mix of state and private schools (see Tables 2.6 and 2.7 on p. 9). Nonetheless the allegiance to state education, even for those who have succeeded in that system themselves, is faltering.[3] The attempts of the New Labour government to make state education more attractive to the middle classes do not seem to have been successful as yet in Battersea (or Stoke Newington: see below). Parents like Monica, cited above, a product of the state system herself, did not see that as a feasible option for her children. However Juliet, herself and her partner, both privately educated, talked positively about the social mix provided by her local state primary school, Goldwater. This particular school, however, is a high achieving school, adopted and colonized by middle-class parents in the area. It is, for many middle-class parents in the locality, the acceptable face of state education and its existence was responsible for attracting a number of the Battersea families into the state system – at least for primary education. The tightly bounded relationship between locality and recruitment in some primary schools makes it possible in some circumstances for middle-class parents to ensure a relatively homogenous educational environment – a form of social closure (see Chapter 4). Butler and Robson (2001) describe a similar 'enclave' in South London's Telegraph Hill area. For these parents and those in our study

[t]he schools are seen as a reflection of the locality and of the parents who send their children to them. This can provide a sort of guarantee, an assurance of success, or a sense of heightened risk. The school is not represented as an independent variable here with qualities of its own separate from its intake and this gives a general indication of the way in which perceptions of schools and perceptions of risk are constructed. In these terms a school can only ever be as good as its intake.

(Ball 2003, p. 155)

There is also a close relationship between house purchase strategies and educational choice here. Juliet describes how she had planned for her child's entry to Goldwater, which is seen as a excellent choice for the moment, as well as keeping other (private) options open for the future:

A huge reason [for having moved] is the school around the corner which is one of the best primary schools in the borough and it's a lovely school and cross our fingers we will be able to take advantage of that. It seems ridiculous thinking five years ahead when you're starting a family but ... if you want to get into the nursery and so on, then it's not five years. About a third of children [from the primary school] go on to competitive private secondary schooling, which is, not that we necessarily want to do that, but it's quite nice to have the option

(Juliet, B)

The differentiation of schools by intake also extends to private schools. We gave the example in Chapter 4 of Philippa who, like several of the other mothers, identifies class fractional differences between the populations of local private schools, and justified her choice on the grounds of relative social diversity (see also Ball 2003):

The parents [at some other private schools] are sort of very City men and sort of flowery women. Hill View wasn't like that. It has for example quite a few black or Asian people in it. It's got some sort of special needs type children

and the avoidance of absolute closure:

we wanted a good education, but we didn't want to be kind of excluding our children from the vast proportion of society

One might argue of course that such distinctions are overly subtle, that the rarefied social environment of any private school will still 'exclude children from the vast proportion of society'. This may be so. Our argument, however, is that it is exactly these sort of nuanced divisions and distinctions that people deploy *within* class groups as well as between them in order to identify 'people like us'. These sorts of comments and related practices indicate a reflexive class awareness – a sense of boundaries, lifestyle and value markers and other distinctions which attract and repel. As Ball (2003, p. 175) argues, 'class identities are not to be found within talk about categories but in practices and accounts of practices – in practices of distinction, and closure and in the "aesthetics of distance"'.

In Stoke Newington, attitudes to education were tangibly different; although as we noted above the proportions of parents who attended private and state schools were similar. There was less adherence to private education, and only one couple (Suzannah and her partner, quoted above) themselves privately educated, were not contemplating state primary education *at all*. There were also far fewer private schools in the immediate area. With the exception of Suzannah, those contemplating private education were far less certain than their Battersea counterparts that this would be the right option:

> My feelings about education really is that we'll do what is appropriate for our kids, I'm not anti-private education, but I'm not kind of automatically pro. I'd prefer – not just for the financial implications – I'd prefer my kids to go through the comprehensive and state systems really – we'll see.
>
> (Jessica, SN)

> I don't know whether or not [daughter] will stay at [private school nursery]. There are several issues. One is that we'll have to pay. [Son] will go there if [daughter] goes there. And so that is something to think about. Whether we can afford it. And also there is the issue of [daughter] going to a school where the majority of people are white and the majority of people have money and this ... isn't very reflective as to where she is coming from. It is not her local school ... It is very different from our local school around here
>
> (Mary, SN)

However, given these ambivalences, there is little in the way of principled championing of state education either, at least not local state education. Practicalities and an ethical pragmatism are in play here; 'putting the family first' (Jordan *et al.* 1994) requires that necessary, if unwelcome, compromises are made:

> People don't stay long [in SN], but people might come here when they have babies and very small children and begin to leave when their children get to three/four. And so my experience is that I met a lot of people when I first arrived who are now virtually moving out, one after the other. And I don't think many people move into Stoke Newington when their children are around school age
>
> (Jo, SN)

I think the schools round here aren't too bad in terms of primary ...
There's about three you'd be happy to send your kids to within the catchment area

(Jessica, SN)

If parents do – or plan to – place their children in a state school, they understand
themselves as having a key role in monitoring their children's experience and
exercising parental voice (Vincent 2001; Vincent and Martin 2002). Such parents
appear well placed to take advantage of modes of engagement which rely upon
the practices of consumption and the skills of assertive talk (Graue 1993).

There is a lot of parental involvement [at primary school]. And there are
whole swathes of middle-class parents who work in the media around
here. There are loads of those parents at school and they put in a lot. And
that's what I'm hoping the experience will be, that we affect change and
we can keep an eye on what's going on

(Madeleine, SN)

As Jessica and Madeleine's words suggest, there have also been attempts by
Stoke Newington parents to capture and adopt local primary schools, although
this has, in several cases, been less securely achieved than in Battersea (see also
Robson and Butler's 2001 account of Brixton).

If perceptions of one primary school attracted Battersea parents to the state
system, then perceptions of a whole sector in Hackney caused Stoke
Newington parents to seek alternatives. The secondary schools in Hackney
were commonly described (by 21 mothers, 68 per cent) as 'appalling', 'dire', a
'nightmare'. Only one secondary school was generally regarded as acceptable,
but is oversubscribed and has a relatively small catchment area, putting it out of
the picture for some of the families.

The secondary schools are notoriously terrible, and I certainly wouldn't
consider, I hope, I don't know how hypocritical I'll turn out to be, but I
wouldn't want to send our kids through the private system, because I don't
believe in that at all. But I think a lot of parents do when it comes to the
crunch or they move out.

(Jessica, SN)

Several families mentioned, either in the first or second interview, that they
would consider moving or had definite plans to do so when or before their child
reached secondary age. As noted, two saw private education as a definite or likely
possibility (and one of these families then moved out of London). Only a small
number of respondents did not mention their concerns with secondary schooling (one of whom was looking for Catholic schools, and the other had her
bilingual child enrolled at a school run by the French government).

In sum, there were local differences around education, with a greater adherence to private education amongst the Battersea families, many of whom saw such a choice as automatic and natural. Stoke Newington parents were more likely to want to educate their child in the state system for a mixture of ideological and financial reasons, but over half the group would move in order to find an acceptable state secondary school. The commonalities between families in the two localities lie in the overwhelming emphasis placed on the importance of education, and their clear willingness, even at this early stage, to consider a range of possible options in order to find a place in a high quality educational institution of an appropriate character for their child. However, for these parents, responsibility for their children's development and education is not left to schools and nurseries. They see themselves as having a role in organizing a whole set of other beneficial activities for their children, and it is to these that we now turn.

Activities

The process of 'making up a middle-class child' involves the children's participation in structured activities to the extent that some in our sample seemed to have little time at home. They are out with their carers, going to commercially run music, gym and swimming classes. If they are in nurseries they are engaged in a range of activities there. This emphasis on 'enrichment' activities was shared by most of the mothers in our sample.

Frank Furedi, in his diatribe against parental anxiety and all its causes, writes of 'contemporary culture's preoccupation with the virtues of constant infant stimulation' (2001, p. 82). And indeed all of this is relatively recent. Tumble Tots, one of the most well known and widely established gym classes, started in 1979. However, there appears to have been a boom in enrichment activities for young children over the last 10–15 years (Crechendo, Tumble Tots' main competitor, started in 1990), and the availability and range of activities in both our case study areas are still increasing. We also glimpse here the use of economic capital in the buying in of development experiences for these children. In effect this is the commercialization of cultural transmissions. As part of the 'under-fives' market (estimated at £4.3 bn in 2002 according to *Business Life*,

Table 7.3 Families mentioning particular activities for their children

	Music	Ballet/ Dance	Gym	French	Drama	Sport
Battersea	23	6	6	7	2	7
Stoke Newington	15	8	1	5	4	5

There was a total of 28 Battersea families and 31 Stoke Newington families, 59 in total. However, children may well do more than one activity, and different children in the family may do different activities, so totals in this table exceed 59.

November 2004, p. 43), enrichment activities are part of a booming area. Research by WAA, the London and Birmingham advertising agency, reveals that the average family spends £1500 per child between the ages of six months and eight years on additional classes and activities (outside school hours). Most activities are given up within five weeks.

It has to be noted that staying in the house with young children except for the occasional trip to the supermarket can be stressful and boring for the adult, a fact long recognized by the Playgroup movement. Attending these activities provides a diversion for carers and a potential opportunity to socialize with other grown-ups. However, the emphasis and range of the activities the children in our sample are involved with goes beyond the simple need for their carers to get out of the house. It is possible to detect a concern amongst our respondents with making up what could be thought of as a 'renaissance child' – one who has been exposed to experiences designed to foster creativity in a number of areas (art, drama, dance, music), physical competence, confidence and good social skills. A sense of necessity, anxiety and expectation is evident in Jessica's comments below – the word 'should' was commonly used by mothers in discussing the commencement of particular activities. Embedded in here is a model of the cultural development of the child and which activities come when:

> She's going to do ballet soon. They do extra lessons at the nursery if you want them so she does an hour a week of drama and an hour a week of music. And then we take them with us [out] on the weekends, but it's not another activity with other kids. And then I think we should think about a musical instrument. Oh God – the violin.
>
> (Jessica, SN, child three-and-a-half years)

Through ballet and other dance classes, particular forms of 'style', 'grace' and 'habit' are invested in the child, embodied in the child,[4] making the child's body readable in a particular way, subject to visible classification. 'The meticulous disciplining of the body enables the conversion of morality into style, aestheticizing virtue' (Skeggs 2004, p. 155). And as Suzannah's extract suggests, the child is also subject to learning manners, or comportment. Important social learning is evident here and the development of early forms of social capital may also be involved.

> [Oldest daughter] does French at [nursery] – it's just a bit of fun – they sit in a little semi-circle and the French teacher … she goes round, asks them things so it's teaching her to take turns and stuff like that. How much French [she learns] I'm not sure, but it's not really the aim. [Youngest daughter] does Tumble Tots and Tick Tock [music group], because what I've tried to do is something for their imagination and something physical … [Oldest daughter] does ballet which is sweet, a really nice ballet teacher who tells them a story

and they pretend to sprinkle stardust and they go on tipitoes. It's not full on … I just think it teaches her to take turns and just learn to get on with the other kids. And I always make sure she puts her ballet costume in her bag herself and just little things like that, just get herself organized

> (Suzannah, SN, children two-and-a-half and three-and-a-half years)

Private nurseries too routinely offer an expanded range of 'extras':

Some of the staff are very good and I think obviously they sort of buy in things like ballet and French and God knows how much French they learn [laughing] it's like kind of to please the parents, that's what the parents expect.

> (Juliet, B)

The emphasis on these activities can be understood as evidence of the planning ahead, the concern with the future that defines the approach of the middle classes to education. As well as being fun for toddlers, enrichment activities have two practical purposes for the future. The first is to formulate the beginnings of a curriculum vitae. A proven track record in music, drama, art or sport can increase a child's attractiveness in a competitive school market. For example, a selective state school in London which is oversubscribed by ten applicants to one place asks Year 6 children to take a series of tests. Without passing these academic tests the child will not be offered a place. However, if they do score well, children can gain extra marks for their participation in extra-curricular activities. The other benefit of these activities is to prepare the child for success at school. For middle-class parents, even being relaxed about the children's development requires thought and planning. There is a fine line between structure and pressure. The structured activities are presented as just 'a bit of fun', ignoring both the social and cultural capital that such activities generate for children and their parents. The pressure for the mother to arrange and finance extra 'enrichment' activities goes unrecognized in the search for the benefits that are felt to accrue to the child. Several of our respondents spoke out against 'pushing' children into formal education at too early an age. Instead enrolling under fives in enrichment activities ensured that children developed physical, social and intellectual skills which would leave them in a state of learning readiness. The providers' scripts focus on this. One London drama school for example claims its classes are specially designed to help develop 'all-round skills in a fun and imaginative way'.

These include a range of social and creative attributes summed up by what we call "the 4 Cs": Confidence, Communication, Concentration and Co-ordination – leading to benefits such as a strong memory, rich vocabulary and high self-esteem.

> (http://www.perform.org.uk).

Get your perfect child here!

Involvement in enrichment activities is a process of 'cultural transmission' serving to inculcate what Bourdieu refers to as 'legitimate taste', legitimate for the social group to which the child belongs:

> Academic capital is in fact a guaranteed product of the combined effectiveness of cultural transmission by the family and cultural transmission by the school, the effectiveness of which depends on the amount of cultural capital directly inherited from the family
>
> (Bourdieu 1986, p. 23)

Here, however, the inherited capital is supplemented by that bought in as activities. These activities contribute to the cultural capital held by and embodied in the family itself, and are part of an accrual of class resources (Skeggs 2004).

To sum up, the emphasis upon enrichment activities was shared across the two research localities, although a higher number of activities is mentioned in Battersea than in Stoke Newington. This may be a reflection of the greater financial capital available in Battersea. It is also interesting that music receives 23 mentions as against 15 in Stoke Newington. It is possible that this reflects an anticipation of the private school experience which awaits many of the Battersea children. Overall, and as with education, one can detect a priority amongst the middle class as a whole to prepare their children for success – in creative and physical as well as purely intellectual arenas.

Conclusion

The analysis of childcare provides a lens through which a whole range of class-related practices come together. In this chapter we have sought to demonstrate some of the ways in which childcare and childrearing practices are joined up within processes of the social reproduction of families. That is, they involve investments within the child, both in the accrual of class resources in Skeggs's (2004) terms, and in terms of the realization over time of particular selfhoods and personalities. These families see things in the long term; they are planning for educational futures for their children, even, in some cases, in their choice of nursery schools and enrichment activities. But of course, they are not only choosing them for their future value: they want their children to be healthy, to have fun, to be happy, to develop social skills and social relationships. However, the work of childrearing can appear to be increasingly intense, increasingly commercialized, and increasingly fraught with concerns about doing the right thing and doing enough for the child.

The choice of childcare, enrichment activities and their relation to choice of school also offers some insights into the generation and maintenance of educational inequalities. In order to come fully to grips with the distribution of academic capital by schools we must look at the work done inside the family in the transmission of cultural capital and in particular 'in its earliest conditions of acquisition … through the more or less visible marks they leave' (Bernstein 2004, p. 18). Childcare and enrichment activities contribute to these 'marks' in various ways. The family's transmission of cultural capital is Bourdieu argues 'the best hidden and socially most determinant educational investment' (2004, p. 17).

Chapter 8

Conclusion

A market in love?

> Improvements in early childhood policies should ideally be accompanied by other developments: radical changes to the world of employment to reduce hours and the intensification of work, men assuming more responsibility for the care and upbringing of children and ... new thinking about school. All of these need vision, not as an optional extra but as a necessity. Because imagining other ways of being is the precursor of struggling to achieve them.
>
> (Moss 2004b, p. 28)

In this concluding chapter we want to draw together and briefly summarize the different concerns, issues, findings and conclusions which make up the earlier chapters, and reinforce our argument for an integrated analysis of childcare. It is difficult to assert any definitive conclusions at this time about the childcare market; it is in transition and undergoing considerable expansion (Hall 2004). Whilst the expansion, especially in state provision, is very welcome, it will be clear by now that we have some reservations about the notion of a large-scale, profit-making private sector as an inherent part of the solution to universal childcare provision. Whilst appreciating that the private sector is not of one piece, and that there is an enormous range of orientations, rationales and positionings among providers, ranging from childminders (many of whom are low paid), through the traditional private providers in this sector, the owner mangers of one or two nurseries (who may make limited profits),[1] to the newer players in the market, the major, chain providers, we remain unconvinced that corporate profit-seeking should be so tightly associated with the care of young children (see also OECD 2001). Yet the nursery industry is still seen by some providers (despite supply outstripping demand in some areas) as capable of generating good profits, and the government is incorporating this impetus as an integral part of its attempts to develop a comprehensive childcare provision. The following quote is from Mark McArdle, the chief executive of the Helen McArdle Group, who in the summer of 2005 sold a large care home business in order to focus on the nursery sector.

We are charging £35 a day for babies and are aiming for young professionals who are more likely to take up a full-time nursery place, rather than
two half-day sessions which is what tends to happen at the lower end of
the market ... In the care home business our fees were pretty much dic-
tated to us as most of the residents were funded by the local authority and
unfortunately they set the fees and that's what we got. In nurseries it is
refreshing that it operates more like a normal market − if people like it
they are prepared to pay the fees you set.

(cited in Vevers 2005b, p. 15)

Furthermore, many of the 'quality' problems associated with daycare outlined
in Chapter 3, although not by any means just located in the private sector, such
as staff retention, staff working conditions, the nature of adult–child relationships and so on, seem, we suggest, irresolvable within the economics of private
sector provision (for one example of quality concerns at a large private sector
chain, see Curnow 2005c). The private sector is an unwieldy and paradoxically
unresponsive tool for achieving coherent and comprehensive childcare provision, at least within metropolitan settings. The childcare market in our two
London localities, Battersea and Stoke Newington, is inflexible and unaccommodating for even our skilled and privileged middle-class consumers. It is a
'peculiar' market. It requires that middle-class consumers are energetic, inven-
tive, persistent, flexible and resilient. They have to deploy the full range of
capitals available to them, economic, cultural and social, to achieve their purposes in this market, but many still have to compromize and rework
arrangements regularly. In part, as a result, the high levels of frustration, anxiety
and guilt which are invested in childcare are heightened still further.

However, it seems that the current 'mixed economy' is highly likely to remain
as the mechanism through which childcare is provided.[2] The childcare sector as a
whole is a highly unusual part of the wider public sector in that it has already
seen an expansion of state provision through Sure Start and, still to come,
through Children's Centres. In stark contrast with health and other education
sectors, new state provision is being put in place as part of achieving universal
childcare targets. However, as we indicated in Chapter 3, the childcare difficulties
experienced by many, particularly low-income families, are not amenable to a
simple expansion of provision (the 'choices' of low-income families are the specific focus of our current research, funded by the Economic and Social Research
Council, award number RES000230770), and, as we noted above, the eventual
'look' of the childcare sector after this period of private and public investment
remains rather unclear. However, we do of course welcome the hugely increased
focus on and attention paid to childcare that only government action can initiate.

There is still much to debate. A recent report (Bell and La Valle 2005) on the
early stages of the Neighbourhood Nurseries initiative suggests that state provision of nursery places does draw into those nurseries families who previously
relied wholly on informal care, or who had had no childcare (two-thirds of

Bell and La Valle's sample fell into these categories). Is this, as is often assumed, unequivocally a good thing? The same survey reported that over 40 per cent of parents said starting to use a Neighbourhood Nursery had enabled them to enter paid work, while more than a quarter said it had helped them to increase their working hours. Are these entirely positive findings? Paid work *can* offer an increase in the family income and other social and personal benefits for the adults. However, if paid work means drawing parents into a low-paid, long-hours work culture and environment, and allowing them less time to spend with their children, then some equivocation seems justified. Our current research exploring how working-class parents choose and use childcare will, we hope, offer some answers here, or at least a more considered asking. For the moment we reiterate Peter Moss's concern that several key questions around childcare provision in the UK are not being asked. These are questions of the value, purpose and benefits of different forms of childcare: what sort of care do we want for our young children? And 'what is our image or understanding of the young child? What is our image or understanding of institutions for young children' (Moss 2004b, p. 20). What should be the priorities for the social, emotional and intellectual development of young children who may be in nurseries or with individual carers? However, the discourse of familialism (see Chapter 3) is still dominant in England, a discourse which asserts that one-to-one care by the mother in the home is the best form of care, and if this is not available, it should be mimicked in other forms of care (see Chapter 3). It seems uncertain that Moss's call for a reinterpretation, a re-creation of the dominant approach to structuring group-based care for young children will be heard in the foreseeable future.

There is unlikely to be one uncontested set of answers to these questions about care. Our sample, drawn from a relatively homogeneous set of middle-class, largely white families living in inner London, still produced a range of responses around what childcare is 'best'. There were mothers who wanted to and believed they should stay at home full-time with their children, others who wanted to work full-time and delegate daily daytime care to others, and a majority in between who worked part-time and juggled convoluted childcare arrangements. For many families, childcare arrangements were in practice a compromise between what would be best and what was possible. We spoke to parents who had chosen (and for most of our sample a considerable degree of choice was involved, albeit constrained by location, availability and cost) nannies, day nurseries, nursery schools and nursery classes in the private, voluntary and state sectors, childminders, au pairs, playgroups and co-operative crèches, as well as complex and fragile mosaics of several of these, held together by the efforts and hopes of the mothers. People's perceptions of 'appropriate' childcare are varied and (at least partly) influenced by spatial and financial constraints and opportunities, as well as their understanding of what 'people like us do', what Holloway calls 'the local moral geographies of childcare' (Holloway 1998; Duncan 2005; Chapter 3 above).

The understanding of 'people like us' amongst the middle classes is complex and nuanced. There is some relationship between class fractions and occupational sectors, but the link is incomplete and unclear, and values and attitudes cannot easily be read off from occupational categories. However, there is a differential distribution of occupational positions in the research localities, with financial occupations prevalent in Battersea and the liberal professions and the arts more in evidence in Stoke Newington (Chapter 4). Space is crucial in understanding the lived experience of class and class fractions, and Stoke Newington and Battersea are areas indicative of some of the more general distinctions and differences amongst the (metropolitan) middle classes. So while there are important areas of commonality across these spatially separated fractions – the persistence of traditional gender relations, the key role accorded to educational success, the understanding of one aspect of 'good' parenting as offering opportunities (enrichment activities) to develop all aspects of the child, there are also significant divergences, such as a preference for state/private education, differing degrees of desire to insulate the child from or expose them to the surrounding urban environment, and more or less positive views on difference and social mix (Chapters 4 and 7). These sociocultural differences map onto other findings from research into middle-class factions, particularly that of Butler with Robson (2003), Savage and Butler (1995), and Bagnal *et al.* (2003). The children in our respondent families are accruing both shared and subtly different class resources and individualities. The differences, we suggest, may prepare and position them in relation to future occupational competencies. These fractional differences may also contribute to different socialities and forms of local social relations; although much more work is needed on these issues before any firm conclusions about such differences and their general social significance can be drawn.

Over and against these more subtle differences there is a striking similarity between middle-class fractions in our sample in the pervasiveness of traditional gendered divisions of domestic responsibility. It is the women in our research who changed their paid work commitments when they had children (the majority moving to part-time work, but even those few who continued working full-time accepted a slower rate of career progression or the curtailment of long hours). The involvement of these women in careers and highly paid jobs is part of what defines them as middle-class. But they are confronted with contradictory expectations and discourses articulating a particular set of new workplace opportunities, and obligations, set over and against a fairly unchanged and traditional articulation of their obligations as mothers. Women's employment and mothering histories can be plotted on an 'investment continuum', where women move between time-investments in their children or in their paid work, in most cases trying to manage the two to the detriment of neither, and being trailed by varying amounts of guilt, responsibility and anxiety (Chapter 5). Mothers involved in the labour market felt acutely that they had 'responsibility without presence' (Uttal 2002, p. 27). As middle-class mothers accepting of their responsibility for all aspects of their child's development, they practised what Hays called 'intensive mothering', and what we have termed 'professional mothering'. 'What looks especially to the childless, like parenting gone mad, is the logical outcome when one interlocks loving a child with feeling responsible for its welfare and being uncertain on how to achieve this' (Beck and Beck-Gernsheim 1995, p. 119). It may even be that if employer attitudes and traditional divisions of domestic labour remain unchanged, the next generation of affluent middle-class women will be, as a result of watching their mothers juggle intense work and family responsibilities, more likely revert to traditional roles, staying at home with the children, and being solely 'professional mothers' (see for example Thomas 2005).

The active involvement of men with their children has gradually attained an accepted place as part of, to use La Rossa's (1988) phrase, the 'conduct' of 'good' fatherhood. But the provider role remains entrenched. Even those fathers who rearrange their work commitments to spend more time with their children, in search of greater levels of emotional intimacy, tend to cede management of domestic and organizational issues to the mother. The responsibilities of childcare, at home and elsewhere, remain almost exclusively with women. When men are involved, at least at home, it is in an adjunct role. There are some middle-class professional men in high-status careers who work very long hours, with detrimental effects on their ability, whatever their desire, to spend more time with their children. The move towards arrangements of work and childcare for parents that are more balanced between mothers and fathers has been achieved in a few families, but is still a long way from redefining the norm of gender roles. It is customary in publications on childcare and the family to include a call for change to work cultures that emphasize presenteeism and long hours (e.g. see Hochschild 1989; Beck and Beck-Gernsheim 1995; Wrigley 1995; Gatrell 2005). With indicators of positive change in this area at best muted (e.g. low take-up of in any case limited 'family friendly' policies introduced in the UK by New Labour governments: see for example Camp 2005), we find the situation too frustrating and intractable simply to add a routine call for change. However, we do find some positives in the 'juggling fathers' and their decisions, encouraged by their partners, to 'spend more time with their families'. Even here though the ingrained expectations of the male provider role weigh heavily in the background and continue to produce tensions for the men involved (see Chapter 5). However, we hope that eventually fathers seeking a work/life balance will be the majority rather than the exceptions (Thompson *et al.* 2005 show clear evidence of a positive attitudinal change by new fathers towards involvement in the care of their baby). As Marchbank notes,

> Childcare is and always has been a radical issue in that it challenges the patriarchal divide of public/private like no other issue, and as such it goes to the root of struggle for gender equality and the public use of resources.
> (Marchbank 2000, p. 2)

We have argued that tensions and uncertainties of another sort are embedded in the relationships of power and control between home-based carers (nannies and childminders) and parents, and are based on class differences, emotional attachments, notions of professionalism and the cash nexus. These relationships are deeply inflected by class, and Wrigley's (1995) formulation of 'choosing difference' and 'choosing similarity' (i.e. class similarity/difference between carers and parents) is useful in making sense of what is happening here. There are significant silences and absences that exist in apparently good working relationships between carers and mothers (mothers are very much to the fore in making and maintaining relationships with carers) in relation to these social and cultural similarities and differences. Mothers and carers occupy antagonistic (although rarely hostile) positions and pursue what are sometimes opposing personal agendas. Therefore dissensions and fractures remain an ever-present possibility. This underlying friction is unlikely to be addressed in situations where dialogue between parents and carers is so limited, and in the conclusion to Chapter 6, we look at the notion of 'storytelling' as a way to fill the communication void, providing a medium for purposeful conversations about and around the child and the child's care and development. These stories may also provide a means for the further development of a grounded language of care.

As indicated already, class and gender come together in various complex ways in the actions of middle-class mothers. We are not here calling up lazy stereotypes of 'pushy mothers' but rather drawing attention to the way in which mothers keenly experience the responsibility for bringing up their children, of wanting an often narrowly defined 'best' for them, and of their anxiety-fuelled efforts to achieve that 'best'. The aggregate effects of these seemingly blameless individual decisions in the area of school choice (the hierarchies and polarization of schools largely on social class grounds, and the further diminution of 'comprehensive' schooling) have been well documented by one of us (Ball 2003; Gewirtz et al. 1995). In Chapter 7 we focused on the question of school choice (actual or planned), particularly on the differing levels of commitment to state schooling between the localities. A willingness, and/or commitment to the idea of the children attending a state school is largely limited to one 'colonized' primary school in Battersea, whilst in Stoke Newington the commitment is stronger and wider at primary level, but weakens considerably at secondary level (cf. Bernstein 1990, p. 81). These commitments are in part contextual and contingent. The experience of exclusive settings for education and care with relatively formalized and 'visible' pedagogies started at two-and-a-half or three years old for some of the Battersea children. Additionally, we have highlighted a rather more neglected outcome of the concern to 'make up' a middle-class child as a rounded and successful educational subject, happy and talented: the proliferation of 'enrichment' activities, primarily, but not confined to, music, art, sport, drama and dance. These require a considerable investment of time, effort and financial capital on the part of mothers organizing their children's participation. These activities offer children fun, enjoyment and the chance to learn new skills, but also limit the amount of free, unsupervised time available to the children. They constitute a part of the children's experience of intensive parenting (see Chapter 7).

One of the joys of writing this book and of doing the research on which it was based, its complexity and many facets, is also the same characteristic that has made presenting the research so challenging. What, finally, is this book about? Is it about social class, parenting, gender, childcare policy, or childcare practice? It is, of course, about all those things. One of the main aims of our analysis has been to show the interrelatedness of care, class, gender and work. Indeed each is embedded in the others. Childcare decisions are intimately imbricated in the economic possibilities and social reproductive concerns of the middle classes, the gender roles within the family, and the work aspirations and opportunities of mothers and fathers. This is, then, a book about, to borrow David Morgan's phrase, 'family practices' (Morgan 1996), about how families act and interact, in both private and public arenas. Morgan defines family practices as being emotionally involving and significant to members of a family, as being constructed by both individuals and broader structures, but seeming natural and inevitable: 'Family practices are not just any old practices. In many cases they appear to have a natural or given character, something which is recognised in many folk expressions about family relations and obligations' (1996, p. 192).

One way of looking at this book is as an exploration, an examination of some facets of the apparently natural and inevitable processes involved in looking after young children, and highlighting the social constructions involved, the classed, gendered and emotional dimensions of family life. We have tried to show how choosing childcare is a highly emotional process, not simply the rational and practical act of consumption it is usually presented as being in policy, and to highlight the gap which exists between the smooth assumptions of policy and the more fractured jagged experience of parents – even these middle-class parents, who are advantaged and skilled consumers in the market place.

We are also presenting the practices of the respondent families as both enactments of and reproductions of structure, of social patterns and distinctions – distinctions between parent and child, mother and father, parent and carer, and between middle-class fractions, and class and ethnic 'others'. We have explored how families socially reproduce their children through decisions about where they live, where and how the child is cared for, and what extra activities are made available to them. As Walkerdine et al. comment, 'class is at once profoundly social and profoundly emotional and lived in its specificity in particular cultural and geographical locations' (2001, p. 53).

Thus childcare is both an *enactment* of class and class relations, focusing on the present and how 'people like us' respond to the need to care for or organize care for a young child, and also an act of *reproduction* focusing on the future, and equipping the child with the social and educational resources deemed necessary by families within particular social groups.

In many respects natural childhood is over and is being replaced by 'staged' childhood ... Staging is not just the parents' personal whim. It is an essential part of 'working to preserve status' (Papanek 1979). Where people feel compelled to protect their place in society by their own exertions, this drive is bound to reach the nursery.

(Beck and Beck-Gernsheim 1995, pp. 32–3)

Our research indicates that it has!

As indicated by Moss's quotation at the beginning of this chapter, it is limiting and simplistic to think about the care of children in isolation from other related 'family' issues such as employment and gender relations, and apart from other social policy areas, such as compulsory education. Our research reinforces this point. It is also necessary to 'think together' childcare and social class. As we have indicated above, the possibilities of who the children are, their subjectivities and individualities – how their days are structured, their activities, their food, their toys – who they mix with, who cares for them, what they learn (in the broadest social sense), and who they might become – are, for these very young children, shaped by the nuances and detail of their parents' classed and gendered locations and practices.

As we indicated in the introduction to this book, childcare has been transformed during the time we have been thinking, researching and writing about it, from a topic characterized by a 'dutiful and dispiriting heaviness' (Riley 1983), a 'political backwater' (Penn 2006), to one central to the contemporary social policy agenda. But the debate about childcare is still being conducted within a narrow framework, and understood to be of interest to limited and bounded constituencies: mainly mothers, early years practitioners and other welfare professionals. In this book we have argued that childcare is neither a specialized nor narrow field of interest, either in policy or academic terms. Rather, in order to fully understand and improve childcare policies and practices and families' experiences of care, an analysis which encompasses class, gender, work and the workings of the childcare market is needed. We intend this book to be a contribution both to the current debates around childcare issues and to changing the framework of considerations within which these debates are conducted.

Notes

Chapter 1

1 Sure Start is a government funded, locally managed programme designed to bring integrated health, welfare, childcare and education services to families with pre-school children living in disadvantaged areas.

Chapter 2

1 Mirza (1998) defines 'placing' as 'the ways in which the personal characteristics of the researcher and researched such as, but not exclusively, class, race/ethnicity and gender, assist the researched in locating the researcher within wider social structures (and vice versa). This is significant as it can have a direct effect upon the developing relationship between the two (pp. 84–5).
2 The book generated a lot of reporting of Stephen Ball's work in newspapers as a critique of 'pushy' mothers.

Chapter 3

1 Bright Horizons Family Solutions, a US based company with global revenues of £254.4 million, is placed fourth in size (summer 2005).
2 Blackburn's 2004 report also notes a rise in vacancy rate nationwide for the second year running. The value of Nord Anglia's shares fell dramatically in March 2005, after a 'sudden and marked decline' in nursery places, as reported on http://www.sharecast.com, accessed 11 March 2005.
3 In Gordon Brown's statement to the House introducing the Spending Review in July 2004, he said:

> But there is one additional reform that has the potential to transform opportunity for every child and be a force for renewal in every community, and on which the government wishes to make further progress today. While the nineteenth century was distinguished by the introduction of primary education for all and the twentieth century by the introduction of secondary education for all, so the early part of the twenty first century should be marked by the introduction of pre-school provision for the under fives and childcare available to all ... as we advance further and faster towards our goal of a Children's Centre in every community and in every constituency in our country.

4 According to Anne Gross, Sure Start Deputy Director, speech to the Laing & Buisson Annual Children's Nurseries Conference, February 2005.

5 Sure Start is focused upon young children and their parents living in the 20 per cent most disadvantaged areas of the UK. There are 524 local programmes, and approximately 400,000 children involved (Moss 2004a). Expenditure will reach £1.5 billion by 2006. For a critique of the conception of Sure Start, see Moss 2004a.

6 The London Development Agency has recently produced 'gap funding' to allow the launch of over 30 Neighbourhood Nurseries, whose appearance was in jeopardy due to the high cost of land and building works in London (*Nursery World*, 15 July 2004, p. 5).

7 The survey was conducted mostly amongst private day nurseries (90 per cent private day nurseries, remainder not-for-profit community nurseries) and the maintained sector does pay a little better. It was conducted by IDS, the information and research service on employment issues in 2004 (reported in *Nursery World*, 5 August 2004, p. 6).

8 Sure Start report (2002/2003) Childcare and Early Years Workforce Survey – day nurseries and other full daycare provision, May 2004 (Sure Start 2004).

9 The 2005 Childcare Bill proposes a new curriculum framework, the Early Years Foundation Stage for children from birth to age 5, which will then link up with the existing curriculum at Key Stage 1 (for children aged 5–7 years). This may be seen as a response to criticism of lack of substance. Critics are however concerned that the bureaucracy and narrowness of learning reflected in the curriculum at Key Stage 1 and above will also affect the Early Years Foundation Stage.

10 In 2004, Ofsted found that 1 per cent of nurseries inspected were 'unsatisfactory', 64 per cent were 'good' and 35 per cent were 'satisfactory'.

11 False kinship is a term Gregson and Lowe use to describe the positioning of nannies by many mothers as 'part of the family'. The risk to the nannies here was that such a relationship can be used to persuade them to do unpaid favours.

12 A similar criticism is often made of parents' relationships with schools, that parents are co-opted as supporters and learners, rather than participants (Vincent 1996, 2000).

Chapter 4

1 The service class is localized and globalized simultaneously, especially within London, a 'world city': they are doubly located, in a local space and a metropolitan one. The former is to the fore in family lives, the latter in their work lives (see Robson and Butler 2001).

2 The private nursery would have adult–child ratios of 1:8 or lower.

3 Parents pay fees for a marketed place in a state nursery, although these fees are generally lower than those of a private nursery. Completely free state provision is only available on the basis on social need.

Chapter 5

1 Local gender cultures of ex-mining communities are given as a specific example here.

2 Monica's quote does assume the professionalism of carers, a view of this low paid female workforce which is not always shared.

3 Thanks to Dr Lora Bartlett from the University of California at Santa Cruz for introducing us to this term.

4 Elsewhere in the interview, she notes that they share cooking and washing, she purees the baby's food, he pays the bills and mends punctures on their bikes, and they have a cleaning lady 'which is essential as he would never do any cleaning'.

5 As these interviews with both parents normally took place in the evening, one parent would sometimes be putting the children to bed as we spoke to the other, thus for some interviews we spoke at different times to each partner separately and to them both together.

6 Hearn notes 'masculinities' has itself been criticized as a concept, for its vagueness, amongst other things.

7 As can be seen from the descriptions, we have included here a successful doctor whose job involves frequent travel, and a senior civil servant who works long hours. Thus, although neither works for private corporations, their jobs require them to be absent from the home for considerable periods whilst working for their organizations.

8 Another respondent, Jeff, talks in similar terms: 'if [the childcare] wasn't right when it happened then we would assess that and change it if we needed to'.

Chapter 6

1 'It's slightly embarrassing – I hadn't gone round nurseries, but I kind of knew it wasn't an option I was keen on ... I know there are great nurseries, but I didn't like, it was really the concept I didn't like. I didn't like the idea of warehousing ... I think warehousing a lot of babies together in a room didn't really seem particularly healthy to me. I don't think from a social point of view it was a particularly natural state of affairs having twelve babies in a room with four adults ... Too many people, too many babies ... That doesn't seem to me to be a particularly natural way for small children to be raised ... There's a lot less chance of a child being battered in a nursery [but] I thought there was quite a high chance of them not getting what I would think of as appropriate love and attention ... People who seem to choose nurseries seem to choose them from a safety angle and because, I don't know how to describe it, but from a jealousy angle. They didn't want one individual forming a close bond with their child ... but I think if you're working five days a week, actually you do need another mummy while you're at work, and that might be painful to admit ... [but] why would you want your children to have anything less than a mummy?'

(Isabel, B)

This quotation illustrates the way in which one woman and one or more children in her home is seen as the most appropriate, indeed 'natural' form of care for small children. Angie echoed Isabel's feelings about nurseries:

She was six months when I went back to work, she was only just sitting up, I just didn't feel comfortable with her going there [day nursery] so I felt like she needed one-to-one care. I just didn't feel like I wanted her to be in that kind of institutional environment, no matter how nice it was ... It's just the routine and environment that's imposed upon them

(Angie, SN)

Also Alice (B), whose child went to a day nursery one day a week from just under a year of age, said:

Personally I wouldn't have wanted that full-time ... I think it's very important to have variety, because, er, I don't know, I just think it's more stimulating for them. However good a nursery is they don't really get one to one attention ... I think, you know, they take them from three months these tiny babies who are basically wailing. I mean I suppose they're not really aware of where they are, but it seems, it's a bit sad you know when they're there all day, but I know sometimes it can't be helped, I really admire people who ... do it everyday

I think [eight months old] is too young for nursery. I think they are too institutionalized, too rigid ... When I was a student nurse we used to do placements in them

and basically I've got bad memories of them. I think they are too rigid ... [Staff at
local nursery] were very, very defensive, very, very defensive. You know if you question or query them about something it's 'this is the way we do it', and that's it ... I
know in these nurseries they decide when they have a nap, or when they eat ...
very inflexible.

(Rosy, SN)

2 Similarly, several nursery chains offer all organic food, and one organization offering
   drama lessons gives the children snacks of organic fruit and mineral water.
3 Because of the small number of carers involved in our study, we are trying to identify
   issues that require further research rather than making definitive statements.
4 As with any London borough, Islington is socially very diverse, and the part of the borough Marcia is referring to does not fit the stereotypical image of Islington as a
   middle-class stronghold.
5 One reading of this incident would be that the mother here appears unhappy with
   Louise's assumption of the role of professional, seeing it as a threat to her own competence and confidence with the child.
6 Nor do Hughes and McNaughton acknowledge what extremely *hard* emotional work
   it is to be involved in meetings where contradiction and disagreement are rife.

Chapter 7

1 A recent survey (conducted for *Mother and Baby* magazine and reported in *The Times*, 5
   November 2003) reported that the average pre-school child attends four activities a
   year.
2 The exceptions in Battersea are the nursery class of Goldwater, the state primary school,
   a nursery attached to a sixth form college (both public sector providers) and a private
   Montessori nursery from which we have insufficient data to allow us to discuss the pedagogical style with any confidence.
3 Parents who had themselves been educated at grammar schools could not easily find
   comparable schools in inner London.
4 Another way of thinking about what is going on here is in terms of Peterson and Kern's
   (1996, cited in Skeggs 2004) 'cultural omnivore' thesis, within which, in the case of
   music for example, elite taste 'is being redefined as an appreciation of every distinctive
   form along with an appreciation of the high arts' (Peterson 1993, p. 169). Skeggs (2004,
   p. 144) suggests that 'time, knowledge, information, bodily investment, mobility across
   cultural boundaries and social networking, all constitute resources for the formation of
   the new middle class omnivorous self'.

Chapter 8

1 These small businesses and voluntary sector providers may be the only providers in areas
   seen as too poor to attract the big chains.
2 Although Margaret Hodge, Children's Minister until the 2005 election, commented
   that she expected 'some of the lower quality stuff to fall by the wayside' (Curnow 2005a,
   p. 4). The new Ofsted inspection categories and procedures are intended to clamp down
   more forcefully on unsatisfactory providers.

Bibliography

Alakeson, V. (2004) '2020 vision', *Nursery World*, 21 October, pp. 10–11.

Anderson, E. (1991) 'The ethical limits of the market', *Economics and Philosophy*, 6 (2): 179–205.

Bagguley, P. (1995) 'Middle class radicalism re-visited', in T. Butler and M. Savage (eds) *Social Change and the Middle Classes*, London: University College London Press.

Bagley, C., Ackerly, C. and Rattray, J. (2004) 'Social exclusion, Sure Start and organizational social capital', *Journal of Education Policy*, 19 (5): 595–607.

Bagnall, G., Longhurst, B. and Savage, M. (2003) 'Children, belonging and social capital: the PTA and middle class narratives of social involvement in the north-west of England', *Sociological Research Online*, 8 (4), http://www.socresonline.org.uk/8/4/bagnall.html, accessed September 2005.

Bailey, L. (1999) 'Refracted selves? A study of changes in self-identity in the transition to motherhood', *Sociology*, 33 (2): 335–52.

Ball, S. J. (2003) *Class Strategies and the Education Market Place*, London: RoutledgeFalmer.

Ball, S. J. (2004) 'Education for sale: A commodification of everything', public lecture, Kings College London, June.

Ball, S. J., Bowe, R. and Gewirtz, S. (1995) 'Circuits of schooling: A sociological exploration of parental choice of school in social class contexts', *Sociological Review*, 43 (1): 52–78.

Ball, S. J., Bowe, R. and Gewirtz, S. (1996) 'School choice, social class and distinction: The realisation of social advantage in education', *Journal of Education Policy*, 11 (1): 89–112.

Ball, S. J. and Vincent, C. (1998) '"I heard it on the grapevine": "Hot" knowledge and school choice', *British Journal of Sociology of Education*, 19 (3): 377–400.

Ball, W. and Charles, N. (2003) 'Social movements and policy change: Childcare and domestic violence policies in Wales', paper presented at 'Alternative futures and popular protest', conference at Manchester Metropolitan University, April.

Ballantine, J. (1999) 'Figuring in the father factor', *Childhood Education*, winter: 104–5.

Beck, U. (1992) *Risk Society: Towards a New Modernity*, Newbury Park: Sage.

Beck, U. and Beck-Gernsheim, E. (1995) *The Normal Chaos Of Love*, Cambridge: Polity Press.

Bell, A. and La Valle, I. (2005) *Early Stages of the NNI: Parents' Experiences*, London: Sure Start.

Benn, M. (1998) *Madonna and Child*, London: Jonathan Cape.

Bernstein, B. (1990) *The Structuring of Pedagogic Discourse*, London: Routledge.

Bernstein, B. (1996) *Pedagogy Symbolic Control and Identity*, London: Taylor and Francis.

Bernstein, B. (2004) 'Social class and pedagogic practice' in S. Ball (ed.) *The RoutledgeFalmer Reader in Sociology of Education*, London: RoutledgeFalmer.

Blackburn, P. (2004) *Children's Nurseries: UK Market Sector Report 2004*, London: Laing & Buisson.

Bottero, W. (1998) 'Clinging to the wreckage? Gender and the legacy of class', *Sociology*, 32 (3): 469–90.

Bourdieu, P. (1986) *Distinction: A Social Critique of The Judgement of Taste*, London: Routledge.

Bourdieu, P. (1987) 'What makes a social class? On the theoretical and practical existence of groups', *Berkley Journal of Sociology*, 23 (1): 1–17.

Bourdieu, P. (2004) 'Forms of capital', in S. Ball (ed.) *The RoutledgeFalmer Reader in Sociology of Education*, London: RoutledgeFalmer.

Bourdieu, P. and Wacquant, L. (1992) *An Invitation to Reflexive Sociology*, Chicago: University of Chicago Press.

Bradley, H., Fenton, S. and West, J. (2003) 'Winners and losers in labour markets: Young adults' employment trajectories', final report for ESRC award R000238215, http://www.esrc.ac.uk/, accessed June 2005.

Brannen, J. and Moss, P. (1991) *Managing Mothers: Dual Earner Households after Maternity Leave*, London: Unwin Hyman.

Brannen, J. and Moss, P. (1998) 'The polarisation and intensification of parental employment in Britain: Consequences for children, families and the community', *Community, Work and Family*, 1 (3): 229–47.

Brannen, J. and Moss, P. (2003) *Rethinking Children's Care*, Buckingham: Oxford University Press.

Brantlinger, E., Majd-Jabbari, M. and Guskin, S. (1996) 'Self-interest and liberal educational discourse: How ideology works for middle-class mothers', *American Educational Research Journal*, 33: 571–97.

Brennan, D. (1998) *The Politics of Australian Child Care*, Cambridge: Cambridge University Press.

Brown, G. (2004) Speech introducing the pre-budget report, http://www.hm-treasury. gov.uk/pre_budget_report, accessed June 2005.

Bunting, M. (2004) 'Nursery tales: Are nurseries bad for our kids?', *Guardian*, http://society.guardian.co.uk/children/story/0,1074,1256461,00.html, accessed June 2005.

Butler, T. (1995) 'Gentrification and the urban middle classes', in T. Butler and M. Savage (eds) *Social Change and the Middle Classes*, London: University College London Press.

Butler, T. and Robson, G. (2001) 'Social capital, gentrification and neighbourhood change in London: A comparison of three South London neighbourhoods', *Urban Studies*, 38 (12): 2145–62.

Butler, T. and Robson, G. (2003) 'Negotiating their way in: The middle classes, gentrification and the deployment of capital in a globalising metropolis', *Urban Studies*, 40 (9): 1791–809.

Butler, T. with Robson, G. (2003) *London Calling*, Oxford: Berg.

CACE (Central Advisory Council for Education) (1967) *Children and their Primary Schools (The Plowden Report)*, London: HMSO.

Camp, C. (2005) 'Right to request flexible working – review of the impact in first year of legislation', report to *DTI*, http://www.parentsatwork.org.uk, accessed September 2005.

Campbell, C. and Whitty, G. (2002) 'Inter-agency collaboration for inclusive schooling', in C. Campbell (ed.) *Developing Inclusive Schools*, London: Institute of Education, London University.

Charlesworth, S. (2000) *A Phenomenology of Working Class Experience*, Cambridge: Cambridge University Press.

Citizens Advice Bureau (CAB) (2005) *Money with Your Name on it?* London: CAB.

Clarke, J. Gewirtz, S. and McLaughlin, E. (eds) (2000) *New Managerialism, New Welfare?* London: Open University/Sage.

Coffey, A. (1999) *The Ethnographic Self*, London: Sage.

Coffey, A. and Atkinson, P. (1996) *Making Sense of Qualitative Data*, Thousand Oaks: Sage.

Collins, P. and Alakeson V. (2004) 'Pennies for the parents', *Guardian*, 3 December, p. 22.

Conle, C. (2000) 'Thesis as narrative', *Curriculum Inquiry*, 30 (2): 189–213.

Connell, R. (1998) 'Men in the world: Masculinities and globalization', *Men and Masculinities*, 1 (1): 3–23.

Cotterill, P. (1992) 'Interviewing women: Issues of friendship, vulnerability and power', *Women's Studies International Forum*, 15 (5/6): 593–606.

Crompton, R. (1992) 'Patterns of social consciousness amongst the middle classes', in R. Burrows and C. Marsh (eds) *Consumption and Class*, Basingstoke: Macmillan.

Crompton, R. (1995) 'Women's employment and the "middle class"', in T. Butler and M. Savage (eds) *Social Change and the Middle Classes*, London: University College London Press.

Crompton, R. (1998) *Class and Stratification: An Introduction to Current Debates*, Cambridge: Polity.

Crompton, R. (2001) 'The gendered restructuring of the middle classes: Employment and caring', in R. Crompton, F. Devine, M. Savage and J. Scott (eds) *Renewing Class Analysis*, Oxford: Blackwell.

Crozier, G. (2000) *Parents and Schools*, Stoke: Trentham Press.

Curnow, N. (2004) 'Council pools funds to level services', *Nursery World*, 7 October, p. 8.

Curnow, N. (2005a) 'Hodge promises funding', *Nursery World*, 3 March, p. 4.

Curnow, N. (2005b) 'PLA plans its role in children's centres', *Nursery World*, 23 June, p. 4.

Curnow, N. (2005c) 'Nursery staff lift lid on poor conditions', *Nursery World*, 15 September, p. 4.

Dahlberg, G., Moss, P. and Pence, A. (1999) *Beyond Quality in Early Childhood Education and Care: Postmodern Perspectives*, London: Falmer Press.

Davies, P., Adnett, N. and Mangan, J. (2002) 'The diversity and dynamics of competition', *Oxford Review of Education*, 28 (1): 91–107.

Daycare Trust (2000) *Child Care for All: The Next Steps – Securing the Future*, London: The Daycare Trust.

Daycare Trust (2001a) *Quality Matters. Ensuring Childcare Benefits Children*, London: The Daycare Trust.

Daycare Trust (2001b) *The UK at the Crossroads: Towards an Early Years European Partnership*, London: The Daycare Trust.

Daycare Trust (2003a) *Parents Eye Project*, London: The Daycare Trust.

Daycare Trust (2003b) *Informal Childcare: Bridging the Childcare Gap*, London: The Daycare Trust.

Daycare Trust (2004a) *Creating Solutions: Guide to Involving Parents and Children in Planning Child Care Services*, London: The Daycare Trust.

Daycare Trust (2004b) 'Tax credits still not plugging childcare cost gap for London parents', http://www.daycaretrust.org.uk/article.php?sid=215, accessed May 2004.

Daycare Trust (2005a) 'Annual childcare costs survey', http://www.daycaretrust.org.uk, accessed June 2005.

Daycare Trust (2005b) 'Childcare facts: Men and childcare', at http:www.daycaretrust.org.uk/mod.php?mod=userpage&page_id=69&menu=10, accesssed 12 September 2005.

Department for Education and Employment (DfEE) (1998) *The National Child Care Strategy*, London: HMSO. Also available at http://www.dfee.gov.uk/childcare/content3.htm, accessed June 2005.

Department for Education and Employment (DfEE) (1999) *Report on Effective Provision of Pre-school Education Project*, London: DfEE.

Department for Education and Skills (DfES) (1998) *Meeting the Childcare Challenge*, London: DfES.

Department for Education and Skills (DfES) (2005) 'Children's workforce strategy: Consultation Document', London: DfES.

Dermott, E. (2003) 'The "intimate father": Defining paternal involvement', *Sociological Research Online*, 8 (4), http://www.socresonline.org.uk/8/4/dermott.html, accessed September 2005.

Devine, F. (1998) 'Class analysis and the stability of class relations', *Sociology*, 32 (1): 23–42.

Diamond, P., Katwala, S. and Munn, M. (2004) 'Introduction: The new politics of the family', in P. Diamond, S. Katwala and M. Munn (eds) *Family Matters: The New Politics of Childhood*, London: Fabian Society.

Doherty, W., Kouneski, E. and Erickson, M. (1998) 'Responsible fathering: An overview and conceptual framework', *Journal of Marriage and the Family*, 60 (2): 277–92.

Duncan, S. (2005) 'Mothering, class and rationality', *Sociological Review*, 53 (1): 50–76.

Duncan, S., Edwards, R., Reynolds, T. and Alldred, P. (2003) 'Motherhood, paid work and partnering: Values and theories', *Work, Employment and Society*, 17 (2): 309–30.

Duncan, S., Edwards, R., Reynolds, T. and Alldred, P. (2004) 'Mothers and childcare: Policies, values and theories', *Children and Society*, 18: 254–65.

Duncan, S. and Irwin, S. (2004) 'The social patterning of values and rationalities: mothers' choices in combining caring and employment', *Social Policy & Society*, 3 (4): 391–400.

Dyck, I. (1996) 'Women's support networks', in K. England (ed.) *Who will Mind the Baby?* London: Routledge.

Edwards, R. (2002) 'Conceptualising relationships between home and school in children's lives', in R. Edwards (ed.) *Children, Home and School: Regulation, Autonomy or Connection?* London: RoutledgeFalmer.

Edwards, R. and Duncan, S. (1996) 'Rational economic man or lone mothers in context? The uptake of paid work', in E. Bortolaia Silva (ed.) *Good Enough Mothering?* London: New York.

Ehrenreich, B. (1989) *Fear of Falling: The Inner Life of the Middle Class*, New York: Pantheon.

Ehrenreich, B. (2003) 'Maid to order', in B. Ehrenreich and A. Hochschild (eds) *Global Women*, London: Granta.

Ehrenreich, B. and Hochschild, A. (2003) (eds.) *Global Women*, London: Granta.

Eisenberg, A., Murkoff, H. and Hathaway, S. (1996) *What to Expect in the First Year*, London: Simon & Schuster.

Esping-Anderson, G. (1990) *The Three Worlds of Welfare Capitalism*, Cambridge: Polity Press.

Esping-Anderson, G. (1999) *Social Foundations of Post-industrial Economics*, Oxford: Oxford University Press.

Etherington, L. (2005) 'South London tribes', *Rise*, April, p. 11.

Evans, M. (2004) 'Age and experience', *Nursery World*, 15 January, pp. 14–15.

Everingham, C. (1994) *Motherhood and Modernity: An Investigation into the Rational Dimension of Mothering*, Buckingham: Open University Press.

Featherstone, M. (1991) *Consumer Culture and Postmodernism*, London: Sage.

Fleming, L. and Tobin, D. (2005) 'Popular child-rearing books: Where is daddy?' *Psychology of Men & Masculinity*, 6 (1): 18–24.

Furedi, F. (2001) *Paranoid Parenting*, Harmondsworth: Penguin Books.

Gatrell, C. (2005) *Hard Labour*, Maidenhead: Oxford University Press.

Gewirtz, S., Ball, S. J. and Bowe, R. (1995) *Markets, Choice and Equity in Education*, Buckingham: Open University Press.

Giddens, A. (1991) *Modernity and Self-Identity: Self and Society in the Late Modern Age*, Cambridge: Polity Press.

Glass, N. (2005) 'Surely some mistake?', The *Guardian*, Society Guardian, 5 January p. 4.

Goldthorpe, J. (1995) 'The service class revisited' in T. Butler and M. Savage (eds) *Social Change and the Middle Classes*, London: University College London Press.

Goldthorpe, J. (1996) 'Class analysis and the reorientation of class theory: The case of persisting differentials in educational attainment', *British Journal of Sociology*, 47 (3): 481–505.

Goldthorpe, J. (2000) *On Sociology: Numbers, Narratives and the Integration of Research and Theory*, Oxford: Oxford University Press.

Grace, M. (1998) 'The work of caring for young children: Priceless or worthless?' *Women's Studies International Forum*, 21 (4): 401–13.

Graue, M. E. (1993) 'Social networks and home-school relations', *Educational Policy*, 7 (4): 466–90.

Gregson, N. and Lowe, M. (1994) *Servicing The Middle Classes: Class, Gender And Waged Domestic Labour In Contemporary Britain*, London: Routledge.

Gregson, N. and Lowe, M. (1995) 'Too much work?' Class, gender and the reconstitution of middle class domestic labour', in T. Butler and M. Savage (eds) *Social Change and the Middle Classes*, London: University College London Press.

Grossman, F., Pollack, W. and Golding, E. (1988) 'Fathers and children: Predicting the quality and quantity of fathering', *Developmental Psychology*, 24 (1): 82–91.

Hakim, C. (2000) *Work-Lifestyle Choices in the 21st Century*, Oxford: Oxford University Press.

Hall, S. (2004) 'Byers presses for end to national childcare lottery', The *Guardian*, 30 April, p. 14.

Hanlon, G. (1998) 'Professionalism as enterprise', *Sociology*, 32 (1): 43–63.

Harker, L. (2004) 'Lessons from Reggio Emilla', *Guardian*, 11 November, p. 22.

Harris, T, La Valle, I. and Dickens, S. (2004) *Childcare: How Local Markets Respond to National Initiatives*, Research report no: RR526, London: DfES.

Hatcher, R. (1998) 'Class differentiation in education: rational choices?' *British Journal of Sociology of Education*, 19 (1): 5–24.

Hatten, W., Vinter, L. and Williams, R. (2002) *Dads on Dads: Needs and Expectations at Home and at Work*, London: EOC/Mori.

Hays, S. (1996) *The Cultural Contradictions of Motherhood*, New Haven: Yale University Press.

Hearn, J. (2002) 'Men, fathers and the state', in B. Hobson (ed.) *Making Men into Fathers*, Cambridge: Cambridge University Press.

Her Majesty's Treasury (HMT) (2004) *Choice for Parents, The Best Start for Children: A Ten Year Strategy for Childcare*, London: Her Majesty's Treasury.

Hill, R. (2004) 'How New Man turned into distant confused New Dad', The *Observer*, 20 June, p. 18.

Himmelweit, S. (2002a) 'Making visible the hidden economy: The case for gender-impact analysis of economic policy', *Feminist Economics*, 8 (1): 49–70.

Himmelweit, S. (2002b) 'Economic theory, norms and the care gap', in A. Carling, S. Duncan and R. Edwards (eds) *Analysing Families: Morality and Rationalities in Policy and Practice*, London: Routledge.

Himmelweit S. and Sigala, M. (2002) 'The welfare implications of mother's decisions about work and childcare', working paper 20, ESRC Future of Work Programme.

Hobson, B. and Morgan, D. (2002) 'Introduction: Making men into fathers', in B. Hobson (ed.) *Making Men into Fathers*, Cambridge: Cambridge University Press.

Hochschild, A. (1979) 'Emotion work, feeling rules and social structure', *American Journal of Sociology*, 85 (3): 551–75.

Hochschild, A. (1989) *The Second Shift: Working Parents and the Revolution at Home*, New York: Viking.

Hochschild, A. (2000) 'Global care chains and emotional surplus value', in W. Hutton and A. Giddens (eds) *On the Edge: Living with Global Capitalism*, London: Jonathan Cape.

Hochschild, A. (2003) 'Love and gold', in B. Ehrenreich and A. Hochschild (eds) *Global Women*, London: Granta.

Hodge, M. (2005) 'Our baby is thriving', *Guardian*, comment, 8 January, p. 22.

Holloway, S. (1998) 'Local childcare cultures: Moral geographies of mothering and the social organisation of pre-school children', *Gender, Place and Culture*, 5 (1): 29–53.

Hondagneu-Sotelo, P. (2003) 'Blow ups and other unhappy endings', in B. Ehrenreich and A. Hochschild (eds) *Global Women*, London: Granta.

Howard, M. (2004) *Tax Credits: One Year On*, London: Child Poverty Action Group.

Hughes, P. and MacNaughton, G. (2000) 'Consensus, dissensus, or community: the politics of parent involvement in early childhood education', *Contemporary Issues in Early Childhood*, 1 (3): 241–58.

Jordan, B., Redley, M. and James, S. (1992) *Trapped in Poverty?* London: Routledge.

Jordan, B., Redley, M. and James, S. (1994) *Putting the Family First*, London: University College London Press.

Kenway, J. and Epstein, D. (1996) 'The marketisation of school education: Feminist studies and perspectives', *Discourse: Studies in the Cultural Politics of Education*, 17 (3): 301–14.

Krieger, S. (1996) 'Beyond subjectivity', in A. Lareau and J. Shultz (eds) *Journeys Through Ethnography*, Bolder: Westview Press.

La Rossa, R. (1988) 'Fatherhood and social change', *Family Relations*, 37: 451–7.

Labour Party (2005) *Britain, Forward not Back: The General Election Manifesto*, London: The Labour Party.

Laing, W. (2005) 'The annual children's nurseries conference: Childcare projections', Paper presented at the Annual Children's Nurseries Conference, London, 9 February.

Laing & Buisson Consultants (2005a) *Children's Nurseries: UK market sector report 2005*, London: Laing & Buisson.

Laing & Buisson Consultants (2005b) 'Childcare', at http://www.laingbuisson.co.uk/childcarestats.htm, accessed June 2005.

Land, H. (2002) 'Spheres of care in the UK: Separate and unequal', *Critical Social Policy*, 22 (1): 13–32.

Lane, R. (1991) *The Market Experience*, Cambridge: Cambridge University Press.

Lawhorn, T. (1996) 'Responsible fathering: An educational approach', *Journal of Family and Consumer Sciences*, 88 (4): 35–40.

Leonard, P. (1997) *Postmodern Welfare*, London: Sage.

Leuifsrud, H. and Woodward, A. (1987) 'Women at class crossroads: Reproducing conventional theories of family class', *Sociology*, 21 (2): 393–412.

Lewis, C. and O'Brien, M. (1987) 'Constraints on fathers: Research, theory and clinical practice', in C. Lewis and M. O'Brien (eds) *Re-assessing Fatherhood*, London: Sage.

Lewis, J. (1992) 'Gender and the development of welfare regimes', *Journal of European Social Policy*, 2 (3): 159–73.

Lewis, J. (2002) 'The problem of fathers: Policy and behaviour in Britain', in B. Hobson (ed.) *Making Men into Fathers*, Cambridge: Cambridge University Press.

Lewis, J. (2003) 'Developing early years childcare in England, 1997–2002: The choice for (working) mothers', *Social Policy and Administration*, 37 (3): 209–38.

Limerick, B., Burgess-Limerick, T. and Grace, M. (1996) 'The politics of interviewing: power relations and accepting the gift', *Qualitative Studies in Education*, 9 (4): 449–60.

Lincoln, Y. and Guba, E. (1985) *Naturalistic Inquiry*, Newbury Park: Sage.

Lockwood, D. (1995) 'Marking out the middle class(es)', in T. Butler and M. Savage (eds) *Social Change and the Middle Classes*, London: University College London Press.

Lyotard, J.-F. (1984) *The Post-Modern Condition: A Report on Knowledge*, Manchester: Manchester University Press.

Mackenzie, S. (1989) *Visible Histories: women and environments in a post-war British city*, London: McGill–Queen's University Press.

Malaguzzi, L. (1993) 'History, ideas and basic philosophy,' in C. Edwards, L. Gandini and G. Forman (eds) *The Hundred Languages of Children*, Norwood: Ablex.

Manicom, A. (1984) 'Feminist frameworks and teacher education,' *Journal of Education*, 166 (1): 77–102.

Marchbank, J. (2000) *Women, Power & Policy*, London: Routledge.

Mason, J. (2002) *Qualitative Researching*, London: Sage.

McKie, L., Bowlby, S. and Gregory, S. (2001) 'Gender, caring and employment in Britain', *Journal of Social Policy*, 30 (2): 233–58.

McMahon, M, (1995) *Engendering Motherhood*, New York: Guildford Press.

McLure, M. and Walker, B. (1999) 'Secondary school parents' evenings', end of award report to the Economic and Social Research Council.

McRae, S. (2003) 'Constraints and choices in mothers' employment careers: A consideration of Hakim's Preference Theory', *British Journal of Sociology*, 54 (3): 317–38.

Mirza, M. (1998) '"Same voices, same lives"? Re-visiting black feminist standpoint epistemology', in P. Connolly and B. Troyna (eds), *Researching Racism in Education*, Buckingham: Oxford University Press.

Mooney, A. (2003a) 'What it means to be a childminder: Work or love?' in A. Mooney and J. Statham (eds) *Family Day Care*, London: Jessica Kingsley.

Mooney, A. (2003b) 'Mother, teacher, nurse? How childminders define their role', in J. Brannen and P. Moss (eds) *Rethinking Children's Care*, Buckingham: Open University Press.

Mooney, A. Knight, A., Moss, P. and Owen, C. (2001) *Who Cares? Childminding in the 1990s*, London: Family Policy Studies Centre.

Morgan, D. (1996) *Family Connections: An Introduction to Family Studies*, Cambridge: Polity Press.

Morgan, D. (2002) 'Epilogue', in B. Hobson (ed.) *Making Men into Fathers*, Cambridge: Cambridge University Press.

Moss, P. (1999) 'Renewed hopes and lost opportunities: Early childhood in the early years of the Labour government', *Cambridge Journal of Education*, 29 (2): 229–38.

Moss, P. (2001) *The UK at the Crossroads: Towards an Early Years European Partnership*, London: Daycare Trust.

Moss, P. (2003) 'Getting beyond childcare: Reflections on recent policy and future possibilities', in J. Brannen and P. Moss, *Re-thinking Children's Care*, Buckingham: Oxford University Press.

Moss, P. (2004a) 'Sure Start', *Journal of Education Policy*, 19 (5): 631–4.

Moss, P. (2004b) 'Setting the scene – a vision of universal children's space', in Daycare Trust, *A New Era for Universal Childcare*, London: Daycare Trust.

Moss, P. and Penn, H. (2003) *Transforming Nursery Education*, London: Paul Chapman Publishing.

Moyles, J. (2001) 'Passion, paradox and professionalism in early years education', *Early Years*, 21 (2): 81–95.

Nagel, T. (1991) *Equality and Partiality*, Oxford: Oxford University Press.

National Day Nurseries Association (2004) *Promoting Quality in the Early Years*, NDNA.

Nelson, M. (1989) 'Negotiating care: Relationships between family daycare providers and mothers', *Feminist Studies*, 15 (1): 7–33.

Nelson, M. (1990) *Negotiated Care: The Experience of Family Daycare Providers*, Philadelphia: Temple University Press.

O'Brien, M. (2005) *Shared Caring: Bringing Fathers into the Frame*, London: EOC.

OECD (2001) *Starting Strong: Early Education and Care*, Paris: OECD.

Ollivier, D. (2005) 'Jealous love', The *Guardian*, G2 section, 1 June.

Padfield, I. and Proctor, M. (1998) *Young Adult Women, Work and Family: Living a Contradiction*, London: Mansell.

Papanek, H. (1979) 'Family status production: The "work" and "non-work" of women', *Signs*, 4 (4): 775–81.

Pearson, A. (2002) *I don't Know how She Does It!* London: Vintage.

Pellegrino, E. (1999) 'The commodification of medical and health care: The moral consequences of a paradigm shift from a professional to a market ethic', *Journal of Medicine and Philosophy*, 24 (3): 243–66.

Penn, H. (2006, in press) 'The UK', in M. Cochran and R. New (eds) *Encyclopaedia of Early Education*, New York: Greenwood Press.

Peterson, R. and Kern, R. (1996) 'Changing highbrow taste; from snob to omnivore', *American Sociological Review*, 61: 900–7.

Phares, V. (1996) 'Conducting non-sexist research, prevention, and treatment with fathers and mothers: A call for change', *Psychology of Women Quarterly*, 20: 55–77.

Phoenix, A. (1991) *Young Mothers?* Cambridge: Polity Press.

Pilcher, J. (2000) 'Domestic divisions of labour in the twentieth century: Change slow a coming', *Work, Employment and Society*, 14 (4): 771–80.

Pleck, J. (1997) 'Paternal involvement: Levels sources and consequences', in M.E. Lamb (ed.) *The Role of the Father in Child Development*, New York: Wiley.

Pollert, A. (1996) 'Gender and class revisited: the poverty of "patriarchy"', *Sociology*, 30 (4): 639–59.

Power, S., Whitty, G. and Wigfall, V. (2003) *Education and the Middle Class*, Buckingham: Oxford University Press.

Pratt, G. (1997) 'Stereotypes and ambivalences: The construction of domestic workers in Vancouver, British Columbia', *Gender, Place and Culture*, 4 (2): 159–77.

Prout, A. (1999) 'Children – a suitable case for inclusion?' Kings College London, CPPR (Centre for Public Policy Research) Annual Lecture.

Raddon, A. (2002) 'Mothers in the academy', *Studies in Higher Education*, 27 (4): 387–403.

Randall, V. (2004) 'The making of local child daycare regimes: Past and future', *Policy and Politics*, 32 (1): 3–20.

Reay, D. (1998) *Class Work*, London: University College London Press.

Reay, D., David, M. and Ball, S. (2005) *Degrees of Choice*, Stoke: Trentham.

Reynolds, T., Callender, C. and Edwards, R. (2003) *Caring and Counting: The Impact of Mothers' Employment on Family Relationships*, Bristol: Policy Press.

Ribbens, J. (1994) *Mothers and their Children*, London: Sage.

Ribbens, J. (1998) 'Hearing my feeling voice? An autobiographical discussion of mother-hood', in J. Ribbens and R. Edwards (eds) *Feminist Dilemmas in Qualitative Research: Public Knowledge and Private Lives*, London: Sage.

Riley, D. (1983) ' "The serious burden of love?" Some questions on childcare, feminism and socialism', in L. Segal (ed.) *What is to be Done About the Family?* Harmondsworth: Penguin.

Riley, S. (2003) 'The management of the traditional male role: A discourse analysis of the constructions and functions of provision', *Journal of Gender Studies*, 12 (2): 99–113.

Roberts, K. (2001) *Class in Modern Britain*, Basingstoke: Palgrave.

Robson, G. and Butler, T. (2001) 'Coming to terms with London: Middle class communities in a global city', *International Journal of Urban and Regional Research*, 25 (1): 70–86.

Russell, G. (1986) 'Shared parenting', *Early Child Development and Care*, 24: 139–53.

Savage, M. (2000) *Class Analysis and Social Transformation*, Buckingham, Open University Press.

Savage, M., Bagnall, G. and Longurst, B. (2001) 'Ordinary, ambivalent and defensive: Class identities in the Northwest of England', *Sociology*, 35 (4): 875–92.

Savage, M. Barlow, J., Dickens, S. and Fielding, A. (1992) *Property, Bureaucracy and Culture: Middle Class Formation in Contemporary Britain*, London: Routledge.

Savage, M. and Butler, T. (1995) 'Assets and the middle classes in contemporary Britain', in T. Butler and M. Savage (eds) *Social Change and the Middle Classes*, London: University College London Press.

Scheurich, J. (1997) *Research Methods in the Postmodern*, London: Falmer Press.

Scott, D. (2000) *Reading Educational Research and Policy*, London: RoutledgeFalmer.

Scottish Executive (2004) *Parents' Access to and Demand for Childcare in Scotland*, Edinburgh: Scottish Executive.

Seale, C. (1999) *The Quality of Qualitative Research*, London: Sage.

Seibold, D. (1995) 'Re-inventing fatherhood', *Our Children*, September/October: 6–9.

Shipman, A. (1999) *The Market Revolution and its Limits: A Price for Everything*, London: Routledge.

Siraj-Blatchford, I., Sylva, K., Taggart, B., Sammons, P., Melhuish, E. and Elliot, K. (2003) *The EPPE project: Intensive case studies of practice across the Foundation Stage: Technical Paper 10*, London: Institute of Education.

Skeggs, B. (1997) *Formations of Class and Gender: Becoming Respectable*, London: Sage.

Skeggs, B. (2004) *Class, Self, Culture*, London: Routledge.

Smith, D. (1988) *The Everyday World as Problematic: A Feminist Sociology*, Buckingham: Open University Press.

Sure Start (2003) *Birth to Three Matters*, London: Sure Start.

Sure Start (2004) *2002/3 Childcare and Early Years Workforce Survey*, London: Sure Start.

Stanley, E. and Wise, S. (1993) *Breaking out Again: Feminist Ontology and Epistemology*, London: Routledge.

Stephens, J. (1999) 'A fight for her time: Challenges facing professional mothers', in L. McKie, S. Bowlby and S. Gregory (eds) *Gender, Power and the Household*, Basingstoke: Macmillan.

Strauss, A. (1987) *Qualitative Analysis for Social Scientists*, New York: Cambridge University Press.

Sullivan, O. (2000) 'The division of domestic labour: Twenty years of change?' *Sociology*, 34 (3): 437–56.

Swift, A. (2003) *How Not to be a Hypocrite: School Choice for the Morally Perplexed Parent*, London: Routledge.

Sylva, K., Melhuish, E., Sammons, P., Siraj-Blatchford, I. and Taggart, B. (2004) *Effective Provision of Pre-school Education (EPPE) Final Report*, London: Sure Start.

Teese, R. (2000) *Academic Success and Social Power: Examinations and Inequality*, Melbourne: Melbourne University Press.

Templeton, T. (2004) 'Best place to be...' *Observer Magazine*, 21 November, pp. 22–3.

Thomas, L. (2005) 'Staying mum', *Guardian*, 4 June, p. 22.

Thompson, M., Vintner, L. and Young, V. (2005) *Dads and their Babies: Leave Arrangements in their First Year*, London: EOC.

Tronto, J. (1996) 'Care as a political concept' in N. Hirshmann and C. DeStefano (eds) *Re-visioning the political: Feminist Reconstructions of Traditional Concepts in Western Political Theory*, Boulder: Westview Press.

Tuominen, M. (2003) *'We Are Not Babysitters': Family Childcare Providers Redefine Work and Care*, New Brunswick: Rutgers Press.

Uttal, L. (1996) 'Custodial care, surrogate care and co-ordinated care: Employed mothers and the meaning of child care', *Gender and Society*, 10 (3): 291–311.

Uttal, L. (2002) *Making Care Work: Employed Mothers in the New Childcare Market*, New Brunswick: Rutgers University Press.

Valentine, G. (1997) '"My son's a bit dizzy." "My wife's a bit soft": Gender, children and cultures of parenting', *Gender, Place and Culture*, 4 (1): 37–62.

van Zanten, A. and Veleda, C. (2001) 'Contexts locaux et strategies scolaires: Clivages et interactions entre classes et classes moyennes danes la peripherie urbaine', *Revue du Centre de recherche en education*, 20: 57–87.

Vevers, S. (2004a) 'By numbers', *Nursery World*, 22 July, pp. 10–11.

Vevers, S. (2004b) 'Feeling the squeeze', *Nursery World*, 29 July, pp. 10–11.

Vevers, S. (2004c) 'Invest in staff first, providers tell MPs', *Nursery World*, 7 October, p. 4.

Vevers, S. (2005a) 'Childcarers list their demands', *Nursery World*, 10 March, p. 5.

Vevers, S. (2005b) 'New arrival', *Nursery Chains*, summer, p. 15.

Vincent, C. (1996) *Parents and Teachers: Power and Participation*, London: Falmer Press.

Vincent, C. (2000) *Including Parents? Education, Citizenship and Parental Agency*, Buckingham: Open University Press.

Vincent, C. (2001) 'Social class and parental agency', *Journal of Education Policy*, 16 (4): 347–64.

Vincent, C. and Ball, S. J. (2001) 'A market in love? Choosing pre-school childcare', *British Journal of Sociology of Education*, 25 (2): 229–44.

Vincent, C., Ball, S. J. and Kemp, S. (2004) 'The social geography of childcare: Making up a middle class child', *British Journal of Sociology of Education*, 25 (2): 229–44.

Vincent, C. and Martin, J. (2002) 'Class, culture and agency', *Discourse*, 23 (1): 109–28.

Wacquant, L. (1991) 'Making class(es): The middle classes in social theory and social structure', in S. McNall, R. Levine and R. Fantasia (eds) *Bringing Class Back In: Contemporary and Historical Perspectives*, Boulder: West View Press.

Walkerdine, V. and Lucey, H. (1989) *Democracy in the Kitchen*, London: Virago.

Walkerdine, V., Lucey, H. and Melody, J. (2001) *Growing up Girl*, London: Palgrave.

Warin, J., Solomon, Y., Lewis, C. and Langford, W. (1999) *Fathers, Work and Family Life*, London: Family Policy Studies Centre/Joseph Rowntree Foundation.

Webb, J. (1999) 'Work and the new public service class?', *Sociology*, 33 (4): 747–66.

Wheelock, J. and Jones, K. (2002) 'Grandparents are the next best thing': Informal childcare for working parents in urban Britain', *Journal of Social Policy*, 31 (3): 441–63.

Windebank, J. (1999) 'Political motherhood and the everyday experiences of mothering: A comparison of the child care strategies of French and British working mothers', *Journal of Social Policy*, 28 (1): 1–25.

Witz, A. (1995) 'Gender and service-class formation', in T. Butler and M. Savage (eds) *Social Change and the Middle Classes*, London: University College London Press.

Wrigley, J. (1995) *Other People's Children*, New York: Basic Books/Harper.

Wynne, D. (1998) *Leisure, Lifestyle and the New Middle Class*, London: Routledge.

Young, I. (1990) *Justice and the Politics of Difference*, Princeton: Princeton University Press.

Young, I. (1996) 'Communication and the other: Beyond deliberative democracy', in S. Benhabib (ed.), *Democracy and Difference: Contesting the Boundaries of the Political*, Princeton: Princeton University Press.

Index